REVIVAL

FIRES AND

AWAKENINGS
Thirty Moves of the Holy Spirit

A CALL TO PRAYER, HOLINESS
AND INTERCESSION FOR REVIVAL

MATHEW BACKHOLER

REVIVAL FIRES AND AWAKENINGS
Thirty Moves of the Holy Spirit
A Call to Prayer, Holiness and Intercession for Revival

UK ISBN 1846853141
978-1-84685-314-2

British Library Cataloguing In Publication Data
A Record of this Publication is available from the British Library

First Published August 2006 by
Exposure Publishing, an imprint of Diggory Press,
Three Rivers, Minions, Liskeard, Cornwall, PL14 5LE, UK
WWW.DIGGORYPRESS.COM

Cover design by Paul and Mathew Backholer

- Jesus Christ is Lord -

Revival Fires and Awakenings

Thirty Moves of the Holy Spirit

A Call to Prayer, Holiness and
Intercession for Revival

'One generation shall praise Your works to another, and shall declare Your mighty acts. Men shall speak of the might of Your awesome acts…they shall utter the memory of Your great goodness, and shall sing of Your righteousness' Psalm 145:4, 6-7.

- Mathew Backholer -

CONTENTS

Section I – An Introduction to Revival

CHAPTER ONE - **What is it Lord?**

Section II – Revival Fires and Awakenings

CHAPTER TWO - **The Hand of the Lord**

CHAPTER THREE - **This is That**

CHAPTER FOUR - **Times of Refreshing**

CHAPTER FIVE - **Rend the Heavens!**

Contents

CONTENTS

CONTENTS

SECTION I

AN INTRODUCTION TO REVIVAL

PREFACE

'And it shall come to pass afterward that I will pour out My Spirit on all flesh. Your sons and your daughters shall prophesy, your old men shall dream dreams, your young men shall see visions; and also on My menservants and on My maidservants, I will pour out My Spirit in those days' Joel 2:28-29.

Within this book a revival is recognised as a localised event, whether in a church, village, town or city; whereas an awakening refers to a move of God which has swept further afield. An awakening is bigger than a localised event, which could affect a district, county or country. They frequently carry on for years or decades and widely affect the moral makeup of society. An awakening could be understood to move in the same way that a forest fire is swept and moved in all directions by the wind. It consumes and covers vast sways of countryside and yet can still leap across roads and ignite on the other side, and be blown as the wind chooses. Revival first and foremost, is for Christians so that they can be revived and live how God desires them to live. Out of this (and during the same period of time) non-Christians come under deep conviction of sin, regardless of whether they are in a church building or within the sound of a preacher or evangelist, they will call upon Jesus Christ to save them.

Dr. Martyn Lloyd-Jones preaching on Exodus 33:18-23, (Moses desiring to see God's glory), said, "That's a perfect description of revival; it's the glory of God passing by. That's precisely what it is, just this glimpse of God as He passes by. The God who is there in the glory, as it were comes down, pays a visit, pours out His Spirit, descends again, and He just passes by us, and we look on and feel and know that the glory of God is in the midst and is passing by, O' it's but a touching of the hem as it were, it's but a vision of the back...a revival I say is just a kind of touch of His glory, a fleeting glimpse of something of what He is, in and of Himself...these things are possible and these things are meant for us, we were never meant to be content with a little." Dr. Martyn Lloyd-Jones then read 2 Corinthians 12:1-6, where the apostle speaks of visions, revelations of the Lord and the third heaven.[1]

The author has diligently studied over one hundred books on revivals, revivalists and awakenings, as well as listening (and watching on video) numerous sermons on revivals some by revivalists themselves. The author has also travelled to locations of revivals (past and present) and spoken to those who witnessed or participated in revival, (or whose parents or friends have). The author, after years of diligent study and prayer for revival is convinced that across the globe, God is always doing a work amongst His people and the nations of the world. God does not slumber nor sleep (Psalm 121:4) and His fires of revival are continually scorching the land and setting hearts ablaze; many of these fires are known only to Him and to those who were blessed to witness and partake of such a Holy Spirit phenomena.

Written history only records certain revivals and no book or library could ever contain such a complete volume of accounts. The author hopes that by reading this book, (understanding the Holy Scriptures, God's covenant promises) and the selection of thirty moves of the Holy Spirit, you too will be stirred to cry mightily unto God. Giving Him no rest, that He would come and heal your land and pour out His Spirit from on high; reviving Christians and turning the hearts of the children to their

Father, and that the desert will blossom and the wilderness will become a fruitful bough.

Popular Christian terminology still records certain revivals as revivals (and not awakenings), such as the Welsh Revival 1904-1905, even though it was more characteristic of an awakening as it swept across the land and ignited fires across the globe. In these instances, the author has retained the historically accepted title of such a move of God.

In this book, unless stated otherwise, the word manifestation(s) refers to physical phenomena, which come from the Spirit of God and not demonic activity which comes from the enemy of God, the spirit of anti-Christ.

The author has not attempted to gloss over or shy away from the more negative aspects of any move of God, as there will always be opposition to the moving of the Holy Spirit, but has aimed at a balanced view, laid before us the historical facts of past revivals and awakenings.

As you read this book, it is best to lay aside any preconceived ideas of what God cannot do and will not do in revival (anyhow, God is God and can do what He wants, how He wants, when He wants without answering to anybody!), but to take a glimpse of what has happened in the past. Historical fact is historical fact. Sadly, some authors of revival books have glossed over some of the facts of revival history, such as physical manifestation (phenomena) and deliverance from demonic powers. The author of this book has not done such a thing, as it is wrong to deny what the Spirit of grace has done, (the enemy is out there to destroy us, but the Lord wants to deliver us). The scribes of the Bible never did such a thing and it is wrong to ignore truth and fact. It not only confuses future researchers on revival, but it wrongly assists incorrect assumption (from some Christians), that a present move of God is not from God, because of certain manifestations, regardless of the fact that there is nothing new under the sun, and that which has been is what will be (Ecclesiastes 1:9). Though there are many similarities, common threads and general features between each revival, there are also distinct differences and variable features as God does things His way and not perhaps how we would like it to happen, or think it should happen. God should not be kept in a box; He is far greater than the box. It is frequently our preconceived ideas and doctrines that are in the box. God and the Bible should shape our thinking and not any pre-programmed mindset, ideas or opinions.

Dr. Martyn Lloyd-Jones said, "You will find that when God manifests Himself and by an outpouring of the Spirit, whose special work and commission it is to manifest the Lord Jesus and His glory and through Him God Himself. You will find, you will often read things like this, that men and women in the presence of this glory and of this presence have literally fallen to the ground, have fainted...don't be interested in nor frightened in phenomena...God Himself has said that the glory is so glorious, that men's physical frame is inadequate [Exodus 33:20-23], so don't be surprised if you read, when you read of these reports, of people fainting, or going of in a kind of a dead swoon. It's the glory of God. It's beyond us, and it is therefore not surprising that sometimes it should lead to these consequences."[2]

The accounts of revivals and awakenings within this book are just a small example of what God can do, 'in the fullness of time' when the conditions have been met. Many a book has been written on most of the revivals which the author has featured; but the author aims to give you a taste of what God has done – He can do again; which will whet your appetite, leave you thirsting for more, and praying harder for revival, in your nation and amongst the nations.

The author in Section I and III has extensively quoted from men of God, both past and present, most of whom partook of the fires of revival and tasted the heavenly glories. Their opinions and experiences hold far greater weight and testimony than anyone who has not been used in revival. When they speak, we should listen and heed the advice of those who walked closer to the Lord than we do now, because if we walked as close to the Lord as they did, then we too would probably see revival! Some of the quotes from yesteryears sound and read slightly antiquated today, but the author, where possible has tried to retain them (when still readable) in their original grammatical formats. Also, some of the quotes are in conversational style which is how they were transmitted; but lamentably the written word cannot reproduce the true personality of the speaker or the atmosphere of the meeting. These revivalists were men of faith, and though the vast majority have passed into glory; being dead they still speak and look down upon us, being part of the great cloud of witnesses. And if they were here, what would they say to their fellow labourers, who are concerned about the present and inspired by the past moves of God?

'Let us lay aside every weight, and the sin which so easily ensnares us, and let us run with endurance the race that is set before us, looking unto Jesus the author and finisher of our faith, who for the joy that was set before Him endured the cross, despising the shame, and has sat down at the right hand of the throne of God. For consider Him who endured such hostility from sinners against Himself, lest you become weary and discouraged in your souls' Hebrews 12:1-3.

ACKNOWLEDGEMENTS AND DEDICATION

First and foremost, I thank God, the Creator of the heavens and the earth and everything in it, the giver and sustainer of life, for keeping me thus far. You are the God of the Holy Bible, the God of wrath and mercy, the One who is a consuming fire, the One who is slow to anger and abounding in love. The One who sends His Spirit, the Holy Spirit to bring about revivals and awakenings, (who convicts, quickens and awakens, Christians and sinners alike to their need of the Saviour, to holiness and guides them into all truth), to glorify Jesus who is the Way the Truth and the Life. The One who can be known as our Heavenly Father who is in heaven, the One with whom mortal man can get to know through a living relationship with Your Son Jesus Christ of Nazareth, who died on the cross of Calvary and rose again after three days, defeating death and conquering sin. Hallelujah! This book is dedicated to the glory of Your name and the majesty of Your splendour for the great things that You have done down through the aeons of history.

A very big thank you to the many persons who have helped in the proof-reading of this book and have given constructive comments, guidance and advice which have been more than helpful and very beneficial.

I give all the glory unto God for giving me the ability to read, study, research, assimilate, write and piece together this revival book over a period of two years. I pray that it will not only be an educational and enlightening read, but a blessing and a challenge to all those that read it – a call to prayer, holiness and intercession for revival. May God be glorified for the great things He has done and may the fire fall once again for His great name's sake.

CHAPTER ONE
What is it Lord? (Acts 10:4)

Then the Lord said: "I have pardoned according to your word; but truly, as I live, all the earth shall be filled with the glory of the Lord" Numbers 14:20-21.

'For the earth shall be filled with the knowledge of the glory of the Lord, as the waters cover the sea' Habakkuk 2:14.

Understanding Revivals and Awakenings

The word 'revival' first came into the English language in 1702; the standard definition being: an awakening in or of evangelical religion. The word 'revival' is used to explain the amazing results of a sovereign outpouring of the Spirit of God, when people are saved and communities are changed and become God-fearing. Firstly, the church gets on fire for God, as the Holy Spirit revives the body of Christ. Secondly, the Holy Spirit convicts the souls of non-Christians, (who become awakened) and shows them their sinfulness and their need of the Saviour, Jesus Christ.

The term 'revival' also incorporates the definitions: an outpouring of the Holy Spirit, a visitation, The Holy Spirit falling, the Spirit of God descending, God coming down, God visiting His people, days of heaven on earth and the presidency of the Holy Spirit in the Church.

A revival can come suddenly or gradually, accumulating in a spiritual climax and either run its course gradually or suddenly end.

During revival people have an awareness of spiritual things as they never have before; there is a solemn awe of God, a reverence and holy fear. Frequently in revival, people are saved outside of the church and are overcome by the power of the Holy Spirit, at home, on the streets, at work or in the fields. Some of whom without ever coming into contact with a Christian who has been revived!

There is a difference between effective evangelism and revival. Evangelist, revivalist and world renown revival historian J. Edwin Orr expressed it well, when he said, "In times of evangelism, the evangelist seeks the sinner, in times of revival the sinners comes chasing after the Lord."

In evangelism the focus is on the evangelist or preacher, and many who profess Christ soon fall by the wayside. But, in revival the focus is on God, and the vast majority of those who profess Christ stay true to Him as abiding fruit, (see Appendix A).

In effective evangelism God may bless the work and people will respond to the call of repentance, and give themselves to Jesus (this sometimes leads to revival or an awakening, see Appendix B). But in revival there is an overpowering presence and move of the Holy Spirit (and regardless of the anointed evangelist or minister pleading and calling for people to repent and to get right with God) the people will be moved by God's Spirit to repent, often breaking down and pouring out their hearts to the Almighty.

I was present at a meeting where a missionary, who was used during the Korean Revival (1960s and 1970s) stated, that when he gave an altar call, so many people responded, that he sent them back to their seats as he thought that they had misunderstood his appeal. He repeated himself the second time, rephrasing his words and still hundreds came forward. After this he stated, that he never made an altar call again, as it was not necessary.

Colin C. Kerr in a broadcast for the BBC from St. Paul's Church, London, England in October 1942 (and was later transmuted into the booklet *How Revival Comes, The Two National Broadcasts*), said, "Missions are the result of great consecrated human activity: publicity drives – great choirs – well-known evangelists – carefully organised plans, and so on. Revival is exactly opposite. The revival creates the activity. Because God has in this special way visited the people, all that is needed just happens. The Movement is its own advertisement, produces its own speakers, singers, halls, churches, finances, everything."

Revivals are Controversial

Revivals can be highly controversial. With many saying, "It's from God" and some believing it's of the devil! While others will say, "It's merely mass hysteria." In Jesus' day there was much murmuring among the people concerning Himself. Some said, "He is good" others said, "No, on the contrary He deceives the people" (John 7:12). Even Jesus' own people thought He was "out of His mind" (Mark 3:20). Now, if they said that about Jesus and His ministry, how much more controversial will revivals, awakenings and those that are involved appear?

In any revival there will be manifestations, physical phenomena, manifestation of the Holy Spirit's convicting power, in healings and other supernatural events. But also the devil will try to influence people, Christian and non-Christians.

It is wrong to say that everything you see in revival is from God, because it's not, there will always be opportunists and exhibitionists. The issue is not to focus on the excesses, but to focus on God and to give glory to Him for the great things He has done and is doing. The Pharisees looked for the negative, even when the miraculous was performed before their eyes. They watched Jesus closely to see whether He would heal on the Sabbath, just so that they might accuse Him! (Mark

3:1-5). This was not a sign of maturity but of immaturity. They went with the wrong attitude and were so blinded in the process that they were unable to see the wood from the trees.

It is also wrong to believe everything you are told or read about another, because even the apostle Paul was slanderously reported as saying, "Let us do evil that good may come" (Romans 3:8). Yet we all know that after his dramatic conversion he led a morally upright life and strived to keep a clear conscience before God and man.

Dr. Martyn Lloyd-Jones (who saw a localised revival in his church at Sandfields, Aberavon, near Swansea, South Wales in 1930, though he himself was reluctant to call it that), minister of Westminster Chapel London said, "The coming of revival has two main effects. One that it blesses all the denominations practically, irrespective of their divisions, and for the time being brings them together in a marvellous unity. There has never been anything that has so promoted spiritual unity as revival. But a revival also invariably has another effect, and that is that it creates a new and fresh division. And why does it do so? It does so for this reason, those who have experienced the blessing and the power of God are naturally one and they come together; there are others who dislike it all and who criticise it all and who condemn it all and who are outside it all and the divisions comes in."[1]

Since the beginning of Christianity enemies of the cross of Christ have denounced godly people believing them to be under the influence of the evil one. Jesus was crucified. Stephen was stoned and the apostle Paul was whipped, beaten, imprisoned and stoned on several occasions. Yet, though the devil can transform himself into an angel of light, he cannot transform someone's character to be more Christ-like and certainly does not encourage them to do so. This is the work of the Holy Spirit working with the believer who has decided to fully give of him or her self to Christ Jesus and to surrender their will to the Holy Spirit.

The real judge of any revival, awakening or move of the Spirit is this: does it line up with Scripture? Is God being glorified? What is the fruit? Are people becoming more Christ-like? Are they walking in the fruit of the Spirit and growing in the grace of God?

What is exceptionally sad amongst the Church is that many Christians proclaim to serve a supernatural and all powerful God, yet when God, the Holy Spirit moves supernaturally they oppose Him and denounce it as of the flesh or of the evil one! In the words of John Wesley's pen: 'They take upon themselves to judge of the things which they know not.' And as the Scripture declares: 'But indeed, O man, who are you to reply against God?' (Romans 9:20). Man's denial and dismissal of the workings of God is wrong. This is ignorance, arrogance and foolishness. The Scriptures (and nearly two thousand years of Church History) clearly reveal the workings of the Holy Spirit since before and after Pentecost which vindicates the servants of the Lord when they move and walk under His anointing.

The most significant thing within Jesus' ministry which demonstrated that the kingdom of God had arrived, was when He cast out demons 'with the finger of God' (Luke 11:20). There were no instances of deliverance (the casting out of demons/evil spirits) in the Old Testament. Jesus gave His disciples the authority to cast out demons and endued this same commission to all subsequent disciples, 'to preach the good news, to make disciples, to heal the sick, to cast out demons and to raise the dead' (Mark 16:15-18). Therefore we should not be alarmed or concerned that people get delivered and set free from demonic powers, as well as healed or raised from the dead, during revival (and outside of revival) when fully surrendered disciples of the Lord Jesus Christ walk in the power and anointing of the Holy Spirit (Matthew 28:18-20, Luke 24:49 and Acts 1:8). By doing this they fulfil Jesus' last command to make disciples and to be witnesses of Him, by their actions and in demonstration of the power of the Holy Spirit (1 Corinthians 4:20 and 2 Corinthians 12:12).

J. Edwin Orr, twentieth century evangelist, who was used in many localised revivals in the mid 1930s from Eastern Europe to Australia (and who also saw revival in Brazil during 1951 and 1952) said, "The key factor in revival is the outpouring of the Holy Spirit. The outpouring of the Holy Spirit results in the revival of the church. That is the work of God with the response of the believers. The outpouring of the Holy Spirit also results in an awakening of the people. That is the work of God with the response of the people. The revived church then engages in evangelising the enquirers and in teaching the disciples, that is those who wish to follow, and by many or by few, in the reforming of society."[2]

Dr. Martyn Lloyd-Jones said, "Revival is a period of unusual blessing and activity in the life of the Christian Church...revival by definition; it is something that primarily happens in the Church of God and amongst believing people, and it is only secondarily something that affects those who are outside of so [the Church]."[3]

Dr. Martyn Lloyd-Jones said, "It is an experience in the life of the Church when the Holy Spirit does an unusual work. He does that work primarily amongst the members of the Church; it is a reviving of the believers. You cannot revive something that has never had life, so revival by definition is first of all an enlivening, quickening and awakening of lethargic, sleeping, almost moribund Church members. Suddenly, the power of the Holy Spirit comes upon them and they are brought into a new and more profound awareness of the truths they had previously held intellectually and perhaps at a deeper level too. They are humbled, they are convicted of sin…and then they come to see the great salvation of God in all its glory and to feel its power. Then, as a result of their quickening, they begin to pray. New power comes into the preaching of the ministers and the result of this is that large numbers who were previously outside the Church are converted and brought in."[4]

Albert Barnes, nineteenth century Bible expositor, in regards to revival said, "That day which shall convince the great body of professing Christians of the reality and desirableness of revivals will constitute a new era in the history of religion and will precede manifestation of power like that of Pentecost."[5]

A Parish Minister at Barvas, Isle of Lewis, UK, during the 1949-1952 revival, in a report wrote: 'The Spirit of the Lord was resting wondrously and graciously in the different townships in the parish. You could feel His presence in the homes of the people, on meadow and moorland and even on the public road. This awareness of God to me is the supreme characteristic, the supreme feature of a God-sent revival.'[6]

A minister who witnessed Revival in Africa in the 1980s wrote: 'Nothing is impossible with God. Revival is about the imparting of authentic hope that comes from a God who loves us. Revival is not simply the migration of a pagan people into the Christian Church. It is also about the release of Christians for a renewing and healing engagement with a broken world. Revival is not about a spiritual knees-up, but an outpouring of the justice and mercy of God which we can expect to see touch the broken and marginalised in our society.'[7]

Colin Dye in his book, *Revival Phenomena* wrote: '...Revival is essentially a manifestation of God. It is a time when He reveals Himself both in His absolute holiness and in great power. It is God rolling up His sleeves – 'making bare His holy arm' – and working in extraordinary power on saints and sinners alike.'[8]

Evan Roberts (used in the 1904-1905 Welsh Revival) in his later years wrote: 'The baptism of the Holy Spirit is the essence of revival, for revival comes from knowledge of the Holy Spirit and the way of co-working with Him which enables Him to work in revival power. The primary condition of revival is therefore that believers should individually know the baptism of the Holy Ghost.'[9]

Willis Hoover who founded the Methodist Pentecostal Church in Chile during the 1909 Chile Revival said, "I believe that the true secret of this whole thing is that we really and truly believe in the Holy Spirit – we really trust Him – we really honour Him – we really obey Him – we really give Him free rein – we really believe that the promises in Acts 1:4-5 and Joel 2:28-29 is for us."[10]

Evangelist Seth Joshua, who was used extensively in Wales in bringing souls to Christ (and especially during the 1904-1905 Welsh Revival) stated in a lecture: 'The world owes everything to the Church and the Church owes everything to revival.'[11]

There are differing views as to how you can see revival. All concerned know that it is the Holy Spirit coming down that affects people, but the differences is in the degree that man has to participate towards seeing a revival. Having read and studied the history of revivals through the ages for more than a decade, I have distinctly seen that there are three prevailing unwritten views:

1. It is a totally sovereign work of God, whilst man makes application of God's promises. Jonathan Edwards, Rev. Duncan Campbell and Dr. Martyn Lloyd-Jones held this view and they saw revival.

2. Anybody can have revival at any time as long as the conditions and promises have been appropriated. Charles Finney, Jonathan Goforth and Edwin Orr held this view and they saw revival.

3. Just preach the pure gospel. George Whitefield, John Wesley (though both of different theological persuasion, see the end of page 40+) and Howell Harris held this view and they saw revival.

Also there are those who had such an anointing on their lives that in many places, regardless of the countries or towns visited, they saw revival. Charles Finney, Jonathan Goforth, Edwin Orr, George Whitefield and John Wesley saw this in their ministries.

My understanding of revival is that the three different views are all part of the same swing of God's revival pendulum; it just depends at which end you are viewing the marvellous work of God. It is the same Holy Spirit that comes down and touches people's lives from different countries in different centuries from varying cultures. God is no respecter of persons, denominations or countries that He works in. The age or gender of the revivalist is immaterial (though 95% of revivalists are male). The common feature amongst revivalists is, they had all fully surrendered their lives to God and had had an encounter with the Holy Spirit. All preached the pure uncompromising gospel, the cross, the atonement, the blood and the Law and grace (the wrath and mercy of God) and they desired that God be glorified in their midst and amongst the graceless. They all saw revival!

SECTION II

REVIVAL FIRES AND AWAKENINGS

CHAPTER TWO
The Hand of the Lord (Joshua 4:24)

The Lord said, "If My people who are called by My name will humble themselves, and pray and seek My face, and turn from their wicked ways, then I will hear from heaven, and will forgive their sin and heal their land" 2 Chronicles 7:14.

'O Lord, though our iniquities testify against us, do it for Your name's sake; for our backslidings are many, we have sinned against You' Jeremiah 14:7.

Examples from Scripture

The Bible does not mention the word 'revival' (depending on your translation), though it does mention on a handful of occasions the word 'revive'. The word 'revival' is like the word 'Trinity'. The word Trinity is not in the Bible, yet we all know that it is a word used to explain the biblical concept of the unity of the Godhead, the Father, the Son and the Holy Spirit. The word revival is the same; we know it means an amazing outpouring of the Holy Spirit, and though the word revival may not be used by direct word of inspiration; in both the Old and New Testament it is by inspired inference.

The Holy Spirit was only poured out after the resurrection of Jesus Christ (John 7:39) as recorded in the New Testament (Acts 1:8 and Acts 2:1-4 etc.); therefore the Old Testament examples of revivals do not have examples of the Holy Spirit falling enmasse, but God's glory did come down when King Solomon dedicated the temple, (1 Kings 8:10-11 and 2 Chronicles 5:13-14). The revivals that are seen in the Old Testament reveal mass repentance under God's conviction and the Spirit's leading as the people returned to the Lord, (or turned to the Lord), often under the influence of a leader, prophet or king.

Frank Bartleman the chronicler of the Azusa Street Outpouring said, "In order to understand what God is going to do, we must understand what He once did."

Old Testament Revivals, Returning to God

1. From the godly line of Seth men began to call on the name of the Lord, and when people start to call upon God, "What must I do to be saved?" then that is an awakening of a group of people (Genesis 4:26).

2. King Asa became king of Judah and did what was right in the eyes of the Lord. He banished the perverted persons (male and female prostitutes) from the land and removed all the idols that his father had set up. He even removed his grandmother from being queen mother because she was an idol worshiper and cut down her obscene image to Asherah. King Asa also commanded his people to seek the Lord God of their fathers and to observe the Law and the commandments (1 Kings 15:9-15 and 2 Chronicles 14:1-15).

3. The prophet Elijah had a spiritual battle on Mount Carmel, before King Ahab and the four hundred and fifty prophets of Baal and four hundred prophets of Asherah. Once the true altar was prepared, a complete offering was given, Elijah called upon his God and the fire fell, and then the people fell on their faces, crying out, "The Lord, He is God! The Lord He is God!" (1 Kings 18:20-40).

4. King Hezekiah of Judah reopened and repaired the house of God which had been shut up and neglected for many years. He made a covenant

before God, the house of God was then cleansed and sanctified with the help of the Levites and the people brought offerings. A big Passover festival was held and celebrated and all the idols, wooden images, high places and false altars were smashed, cut down and destroyed. The temple worship was reinstated and the Levites got their old jobs back (2 Kings 18:1-8 and 2 Chronicles chapters 29-31).

5. King Josiah, son of evil King Amon (who was the son of evil King Manasseh) brought about revival in the land when the Book of the Law was found and he acted upon It – by repenting and humbling himself before God. King Josiah called the elders of the land and made a covenant before the Lord to obey His commandments as did the people of Judah. The temple of the Lord was cleansed and all the false altars and temples etc. were destroyed and they celebrated with a huge Passover festival (2 Kings chapters 22-23 and 2 Chronicles chapters 34-35).

6. Jonah the son of Amittai was called to preach in Nineveh to the notorious cruel Assyrians, but he fled from the call of God. Eventually the prophet Jonah preached in this large Gentile, pagan city shouting, "Yet, forty days, and Nineveh shall be overthrown!" The people of Nineveh believed the word of the Lord, they declared a fast and wore sackcloth as a sign of humility. The king also clothed himself in sackcloth, sat in ashes, and proclaimed that no man or beast should eat or drink; should be clothed in sackcloth and that all men should cry mightily to God and turn from their evil ways. God saw their humility and contrition and judgment was avoided which upset Jonah! (The book of Jonah).

The revival at Nineveh is unique, in that God did not come to revive His people first (the Israelites), but He came to give life to those who had previously not known life who were dead in trespasses and sins.

New Testament Heaven-Sent Blessings, Revivals and Awakenings

1. The Holy Spirit fell on the Day of Pentecost and people began to speak in tongues. Peter stands up to preach and about three thousand people were 'cut to the heart,' under conviction of sin, they believed on the Lord Jesus Christ, repented and were baptised in the name of Jesus (Acts chapter 2).
2. Peter and John preached and around two thousand people (five thousand less three thousand) were added to the church (Acts 4:1-4).
3. Through the hands of the apostles many signs and wonders were performed and multitudes became believers in Christ Jesus (Acts 5:12-14).
4. The number of disciples of Jesus multiplied greatly in Jerusalem including many of the priests (Acts 6:1-8).
5. Philip went down to the city of Samaria, preaching with miracles following and multitudes with one accord heeded what he said and became followers of Jesus and there was great joy in that city (Acts 8:5-8).
6. Peter visited Joppa and raised Dorcas from the dead; as this fact became known throughout Joppa, many believed on the Lord Jesus (Acts 9:36-43).
7. Peter and some brethren went to Caesarea to meet the centurion Cornelius, Peter preached to him, his relatives and friends and the Holy Spirit falls upon them all and they spoke in tongues (Acts 10:23-48).

8. Some of the disciples of Jesus (not the twelve) preached at Antioch to the Hellenists and a great number believed and turned to the Lord (Act 11:19-21). When news of this revival reached the church at Jerusalem they sent Barnabas to assist in the work and more people were added to the faith (Acts 11:22-24).

9. The apostle Paul and friends preached to the Jews in the synagogue in Antioch at Pisidia. Many of the Jews and devout proselytes followed the teaching of Jesus Christ. The Gentiles then begged that they also may hear this preaching on the following Sabbath and almost the whole town came to hear, which upset the elders of the city but nonetheless the word of the Lord spread throughout that region (Acts 13:14-50).

10. The disciples preached at Iconium in the synagogues and both Jews and Greeks believed the message. Signs and wonders were performed and the city was divided against the Jews and the apostles (Acts 14:1-4).

11. Paul and the apostles travelled, the churches were strengthened in the faith and the church increased in numbers daily (Acts 16:1-5).

12. Paul and Silas went into the synagogue in Thessalonica and preached. A great multitude of devout Greeks and many of the leading women followed them, which led to a riot as people said, "These who have turned the world upside down have come here too" (Acts 17:1-9).

13. Paul and Silas were sent to Berea and they preached in the synagogue. Many believed, both Greeks and prominent women of the city, but Jews from Thessalonica stirred up the crowd and another riot began! (Acts 17:10-15).

14. Paul preached on Mars Hill, in the midst of the Areopagus in Athens to the pagans, some

mocked, but other joined them and believed (Acts 17:22-34).

15. Paul, Silas and Timothy travelled to Corinth and spoke at a house meeting of Justus who lived next door to the synagogue. Crispus the synagogue ruler and his entire household believed along with many of the Corinthians. They stayed there for six months, teaching the new converts (Acts 18:7-11).

16. Paul teaches in the school at Tyrannus for two years and all who dwelt in Asia (Minor) heard the word of the Lord, both Jews and Greeks, but some were hardened and spoke evil of the Way (Acts 19:8-9).

17. In Ephesus, after hearing and seeing the power of God working through the apostle Paul, fear fell on the Jews and Greeks, Jesus was magnified; many who had believed on Jesus Christ publicly confessed their sins and deeds and those who had practised magical arts publicly burned their expensive books (Acts 19:11-20).

18. Paul after being arrested and having been shipwrecked lands on the Island of Malta. Many people were healed as Paul prayed and laid his hands on them including the father of the leading citizen of the island (Acts 28:1-9). There is no recorded mention of conversions but undoubtedly there were many who would have believed his message as they thought him to be a god (verse 6) as neither shipwreck nor a snake bite could kill him.

God said, "Take heed to yourself, and diligently keep yourself, lest you forget the things your eyes have seen, and lest they depart from your heart all the days of your life. And teach them to your children and your grandchildren" Deuteronomy 4:9.

CHAPTER THREE
This is That (Acts 2:16)

'Lord who may abide in Your tabernacle? Who may dwell in Your holy hill? He who walks uprightly and works righteousness, and speaks the truth in his heart; he who does not backbite with his tongue, nor does evil to his neighbour, nor does he take up a reproach against his friend' Psalm 15:1-3.

'Who may ascend into the hill of the Lord? Or who may stand in His holy place? He who has clean hands and a pure heart, who has not lifted up his soul to an idol, nor sworn deceitfully. He shall receive blessing from the Lord and righteousness from the God of his salvation. This is Jacob, the generation of those who seek Him, who seek Your face' Psalm 24:3-6.

Dating a Revival

The dates of the revivals or awakenings are considered when the main 'fire' fell but the 'afterglow' in some cases carried on for years or decades and in some cases has been re-ignited. This is especially true of the Nagaland Revival (north-eastern corner of India) where it is reported that 99% of the population (under two million) are now Christian after revival broke out in 1952, 1956, 1966, 1972 and 1976, and the fires are still being felt today (in 2006) where former head-hunters are now soul-hunters, and many have become missionaries throughout India and Asia.

As stated previously a revival is generally referred to as a localised event, in a church, village or town, but an awakening refers to a move of God which has swept further afield, (and is bigger than a localised revival); in the same sense that a fire that is swept by the wind consumes and covers vast sways of countryside.

God is unchanging and what He has done, He can do again.

Dr. Martyn Lloyd-Jones said, "In revival you get this curious strange mixture as it were, of great conviction of sin and great joy, great sense of the terror of the Lord, great thanksgiving and praise. There is what somebody once called a 'divine disorder' always in revival, some groaning and agonising under conviction, others praising God for the great salvation. And all this leads to crowded and prolonged meetings, time seems to be forgotten, people seemed to have entered into eternity...time, the body, and the needs of the flesh are all forgotten. So then what really is revival? Days of heaven on earth."[1]

'Isaac dug again the wells of water which they had dug in the days of Abraham his father, for the Philistines had stopped them up after the death of Abraham. He called them by the names which his father had called them' Genesis 26:18.

Jonathan Edwards, Northampton 1734-1735
Jonathan Edwards had a revival in his parish of around 220 families in December 1734, in Northampton, Massachusetts, New England (America). It started when five or six people got wonderfully converted and a young lady started telling everyone about how she met the Saviour, who had given her a new heart; it had been truly broken and she was now truly sanctified. Edwards said, "The Spirit of those that have been in distress for the souls of others, so far as I can discern, seems not to be different from that of the apostles who travailed for souls."
On the evening of the day preceding the outbreak of revival, some Christians met, and spent the whole night in prayer. The whole town was affected. Edwards wrote:

'The work of conversion was carried on in a most astonishing manner, and increased more and more; souls did as it were come by flocks to Jesus Christ.'

Within six months around three hundred people were saved, to include children, adults and elderly alike and later on, 620 people were entitled to take communion at his church, including almost all the adults of the town. Some people came under such conviction that they were unable to sleep at night knowing the damnation that awaited them in hell!

The work of God was so great that by the second year. Edwards wrote: 'The town seemed to be full of the presence of God; it was never so full of love, nor of joy, and yet so full of distress, as it was then. There were remarkable tokens of God's presence in almost every house...The goings of God were seen in His sanctuary, God's day was a delight, and His tabernacles were amiable.' At the height of the revival at least four souls were saved each day, an average of thirty each week for five or six weeks during March and April 1735.[2]

American Great Awakening 1735-1760

The Great Awakening began in 1735, which was largely a continuation of Jonathan Edwards ministry in Northampton, New England. It continued for about twenty-five years and was powerful in many of the American States. The leaders were mainly Edwards, the Tennents, Davenport, and George Whitefield. From Northampton the revival spread to South Hadley, Suffield, Sunderland, Green River, West Springfield, Long Meadow, Enfield and Northfield. From these towns as the epicentre it spread throughout New England and the Middle States.

The preaching of Whitefield stirred the whole country, but he was preaching to those whose hearts were already prepared to meet with God and knew their need of a Saviour.

William Conant wrote: 'It cannot be doubted that at least 50,000 souls were added to the churches of New England, (those who could prove a confession of faith) out of a population of 250,000. A fact sufficient, as indeed it did, the religious and moral character, and to determine the destiny, of the country. Not less than 150 new Congregational churches were established in twenty years. The increase of Baptist churches in the last half of the century was still more wonderful, rising from nine to upwards of four hundred in number, with a total of thirty thousand members.' There was similar growth in the Presbyterian and other churches.

In this revival many people were stirred to share the good news with their neighbours, 'warning every man and exhorting them to turn to the Lord. There was a deep conviction of the evil of sin, and of peril of a rebellious state. The earnest appeals of those involved made the stout hearted tremble, awed many a reprobate into silence, and wrung tears from daring and hardened offenders...some of the most powerful preachers immigrated to other States and wherever they went, the floods of blessing poured over the land.'[3]

Howell Harris, Wales

In 1735 there arose an Elijah of his day amongst the Welsh valleys and mountains, Howell Harris (the son of a farmer), began to traverse the country of Wales, UK, in this year (the year of his conversion) and to his assistance came Daniel Rowlands, 'the thunderer' as he was called.[4]

Howell Harris was a young praying man and was baptised in the Holy Spirit early on from his conversion and instantly began to do the work of an evangelist, telling his former companions of the saving work of grace. He went from house to house and then into other villages and multitudes came to Christ. As a lay preacher (he was four times refused ordination!) he preached for hours at a time, even six hours! Howell Harris was a good organiser and formed Societies where his converts met for fellowship (this led to the beginning of the Welsh Calvinistic Methodism); Whitefield states that by 1739 there were thirty such Societies.[5]

Howell Harris met George Whitefield in 1739 (and they preached together in their respective languages). Howell Harris visited John Wesley in Bristol, England on the 18 June of the same year. Initially, Harris had been quite reluctant to meet the father of Methodism due to the many evil reports that had been given to him, but said after hearing him preach, "As soon as I heard you preach, I quickly found what spirit you were of. And before you were done, I was so over powered with joy and love that I had much ado [trouble] to walk home."[6]

John Wesley visited Wales in October 1739 and in his *Journal* wrote: 'I preached in the morning at Newport…to the most insensible ill-behaved people I have ever seen in Wales. One ancient man, during a great part of the sermon, cursed and swore almost incessantly; and, towards the conclusion, took up a great stone, which he many times attempted to throw. But that he could not do.' Wesley continued writing on another day, 'Most of the inhabitants are ripe for the Gospel, they are earnestly desirous of being instructed in it; and as utterly ignorant of it they are, as any Creek or Cherikee Indian. I do not mean they are ignorant of the name Christ. Many of them can both say the Lord's Prayer and the Belief, nay, and some all the Catechism: but take them out of the road of what they have learned by rote, and they know no more (nine in ten of those with whom I conversed) either of Gospel salvation, or of that faith whereby alone can we be saved, than Chicali or Tomo Chachi [American Indian tribes]. Now what spirit is he of, who had rather these poor creatures should perish for lack of knowledge, than that they should be saved, even by exhortations of Howell Harris, or an itinerant preacher?'[7]

In 1752 Howell Harris turned his New House in Trevecca, North Wales into a centre for revivalist activity. He later became associated with the Countess of Huntington, who after 1768 sent her own students for the ministry to Trevecca for training.[8]

The British Great Awakening 1739-1791

The British Great Awakening is also known as the Evangelical Revival, the Methodist Revival or the Wesleyan Revival. During this time a quarter of the population, approximately 1.25 million people were converted to the Lord Jesus Christ. Over a period of time many places, villages and towns were completely transformed, so much so that the whole character of the nation was changed. Many historians believe that it was because of this move of God that Britain did not have revolution like what happened with the French.

Prior to the time of the Great Awakening in Great Britain, the nation was in a desperate state, and the Church was just as bad. As Edward Miller, in his book, *John Wesley The Hero of the Second Reformation* wrote: 'When the Church fails in her mission, the whole of society becomes corrupt.'

Across Britain, before the Great Awakening there was a rise in deism, a decline of Christian observances, a massive rise in gin consumption and other alcoholic beverages which led to poverty and abuses within many families. Every sixth house in London was a grogshop (where spirits were sold, gin, rum etc.) and you could get drunk for a penny and dead drunk for two pence and even straw would be provided in the cellar to aid recovery from your carouse. In 1714, two million gallons of spirits was distilled; by 1742, it was seven million gallons and by 1750, it was more than eleven million. Vast sways of the Church were corrupt and the historian Montesquieu, stated that only four or five members of Parliament were regular attendants at church. The population had doubled (just under five million) since the settlement of the Church under Queen Elizabeth I, towns and cities had expanded greatly, but no endeavour had been made for any adequate religious instruction for these great masses.

This was the land and age of highway men in the countryside, burglars in the cities, profanity, bear-baiting, bull-baiting, prize-fighting, cock-fighting – the amusements of all classes were calculated to create a cruel disposition. It was the age of mobs and riots and the state of the criminal law was cruel in the extremes. There were no fewer than one hundred and sixty crimes for which a man, woman or child could be hanged! In the remote regions of England, such as Cornwall in the west, Yorkshire and Northumberland in the north and especially in the midland Staffordshire, the manners were wild and savage, passing all conception and description.[9]

In 1736, Archbishop Secker, Bishop of Oxford said, "That an open and professed disregard to religion is become, through a variety of unhappy causes, the distinguishing character of the present age; that this evil is grown to a great height of the nation and is daily spreading through every part of it."

Parliamentary life was rotten through and through. Walpole, the great leader, laughed aloud at appeals to the loftier motives of action. There was a great and growing neglect of Sunday among the ruling elite. Cabinet dinners, and even cabinet councils, were constantly held on that day. Sunday concerts and card-parties were common. Drunkenness was almost universal, and the drunkards walked unashamed.

In the higher ranks the young "Bloods" [nobility] often banded themselves together and paraded the streets in search of victims for what they were pleased to call their wit. Many a man, and many a woman died in their hands, in consequence of their ferocious treatment.[10]

In 1728, at Oxford University, Charles Wesley [the hymn writer and preacher] was called a "Methodist" because of his methodical study habits. Charles was to help found a holy club with his brother John. The Methodist Awakening was born in the power of the Holy Spirit. Wesley in his journal for the 1 January 1739 wrote: 'Mr Hall, Kinchin, Ingham, Whitefield, Hutchins, and my brother Charles, were present at our love-feast in Fetters Lane, with about sixty of our brethren. About three in the morning, as we were continuing instant in prayer, the power of God came mightily upon us, insomuch that many cried out for exceeding joy, and many fell to the ground. As soon as we were recovered a little from that awe and amazement at the presence of His Majesty, we broke out with one voice, "We praise thee, O God, we acknowledge thee to be the Lord." ' Of this love feast George Whitefield said, "It was a Pentecostal season indeed, sometimes whole nights were spent in prayer. Often we have been filled as with new wine, and often I have seen them overwhelmed with the Divine Presence, and cry out, "Will God, indeed, dwell with men on earth? How dreadful is this place! This is none other than the house of God, and the gate of heaven!" '

The Great Awakening began on the 17 February 1739, when George Whitefield preached to the colliers at Kingswood near Bristol in the open air as there was no church or school in this area. One writer wrote: 'Here lived a godless, ferocious race – men living beyond the pale of religion or even the law...they were a people apart, a byword for vice and crime.'[11] Two hundred people attended. Whitefield wrote: 'I thought I might be doing the service of my Master.' The second time he preached there were two thousand! Thousands of people heard him, and were deeply moved by his preaching. Soon ten or twenty thousand flocked to hear him. A gentleman lent him a large bowling green in the centre of Bristol and for six weeks he preached to vast congregations. Whitefield encouraged John Wesley to take charge of the work in Bristol and Kingswood whilst he visited other places. Wesley was preaching in London and finally relented and came to Bristol (even though he was preaching to hundreds in crowded churches and in the fields after service at St. Katherine's, Islington's and others places).

In London, John Wesley preached at Blackheath in mid-June 1739 (Whitefield was present) where twelve or fourteen thousand people had assembled. At 7am on a Sunday he preached in Upper Moorefield's to six or seven thousand people (Charles Wesley says, "above ten thousand as were supposed"), and at five in the evening to fifteen thousand at Kennington Common. The next Sunday Charles began field preaching having been driven from his curacy at Islington by the action of his churchwardens.[12]

Whitefield crossed the Atlantic thirteen times in total (he was also a major player in the American Great Awakening) and travelled extensively around the British Isles. He preached a total of 18,000 sermons in his lifetime. Wherever he went thousands gathered to hear the word of the Lord. He lived constantly with a clear realization of the reality of eternity: of heaven and hell, and that the eternity of souls was in the balance. Whitefield once said, "It is not for me to tell how often I use secret prayer; if I did not use it, nay, if in one sense, I did not pray without ceasing, it would be difficult for me to keep that frame of soul, which by Divine blessing, I daily enjoy."

John Wesley began preaching Methodism at Bristol in April 1739. The first Methodists conference was held in 1744. Wesley was banned from most public pulpits for his fiery sermons, preaching "justification by faith" and rode around the country preaching; revivals broke out everywhere. He rode annually between four-five thousand miles and would preach at 5am to crowds in excess of twenty thousand! He established in England more than one hundred preaching circuits and enlisted three hundred ministers and thousands of local lay preachers were making Jesus known.

John Wesley had three main bases, Bristol, London and Newcastle, and from these he pushed year after year, into remote and inaccessible corners of the kingdom, visiting the Channel Islands, crossing also into Ireland and penetrating far into Scotland and in his later life he visited Holland twice.

Methodism took root in North America where ideas of political independence from Britain were to merge with ideas of religious independence from the Church of England.

Wesley on his return from Georgia, America in 1738 until his death in 1791 preached 42,400 sermons, which was an average of fifteen per week for fifty-three consecutive years. 'Cheaper shorter, plainer books' was his motto and he kept up a constant supply of tracts pamphlets and sermons. Wesley was probably the most widely read person of his day and felt it his duty after reading a book to make comment on it and the author. His last words were, "The best of all is God is with us, farewell."

By 1791 there were seventy-nine thousand Methodists in England; in America, fifty thousand. In the various English preaching circuits there were three hundred preachers. And as one man once said, "The world has yet to see what God can do with one man who is wholly consecrated to Him."

There is one main blight on the history of the British Great Awakening and it was this, the doctrines of 'Election' (Calvinism) as preached by Whitefield, verses 'Free Grace' (Armenianism) as preached by the

Wesley's. This led to two camps being birthed within Methodism. The ironic thing is that these men of God were striving for the same goal, to preach Christ and to see men turn back to God, and regardless of their theology, God brought about revival wherever they went.

At the end of March 1741, Wesley went to hear Whitefield preach, having heard much of his unkind behaviour since his return from Georgia, New England (though this debate had been going on in private between them, Charles, the Moravians and their close associates for over a year). Wesley in his *Journal* wrote: 'He told me, he and I preach two different gospels; and, therefore, he not only would not join with, or give me the right hand of fellowship, but was resolved to publicly preach against me and my brother, wheresoever he preached at all.'

Whitefield then wrote a letter to John Wesley, which had been printed, without either party consenting and was distributed in great numbers. The Methodists foolishly decided to embrace one and denounce the other, so the Societies were divided. Whitefield then decided to print a letter that he had written in answer to Wesley's *Sermon on Free Grace*. Wesley in his *Journal* wrote: 'It was quite imprudent to publish it at all, being only the putting of weapons into their hands who loved neither the one nor the other.' Wesley also stated that if he wanted to write anything then he should not have called his name into question. Wesley continued, 'He has said enough of what wholly foreign to the question, to make an open (and probable, irreparable) breach between him and me; seeing "for a treacherous wound, and for the bewraying [betraying] of secrets, every friend will depart." ' Though they both met again in May 1742 when they were summoned before the Archbishop of Canterbury and the Bishop of London.[13]

In August 1743 John Wesley tried to arrange a conference, where he and his brother would be present along with Whitefield and the Moravians. He was even prepared to make concessions for the sake of the peace; but as neither Whitefield nor the Moravians would take part in the conference, the whole matter fell through.[14]

Within a decade their friendship had been healed as John Wesley in his *Journal,* on the 28 January 1750 wrote: 'I read prayers, and Mr Whitefield preached. How wise is God in giving different talents to different preachers.'[15]

George Whitefield died on the 10 November 1770 and by request of his executors (of his will) John Wesley preached at his funeral service a week later.[16]

Physical Manifestations

Under John Wesley's preaching (and George Whitefield's) there were physical manifestations, (as there has been in all revivals). Charles Wesley wrote: 'Many, no doubt, were, at our first preaching struck down, both soul and body, into the depth of distress. Their outward affections were to be easily imitated.'

Some of these manifestations were of the flesh (to which John Wesley rebuked), the majority were of God, when those under deep conviction of sin cried out, in screams and deep anguish of soul, some slumped to the ground, while others convulsed, shook, or trembled. Some of the manifestations were clearly demonic and the people concerned were delivered from the oppression of the devil when they cried out to God.

The first occurrence of these manifestations was on the 21 January 1739, when a well-dressed middle-aged woman cried out as in the agonies of death, which continued for some time. The doctors and clergy prior to this had thought she was mad, but the next day she told John Wesley that she had been under conviction of sin for three years but under Wesley's preaching had found hope.

Often in meetings, John Wesley would have to stop preaching because of the cries and groans of those under conviction of sin. Sometimes violent trembling seized its hearers and they sank to the ground. A Quaker who was greatly displeased at these sights dropped down in a moment. His agony was terrible to witness. Prayer was made and he soon cried out, "Now I know thou art a prophet of the Lord." Similar convulsion seized some of the John Wesley's hearers in Newcastle and London.

A physician who suspected that fraud had much to do with these manifestations was present at a meeting in Bristol. One woman who he knew, broke out 'into strong cries and tears.' He stood close to her observing every symptom, till great drops of perspiration ran down her face, and all her bones shook. He was puzzled at once, because he saw that this was neither fraud nor any natural disorder. When both body and soul were healed in a moment the doctor acknowledged the finger of God.[17]

John Wesley, noted in his *Journal* on the 15 June 1739 that whilst he was preaching at a society at Wapping, and 'earnestly exhorting sinners to "enter into the holiest" by this "new and living way" [Hebrews 10:19], many of those that heard began to call upon God with strong cries and tears. Some sunk down, and there remained no strength in them; others exceedingly trembled and quaked; some were torn with a kind of convulsive motion in every part of their bodies, and that so violently, that often four or five persons could not hold one of them. I have seen many epileptic fits, but none of them were like these in many respect. I immediately prayed that God would not suffer those who were weak [in the faith] to be offended. But one woman was greatly offended; being sure they might help if they would – no one should persuade her to the contrary; and was got three or four yards, when she also dropped down in as violent agony as the rest. Twenty-six of those who had been thus affected (most of whom, during the prayers which were made for them, were in a moment filled with peace and joy) promised to call on me the next day. But only eighteen came; by talking closely with whom, I found reason to believe that some of them had gone home to their house justified [saved and converted]'[18]

John Wesley on the 7 July 1739 had to talk to George Whitefield 'of those outward signs which had so often accompanied the inward work of God.' Wesley continued in his *Journal,* 'I found his objections were chiefly grounded on gross misrepresentations of matter of fact. But the next day he had opportunity of informing himself better: for no sooner had he begun (in the application of his sermon) to invite all sinners to believe in Christ, than four persons sunk down close to him, almost in the same moment. One of them lay without sense or motion. A second trembled exceedingly. The third had strong convulsions all over his body, but made no noise, unless by groans. The fourth equally convulsed, called upon God, with strong cries and tears. From this time on I trust, we shall all suffer God to carry on His work in the way that pleaseth Him.'[19]

Deliverance from demons

Wesley records in his *Journal* many instances of people being tormented and delivered from demons. On one occasion in November 1739 Wesley preached at a Society in Bristol. Five people were severely tormented and were ordered to be removed to the door as their cries were drowning out the preaching and interrupting the attention of the congregation. After the sermon Wesley and his companions prayed with them from evening till nine the next morning! Wesley wrote: 'Three of them sang praises to God; and the others were eased, though not set at liberty.'[20]

One lady who was about twenty, was being held down by three people, her face was deadly pale and into which was seen her anguish and horror. Wesley stated 'that it was a terrible sight...the thousand distortions of her whole body showed how the dogs of hell were gnawing her heart. The shrieks intermixed were scarce to be endured. She screamed..."I am damned, damned; lost forever...I am the devil's now. I have given myself to him. His I am. Him I must serve. With him I must go to hell." She then began praying to the devil.' Wesley stated that he and his companions prayed and called upon God, whilst another lady in the room began to roar out as loud as she could. Five hours later, 'God in a moment spoke peace into the soul, first of the tormented, and then of the other.'[21]

One man, John Haydon, a weaver, a godly churchman regular in all his life and habits heard of these strange fits and came to investigate. After the meeting he tried to persuade his friends that it was all a delusion of the wicked one. The day after the meeting he was at home reading a sermon, *Salvation by Faith* and as he read the last page, he changed colour, fell from his chair and began screaming terribly and beating himself against the ground. The neighbours flocked to see what was happening. Mrs Haydon tried to keep the people outside, but Mr Haydon said, "No; let them all come; let the world see the judgment of God." John Wesley was called for and saw Mr Haydon, on the floor being restrained by three men. Stretching out his hand John Haydon cried, "Ay this is he who, I said was a deceiver of the people. But God has overtaken me. I said it was all a delusion; but this is no delusion. He then roared out, "O thou devil! Thou cursed devil! Yea thou legions of devils! Thou canst stay. Christ will cast thee out. I know His work is begun." He then began to beat himself on the ground and perspired greatly as his chest heaved. Wesley and his friends prayed for him until he was set free.[22]

Transformation of a Nation

During and after the British Great Awakening, much has been recorded, how a collection of nations, England, Wales and Scotland were transformed to the glory of God, Ireland did not join Britain until 1801.[23] John Wesley preached in Scotland, but the Scots were not quite as affected as the rest of the Brits (see Appendix E).

Isaac Taylor said, "No such harvest of souls is recorded to have been gathered by any body of contemporary men since the first century;" and on the grounds of "expansive and adventurous Christian philanthropy," he held that the founders of Methodism had no rivals.

C. Grant Robertson, in his book, *England under the Hanoverians* wrote: 'Methodism and the French Revolution are the two most tremendous phenomena of the century [eighteenth century]. Wesley swept the dead air with an irresistible cleansing ozone. To thousands of men and women his preaching and gospel revealed a new heaven and a new earth; it brought religion into soulless lives and reconstituted it as a comforter, an inspiration and a judge. No one was too poor, too humble, too degraded, to be born again and share in the privilege of divine grace, to serve the one Master, Christ, and to attain the blessed fruition of God's peace. Aloof alike from politics and the speculations of the schools, Wesley wrestled with the evil of his day and proclaimed the infinite power of a Christian faith based on personal conviction, eternally renewed from within, to battle sin, misery and vice in all its forms. The social service that he accomplished was not the least of his triumphs.

'It is certain that into the moral fibre of the English people, even in the classes most anxious to repudiate the debt, were woven new strands by the abiding influence of Methodism…'

Bishop Ryle, (from the nineteenth century) said, "These times were the darkest age that England has passed through in the past three hundred years. Anything more deplorable than the condition of the country, as to religion, morality and high principles, it is very difficult to conceive."

British Prime Minster, David Lloyd George on the 20 June 1922 said, "I come from a country that owes more to the Methodism Movement, of which Wesley was the inspirer and prophet and leader, than to any other movement in the whole of its history. He was undoubtedly the greatest religious leader the Anglo-Saxon race ever produced, and the movement of which he was the leader, probably the greatest religious movement in the past 250 years at least. Its influence, just like that of the Reformation – its indirect influence was probably greater than even its direct influence. That is the story of all great religious reformations. He founded a great religious community." Methodism "gave a new spiritual life to the whole community."

E. Paxton Hood in his book, *Vignettes of the Great Revival* wrote: 'There was a deeper upheaving of religious life, and far more widely spread, than perhaps any age of the world since the time of the apostles had known before.

'A change passed over the whole of the English society. The language of impurity indulged with freedom by the dramatists when the revival arose, and read aloud, by ladies and young girls in drawing-rooms, or by parlour firesides, became shameful and dishonoured. In the course of fifty years, society, if not entirely purged – for when may we hope for that blessedness? – was purified. A sense of religious decorum, and some idea of religious duty, took possessions of homes and minds which were not all impressed either by the doctrines or the discipline of Methodism. All this arose from the new life which had been created.

'It was a fruitful soil upon which the revivalist worked. There was a reverence for the Bible as the word of God, a faith often held very ignorantly, but it pervaded the land. The Book was there in every parish church, and in every hamlet; it became a kind of nexus of union for true minds when they felt the power of Divine principles.'

For me personally, I draw great encouragement from reading about the British Great Awakening. I have heard it often said that today's society is the worst that it has ever been. But Wesley's *Journal* completely debunks this myth – just read it for yourself. Whilst there is much evil in society today, godlessness and false spirituality, society in general has improved since the days of Wesley and Whitefield, though we still have a long, long way to go. In those days there was not even a police force, missionary society or welfare system. Mankind is still incredibly evil and rebellious towards God, but where sin abounds grace abounds more. Personally, I believe that the next revival within the United Kingdom (according to the prophets and revelations {some of which are recorded in chapters seventeen and eighteen} will flow from the north of Scotland, to the south of England and into Europe and beyond) and will surpass the Wesleyan Revival, in percentage of conversions per head of population. God is willing, God is able, but are we prepared to pay the price?

"The glory of this latter temple shall be greater than the former, says the Lord of Hosts. 'And in this place I will give peace,' says the Lord of Hosts" Haggai 2:9.

CHAPTER FOUR
Times of Refreshing (Acts 3:19)

'Unto You I lift up my eyes, O You who dwell in the heavens. Behold, as the eyes of servants look to the hand of their masters, as the eyes of a maid to the hand of her mistress, so our eyes look to the Lord our God until He has mercy on us' Psalm 123:1-2.

'For the Lord will not cast off His people, nor will He forsake His inheritance' Psalm 94:14.

Dundee and Kilsyth 1839

Rev. William Chalmers Burns, a missionary in waiting, preached for a time in the church of Mr Robert McCheyne, at St. Peter's, Dundee, Scotland, UK. In April 1837 McCheyne due to his strenuous work load had a break down and developed heart trouble and so went to Edinburgh to recuperate. He then travelled on to Palestine (modern day Israel). Whilst away from his flock he did not cease to pray for them in agony of soul and travail. It was one day while he was on the brink of eternity in far-off Bouja that the great showers of blessing began to fall in Dundee.[1]

Prior to the outpouring in Dundee the Rev. Burns went to the communion at Kilsyth, a quiet country village, where on the 23 July 1839 the Lord began to employ him in a way so remarkable for the awakening of sinners. As he preached in the market place a large assembly gathered, but as the rains came they entered the church which was soon filled to overflowing, even the porch was blocked with eager listeners. Solemn prayer was offered and Rev. Burns preached from Psalm 110:3 after having read from Acts chapter two. As he spoke hearts were melted and tears began to flow. At the close of the meeting he retold the story of the Shotts Revival in 1630; how John Livingstone a native of Kilsyth, in preparation for an after-communion service, spent a whole night in prayer and that the following day five hundred people were converted after hearing him preach. As the Rev. Burns was speaking he could see that the Spirit was moving and felt compelled to urge his hearers to accept Christ there and then and closed with the words, "No cross, no crown." Suddenly the whole audience broke down and cries of mercy went up before God. Some remained under conviction for days and the church was open daily for services for many months. In the market place and in the church yard crowds of up to four thousand would gather to hear the word of the Lord. The whole town was changed as the vice of drinking took a fatal blow and loom shops became a place of prayer.[2]

On returning to Dundee, a large manufacturing town, amidst such a continued spiritual awakening, Rev. Burns decided to defer his missionary call, but not relinquish and to remain where he was, to fulfil the work which God was laying upon him with His mighty hand. On the 10 August, a week day prayer meeting, he spoke of the wonder that he had witnessed at Kilsyth and challenged those present to stay behind 'who felt the need of an outpouring of the Spirit to convert them.' About one hundred waited behind and the Spirit came as Rev. Burns spoke and the entire congregation was bathed in tears. This work of God carried on for four months, the church became packed night after night and the whole city was moved. A great spirit of reverence came upon the community, and sin was greatly restrained.[3]

A member of the congregation of St. Peter's wrote: 'Scarcely had Mr Burns entered the work at St. Peter's here, when his power as a preacher began to be felt. Gifted with solid and vigorous understanding, possessed of a voice of vast compass and power, and withal fired with an ardour so intense and an energy so exhaustless that nothing could damp or resist it, Mr Burns wielded an influence over the masses which was almost without parallel since the days of Wesley and Whitefield. Crowds flocked to St. Peter's from all the country round; and the strength of the preacher seemed to grow with the incessant demands made upon it. He was frequently at Kilsyth, labouring in connection with a remarkable religious awakening which was going on there. The word of the Lord mightily grew and prevailed. Mr Burns was full of prayer; his preaching was sensible, clear, orthodox, unobjectionable; and in that he never altered, for in the midst of all the excitement there was never any eccentricity or extravagance. He never expected conversion by any means but the plainly-stated gospel, and the power of the Divine Spirit to accompany it.'[4]

Mr Bonar in his memoirs of Mr McCheyne, wrote: 'For some time before, Mr Burns had seen the symptoms of deeper attention than usual, and real anxiety in some that had hitherto been careless. But it was after his return that the people began to melt before the Lord.' Mr McCheyne returned from the Holy Land in late November 1839, when Rev. Burn's connection with St. Peter's ceased.

In Dundee the scenes at Kilsyth were repeated. Mr Bonar wrote: 'The crowded and deeply attentive assembled in the church from night to night, for months together; the eager throngs of enquirers, sometimes so numerous as to be really themselves a congregation; the varied and weighty instructions of ministers, followed generally by more special counsels and prayers for those whose overmastering anxiety constrained them to remain behind; the numberless prayer meetings (one author puts the prayer meetings at thirty-nine, which were held weekly in connection with the church, five of these were carried on wholly by children![5]) of old and young, in private rooms, in workshops, in retired gardens, in open fields; the nightly journey of thirsty souls from far distances in the outskirts of the city, and in the rural parishes around; the general sensation and spirit of inquiry were here as none who live through it, and entered in any measure into the feeling of it can never have forgotten.'[6]

'...I will remember the years of the right hand of the Most High. I will remember the works of the Lord; surely I will remember Your wonders of old. I will also meditate on all Your works, and talk of Your deeds' Psalm 77:10b-12.

Awakening in America 1857-1858

This awakening in America is also known as the Prayer Meeting Revival. Within the space of two years, during the awakening in America one million people had become "born again" and another one million church members were set ablaze.

The Prayer Meeting Movement in New York started when Mr Jeremiah C. Lamphier, (some authors spell his name with an 'n' Lanphier) a lay missionary was greatly burdened for souls. Most days he would be found in the lecture room of an old Dutch church on Fulton Street, New York City. He decided to invite others to join him and then announced a weekly meeting to be held at noon, beginning on the 23 September 1857. Before long, due to the numbers attending the meeting was held daily.

The autumn of 1857 was signalised by a sudden and fearful convulsion in the commercial world, as sources of prosperity dried up. Thousands lost their jobs, masses of people tramped the streets with banners demanding bread. People started to attend the established prayer meetings, many searching for salvation, others killing time. The Fulton Street hall grew too small so the meeting was moved to the largest hall in the city with seating capacity for four thousand!

Other prayer meetings were birthed in New York, Philadelphia and beyond and many businessmen and workers would take their lunch hour and go to these prayer meetings which lasted exactly an hour. In other places daily prayer meetings were held in the evenings. In New York, a hymn would be sung and then prayer began, along with prayer requests and testimony of answered prayer. No person was permitted to openly pray for more than five minutes, so that others present would have an opportunity. Prayer was for conversions, for their city, for help in honest dealing in business, for healing etc. Many merchants and businessmen got right with God and started to deal honestly, even debts of more than two decades previous were repaid in full and those who had overcharged made restitution. One merchant within New York told the people that 50,000 professed to be Christians within this city and the way to reach the 1,000,000 residents was to take an individual or family under ones special supervision and to lead them to Christ.

Even the crime rate during the winter of 1857-1858 dropped, and under the circumstances of mass unemployment it could have been expected to rise. The wealthy looked upon the under classes as their brothers and sisters in Christ and their physical needs were met, but their spiritual needs were deemed more important.

In 1859, on the second anniversary of the first noon prayer meeting a convention was assembled in Cooper Institute, New York City, to consider the means to sustain and enlarge the influence of the meetings. Representatives came from as far away as San Francisco. In Boston a man stood up in one of the meetings and said, "I am from Omaha, Nebraska. On my journey east I have found a continuous prayer meeting. We call it about two thousand miles from

Boston to Omaha, and here was a prayer meeting about two thousand miles in length."[7]

The New York dailies (newspapers) published several extras filled with accounts of the progress of the work in various parts of the land. In Pennsylvania some lumbermen visited Philadelphia where Charles Finney was holding evangelistic meetings and they got converted. They returned home to their kinsfolk which was known as the lumber region and five thousand people were converted along an area of eighty miles and there was not a single minister of the gospel there![8]

Charles Finney stated of this revival that the winter of 1857-1858, will be remembered as a time when a great revival prevailed. It swept over the land with such power, that for a time it was estimated that no less than 50,000 conversions occurred weekly. The lay influence predominated to such an extent that ministers were overshadowed. This awakening was not a remote piety in little corners of churches, but to the fore of everyday business life, college life and home life. It was right there in the nitty-gritty of everyday work, not just a Sunday affair. The awakening became known as the Prayer Meeting Revival, as from its beginning it was marked far and wide with fervent prayer.

Promoter of genuine revival J. Edwin Orr after long and careful research endorsed the estimate that one million people were fully converted out of a population less than thirty million in the period of 1858-1859. These converts were solid, lasting, genuine converts.[9]

During the American awakening, The *Methodist advocate* – January 1858 reported ten noteworthy features of the revival: 1. Few sermons were preached; 2. Lay brethren were eager to witness; 3. Seekers flocked to the altar; 4. Nearly every seeker had been blessed; 5. Experiences enjoyed remained clear; 6. Converts were filled with holy boldness; 7. Religion became a day-time social topic; 8. Family altars were strengthened; 9. Testimony given nightly was abundant; 10. Conversation was marked by a pervading seriousness.[10]

Welsh Revival 1859-1860

Rev. Humphrey R. Jones (a Wesleyan) and Rev. David Morgan (a Calvinistic Methodist), were the main instigators of this Welsh revival. It was estimated that 300,000 people were saved and at least 50,000, who could prove a confession of faith became a member of an established church. At the same time in 1859, a revival was underway in Ireland which later broke out in parts of Scotland and England, as the blessing of the manifold presence of the Holy Spirit came and convicted sinners of their need for the Saviour.

The Rev. Jones had been touched in America during the 1858 revival and wanted to see the fire fall in Wales. As reports filtered through from America, many Welsh churches held a day of prayer for revival on the first Sunday in August 1858. The Rev. Jones returned in September with glowing reports to tell. The two ministers, Jones and Morgan and their churches came together for prayer, to hold joint services and to arouse the country in prayer. The Rev. Morgan received a remarkable endowment of power from on high and became the main leader (amongst many) and thousands were converted. As other churches heard these good reports, they sent for these men and revival broke out around the country and by August 1859 most of the southern counties of Wales were crowded on a Sunday and week days. Prayer meetings, morning and evening were held everywhere.[11]

Some of the young converts from a local church near Morlais Castle decided to invade the devil's territory, where every Sunday men from the local iron works used to congregate to get drunk and fight. As they made their intentions known to pray and praise, the intoxicated men jeered and laughed them to scorn. But the faithful believers knew who had the victory and began to sing a Welsh hymn, which was rich and melodious. The men were so overcome by the Spirit of God that tears rolled down many a hardened face and the beer was thrown away. Within one month hundreds were holding revival meetings on the highest summit of Morlais Castle.[12]

'...For He is good, for His mercy endures forever' 2 Chronicles 7:3.

Irish and Scottish Revivals 1859-1860

The Irish Revival (also known as the Ulster Revival) had its beginning when four young men who lived in different villages became so encouraged by the work of faith in the life of George Müller in Bristol (with his orphanages) that they began to meet together for secret prayer and fellowship. These men were already attending the Tannybrake Sabbath-School weekly prayer meetings which had begun in 1857, and as a result they soon noticed a marked increase of attention amongst the children which encouraged them to step out deeper. The men began meeting together in the neighbourhood of Kells, (a central location) in September 1857 (some sources state in October), the same month and year as Fulton Street, New York City, prayer meeting began, though unknown to each other. They prayed that, "Their labours and that of others might be eminently owned by God." From this prayer meeting many were birthed, but it took nearly two years before large numbers of visible results were seen as sinners came under deep conviction of sin.

The Rev. J. H. Moore of Conner, inspired by the revival in America encouraged his flock to pray for revival. He preached and taught his congregation on the subject of revival and read accounts of past revivals; the idea of God coming down and touching the people finally gripped his congregation and it became a subject for serious prayer. The Rev. Moore later reported, 'that there was no human leader in this movement; the Holy Spirit was the leader.'

Ulster alone saw 100,000 profess Christ as Lord and Saviour. From Ulster the revival spread to Cavan County. In Corglass, a church was crowded inside and outside. As the preacher preached, people fell to the floor slain under conviction of sin. The entire graveyard was full of prostrate people in deep weeping and anguish of soul, and that at ten o'clock at night!

In Coleraine upon seeing the fire fall in Ballymena, both churchmen and dissenters forgot their differences and joined in united prayer for the blessing of God.

The west of Scotland is closely related to the north of Ireland and from Ireland the fires flowed to Scotland. As visitors told of the stories from Ireland, the Scots started prayer meetings and prayed like never before. On the 10 August 1859, the General Assembly of the Free Church of Scotland sent out a call to prayer. It said, "The Commission also feels the deep solemnity of our position as a church in such circumstances. These events which have recently taken place in America, in Wales, in Ireland and to a small extent in Scotland, strikingly illustrate the Sovereign Power of the Holy Spirit and the efficacy of believing prayer and ought to encourage us to attempt great things for God and to expect great things from God, and they call upon all ministers and people of this Church earnestly to pray that God may be graciously pleased to pour out His Holy Spirit abundantly upon our land that His work may be revived everywhere." People began to pray in churches, at home, in shops and even in the University of Edinburgh.

In Scotland, it was estimated that ten percent of the population were converted! That was 300,000 conversions out of a population of three million Scots![13]

An Ulster minister wrote, 'After examining the facts as far as I could gather them, I judge that not less than 100,000 persons in Ulster were brought under gracious influence during that time. The revival had the help of almost the entire secular press. It was not confined to any one denomination, but embraced all evangelical churches; and up till the present time, all those have maintained unprecedented unity. I consider it the most glorious work of God ever known in this country in so short a time.'[14]

'At the Quarter-Sessions for Londonderry, in April 1860 held before Wm. Armstrong, Esq., Assistant-Barrister, there was no criminal business, and his worship was presented with a pair of white gloves.'[15]

Towards the end of the revival in Ireland in 1860, the effects of the revival were renewed and summarised as follows: 1. The preaching services were thronged; 2. Numbers of communicants were unprecedented; 3. Prayer meetings were abundant; 4. Family prayers were increased; 5. Scripture reading was unmatched; 6. Sunday schools were prosperous; 7. Converts remained generally steadfast; 8. Liberality seemed greatly increased; 9. Vice was abated; and 10. Crime was much reduced.[16]

English Revival 1859-1860

England was the last place in the Anglo-Saxon world to experience the revival which swept the world. Reports from America and other parts of Great Britain stirred the hearts of the English. The revivals were reported in many of the religious periodicals in England. Early in June 1858, a prayer meeting of forty people soon grew to four hundred in Exeter as the faithful sought God to pour out His Spirit from on high.

On the 29 November 1858, the Lodiani Mission in north India held its twenty-third annual conference. The theme was revival and how could they receive the same blessing like America. This led them to issue a worldwide proclamation for a week of prayer for revival for the second week of 1860. In November 1859, a circular letter was issued containing the Lodiani invitation and the endorsement of forty-one ministers of England. In London during the week of prayer, January 1860, there were at least two hundred prayer meetings in the capital alone. After the week of prayer many continued to seek God and beseech Him for His mercy to rain down from on high.

In Newcastle-on-Tyne, a united prayer meeting was held for over a year before any great results were seen. In Leeds, within a month one church had received one hundred new members after the union prayer meetings had begun and were still going strong by February 1860. In Staffordshire, prayer meetings and Bible studies were held in the mines as hundreds of colliers were converted, along with drunks and a multitude of vices were stopped. Daily meetings for prayer and Bible readings were held right in the pits! In one locality 500 people professed conversion.

An eye-witness from Bicester said, "It is not asserting too much to say that a greater number of sinners have been converted to God in Bicester, and within eight miles of it, during the last ten months than have made an open profession of religion during the last two hundred years."[17]

Charles H. Spurgeon, London, England
Charles H. Spurgeon, the 'Prince of Preacher,' saw hundreds come to Christ in his 6,000-seat Metropolitan Tabernacle during the 1859-1860 English Revival.

During his ministry in London it has been estimated that 14,000 new members joined his congregation which resulted in many churches being planted around the city.[18]

Charles H. Spurgeon in his autobiography reveals the secret of his ministry. He said, "When I came to New Park Street Chapel [London, in 1854], it was but a mere handful of people to whom I first preached; yet I can never forget how earnestly they prayed. Sometimes they seemed to plead as though they could really see the Angel of the covenant present with them, and as if they must have a blessing from Him. More than once, we were all so struck with the solemnity of the meeting, that we sat silent for some moments while the Lord's power appeared to overshadow us; and all I could do was to pronounce the Benediction, and say, 'Dear friends, we have had the Spirit of God here very manifestly tonight; let us go home and take care not to lose His gracious influences.'

"Then came down the blessing; the house was filled with hearers, and many souls were saved. I always give the glory to God, but do not forget that He gave me the privilege of ministering first to a praying people. We had prayer meetings that moved every soul...each one appeared determined to storm the Celestial City by the might of intercession; and soon the blessing came upon us in such abundance that we had not room enough to receive it."[19]

CHAPTER FIVE
Rend the Heavens! (Isaiah 64:1)

'Restore us, O God of our salvation, and cause Your anger towards us to cease. Will You not revive us again that Your people may rejoice in You? Show us Your mercy, O Lord and grant us Your salvation.' Psalm 85:4, 6-7.

'Restore us, O God; cause Your face to shine, and we shall be saved!' Psalm 80:3.

Revival in Cornwall 1861

William Booth's love for God and his fellow man led him into the Methodist Church, but the Methodist's later kicked him out of the church and withdrew his membership as they found it hard to accept his fiery open-air preaching at Kennington Common.

In 1855, aged twenty-six, Booth was sent out as a travelling evangelist under more spiritual Methodists. As a circuit preacher, God's hand was very evident upon him as he saw on average, twenty-three new converts a day!

In 1858, Booth was ordained as the Rev. William Booth, and became a Methodist pastor of a large church in Gateshead.

In 1860, his wife Catherine started to preach as she felt compelled by the Spirit of God and could not stay silent any longer; her husband was so impressed by her anointing that his views on women preachers radically changed.

A turning point in the life of Rev. Booth was when he had a vision of a black dark stormy sea of the perishing lost which he never forgot. In the vision he saw and heard the screams and shrieks of those bobbing and struggling for air, as the waves crashed over them and the lightning and the wind struck and howled overhead. Out of the sea rose a great rock where survivors had clambered but stayed in leisurely pursuits and pastimes, not caring for those who were struggling around the base. Some even argued about how best to save the drowning but still did nothing. But there was the Wonderful Being, who came to aid those who were drowning and He beckoned to the other survivors to assist Him but they wanted to be comforted, and wanted Him to come to them to give them more reassurance.

In 1861, Rev. Booth, whilst at the Methodist New Connexion's Annual Conference, asked to be released from his duties so as to be able to evangelise more, but the committee wanted to promote him to the Superintendent of the whole Newcastle District. Within two months Rev. Booth resigned his positions due to the burden of administration which was not as important as the burden he had for souls. Booth and his wife Catherine headed for Hayle, Cornwall where 7,000 Cornishmen were converted in just eighteen months.[1]

By 1865, Booth was in the East End of London preaching to crowds in the streets when he was invited to hold an evangelistic campaign on an old burial ground in Whitechapel. Rev. Booth later to be known as General Booth founded The East London Christian Mission which was renamed in May 1878, The Salvation Army.

Revival in Ghana 1875-1877

English born Thomas Birch Freeman (1809-1886) was the free son of a slave, (hence the surname), of supposed West Indian origin. In January 1838, he began his pioneering work along the Gold Coast of West Africa (modern day Ghana, Togo, Benin and Nigeria) and laboured there as part of the Wesleyan Missionary Society until he resigned due to differences.

His pioneering work lasted nearly fifty years of service amongst fierce tribes, fetish priests, native kings and their customs, and the cruel, inhuman rituals of human sacrifice and slavery for profit.

In October 1875, Bishop Freeman visited Kuntu, an outstation of Anamabu, where he found the Christians greatly quickened and in great spiritual expectancy. During his preaching the people were moved and cried aloud. As they knelt penitently at the communion rail, many trembled exceedingly, and clutched the rail to prevent them from falling. A few days later communion was conducted at Anamabu where three hundred partook. In the same month Freeman visited Cape Coast, and alongside the native minister Andrew W. Parker, a special meeting was conducted for penitents. Cries of mercy resounded around the school-room. Many found the peace of God and the others moved to a house and continued all night in prayer. At Salt Pond and Accra the same happened as the churches burst at the seams and spilled into the streets.

At Elmina, the chapel was full, as people stood outside by the doors and windows. Freeman wrote: 'There was a gracious influence resting on the congregation. We invited the penitents to the communion rail, to which they came in crowds. The Blessed Spirit brooded over us, and we had a fine revival meeting. Scores of the congregation were in tears and crying for mercy and many found peace and joy in believing. At Kormantine, the people 'cried mightily to the Lord for salvation.' Leaving the chapel Freeman preached to the fishermen in the open air, 'who were greatly moved by the truths declared.'

One lady had to have her wedding delayed by a few hours, as in the morning prayer meeting she was prostrate on the floor in intercession for souls. Such were the number now attending church at Cape Coast, discussion commenced about enlarging the Wesleyan

Church. Freeman warned his leader about excesses and advised them how to act during the revival. 'Less the people come to think that loud cries and trembling as a necessary part, or as adjuncts to conversion.'

In Anamabu, Freeman's wife wrote for him to return as the chapel was overflowing into the streets. She wrote: 'While one girl was praying and crying all that were in the chapel trembled.' Another letter said, 'One of our sisters, as she was passing along the street, met a group of about twelve heathen people, men and women, from the fishing quarters of town, who were saying, "We will go to chapel to be Christians; we will go and give ourselves to God omnipotent." '

In early December 1875, Freeman revisited Salt Pond, where the candidates for baptism, occupied a line of benches forty-seven paces long. On the same day he returned to Anamabu where two hundred and twelve people were baptised in the presence of hundreds. The author continues that there were many extraordinary cases of people trembling violently, loud cries, which might rank with some recorded in John Wesley's journal.

One day in January, Freeman baptised two hundred and sixty adults and children, one of whom was the head of a pagan family who was formerly an extravagant drinker of rum, which was connected as part of a ritual with the burial of the dead.

On the 9 April 1876, one thousand Christians flocked to the Gold Coast, at Great Kormantine village camp meeting. Fifteen hundred people partook of the love feast later that day. Freeman remarked, "It may be deemed important to notice that the extraordinary meetings in *feeding the revival* has been their suitableness to the national genius of the people. In their pagan life they are accustomed to frequent and extensive gatherings in their occasional and annual customs. Thus the national habits have been utilised to promote the spread of the gospel, and to uplift the Church of Christ into a higher atmosphere of Christian life."

In 1876, four thousand five hundred natives were baptised. Whole villages forsook their pagan ways and idols to serve the Living God. By the end of 1877, no less than three thousand more persons had been added to the church and fifteen hundred had been baptised by Freeman himself and still the revival continued.[2]

China and Japan 1885

In February 1885, the Cambridge Seven departed London, England and arrived in Shanghai, China after a six week journey. The Rev. W. W. Cassels, one of the Seven wrote: '[there was] an almost overwhelming thought of the enormous work which has to be done here. Even in a place like Shanghai, which I suppose to be the centre of missionary activity, how many thousands there are entirely untouched by the efforts at present put forth! If this is of Shanghai what shall we say of the rest of the country. We felt more than ever that nothing but a mighty outpouring of the Spirit of God can be of any use…how one longs to be able to speak the language and talk to these dear people!'[3]

Mr Montagu Beauchamp, another of the Seven in a letter from Shanghai dated 25 April 1885 wrote: 'We had meetings twice and sometimes three times a day. We were quite a large gathering; no less than sixteen of us…we took as our subject "In Christ." One Sunday evening we had the Lord's Supper, which was a very precious time together…we were abundantly rewarded by a special manifestation of the presence of the MASTER Himself. At this meeting we may attribute special blessing to the fact that every one present contributed something to the edifying of the Body; though in some cases it was only a Scripture…'

A circular letter from missionaries in Peking dated 22 June 1885, 'Dear brothers...in the afternoon meetings [two hours each] they dwelt largely on the theme that the baptism of the Holy Ghost was promised to all believers...our object in these has been, first, the baptism of the Holy Spirit on our hearts, giving power for our work, and second, the outpouring of the Spirit on China. The present revival in Japan began with a daily prayer meeting. If we would all unite, have we not faith to believe that God would shake China with His power? Yours in the Gospel. Signed by twenty-five missionaries of eight different organisations, including the Inspector-General of I.M. Customs, Peking.[4]

Prayer for World Revival 1885

In August 1855, Dwight L Moody, with several hundred delegates attended a ten day convention in Northfield, America where they discussed and prayed for world revival. On the 10 August, the sixth day, Dr. Pierson warmly contended that the promise of supernatural power with the preaching of the gospel, accompanied by supernatural signs, is as binding today as when it was made by the departing Saviour. A circular letter was soon prepared, made by resolution and carried by acclamation in the name of the convention to all believers throughout the world. The letter went as follows, 'To fellow believers of every name scattered through the world, greetings: Assembled in the name of our Lord JESUS CHRIST, with one accord in one place, we have continued for ten days in prayer and supplication, communing with one another about the common salvation, the blessed hope, and the duty of witnessing to a lost world.

'It was near our place of meeting that in 1747, at Northampton, Mass, Jonathan Edwards sent forth his trumpet peal calling upon all disciples everywhere to unite in prayer for an infusion of the Spirit upon the whole habitable globe. That summons to prayer marked a new epoch in the Church of God. Praying bands began to gather in this and other lands. Mighty revivals of religion followed; immorality and infidelity were wonderfully checked [put to an end]; and after 1,500 years of apathy and lethargy, the spirit of mission was reawakened. In 1792, the monthly concert was begun, and the first missionary society was formed in England. In 1793, William Carey, the pioneer missionary sailed for India. Since then over 100 missionary boards [societies] have been organised, and probably no less than 100,000 missionaries including women have gone out into the mission field...results of missionary labour in the Hawaiian and Fiji islands, Madagascar, in Japan, probably have no parallel even in apostolic days, while even Pentecost is surpassed by the ingathering of 10,000 converts in one station in India within sixty days in the year 1868...God has thus in answer to prayer opened the door of access to the nations...The first Pentecost covered ten days of united, continued supplication. Every subsequent advance may be divinely traced to believing prayer, and upon this must depend a new Pentecost. We therefore earnestly appeal to all disciples to join us in importunate and daily supplications for a new and mighty infusion of the Holy Spirit on all ministers, missionaries, pastors, teachers, and Christian workers and upon the whole earth, that God would impart to all Christ's witnesses the tongues of fire, and melt hard hearts before the burning message. It is not by might, but by the Spirit of the Lord that all true success must be secured; let us call upon God till He answereth by fire! What we are to do for the salvation of the lost must be done quickly, for the generation is passing away, and we with it...'Thy Kingdom come.' '[5]

Edwin Orr was asked by a Danish newspaper editor, "What in your opinion is the greatest hindrance to world-revival?" To which he responded, "...the indifference of believers themselves. Revival will come to us – only by the way of obedience to the word, of living faith, and of unceasing prayer – when as Paul wrote in Romans 12:2, we present our bodies as a living, holy, and God-acceptable sacrifice"[6]

The Welsh Revival 1904-1905

Wales has long been known as the 'Land of Revivals.' Between 1762 and 1862 there were at least sixteen outstanding revivals. Some were localised, while others were far reaching in their effect. 'Many of the famous preachers of Wales attributed their spiritual birth and their ministerial power to movings of the Spirit felt at such times,'[7] whilst for others it was a vitalisation, a recharging, a fresh impetus for their already successful ministry.

In 1904 revival broke out in Moriah Chapel, Lougher, South Wales, UK on the 31 October; as Evan Roberts' call went forth to the Lord in the presence of the youth meeting, "Send the Spirit now for Jesus Christ's sake" and the youthful congregation of seventeen persons followed suit. Within a week the local and national papers got a hold of the move of God and free advertisement through its reporting began to spread, which drew people who were hungry for God from across the globe.

Of all the revival locations I have visited, Moriah Chapel is the one I have most frequented over the years and have always been met with a warm reception from the elders and congregational members. The revival itself actually broke out in the small school room which is adjacent to the main Chapel. In 2004 the centenary celebration of the Welsh Revival was held in the main Chapel and was packed to maximum capacity which it had not seen since March 1969, the sixty-fifth anniversary of the 1904-1905 Welsh Revival when Dr. Eifion Evans preached in English in the morning service and Dr. Martyn Lloyd-Jones preached in Welsh at the evening service. Evan Roberts is buried in the graveyard in the family plot which is located behind the chapel. The Presbyterian Church of Wales erected a granite memorial column outside the chapel with an inscription in Welsh and English to the memory of Evan Roberts and the Welsh Revival, as a testimony for future generations.

At around the same time, as the revival which began at Lougher spread south, revival broke out in Rhos, South Wales, and spread north. The Wrexham Advertiser (newspaper) reported, 'The prayer meetings are so crowded that the places of worship are inadequate to contain them. Some last eight hours, with no cessation in prayer or singing! From the lips of the humblest and lowliest put forth petitions which thrill the whole being – the spell of earthly things seem to be broken. In the streets, in the train, in the car, even in public houses, all this is, in hushed and reverential tones, the theme of conversation.'[8]

Evan Roberts received invitations from numerous churches and chapels around South Wales and beyond. Within six weeks, 100,000 souls were swept into the Kingdom of God (some authors incorrectly state that 100,000 souls were converted in total) at the time the population of Wales was only around one million and within eight months 150,000 had made application for church membership. Revival historian, J. Edwin Orr stated that as many as 250,000 people could have been converted during this revival, those who emigrated, moved away to other towns outside of Wales or who attended a non-established church (Mission Halls etc.) would not have been recorded on official church membership roles.

Sadly many churches and Christians rejected the revival and doors were bolted shut to Evan Roberts. As the Holy Spirit flowed through the valleys, some villages were entirely bypassed.[9]

Leonard Ravenhill stated that when Evan Roberts visited Anglesey, North Wales, there were open manifestations of the Spirit of God in at least five places. Roberts knew that God was there and simply told the people, "Obey God" and left them to it.[10]

The daily shifts at the mines soon started with a word of prayer. Miners would become aware of the presence of God while deep in the mines and fall on their knees in repentance. The mineshafts resonated with the hymns of the converted miners who were so taken up into glory and this was whilst doing their hard labour and intensive work. Some of the miners were so changed by God that the pit ponies which were used to being commanded by the unconverted foul mouths refused to work as they could not recognise the sanctified tongues! Many of the workers drinking songs had their lyrics changed and sanctified to suit the well known and popular tunes. In church services people would cry out, 'What must I do to be saved?' others would cry out 'O God forgive me' as the weight of their sins came upon them in deep reality.

In the Rhondda Valley and beyond, the magistrates were given white gloves (a symbol of purity) as there were so few cases to hear – God's Spirit that brought conviction of sin (which eventually led to salvation as people called upon God), brought about changed lives, sobriety and restraint. White gloves were also handed out in Swansea County Court; Aberdare and on Christmas Eve, Aberdare was almost entirely free from drunkenness and on Christmas Day there were no prisoners at all in the cells. At Abercarn Police Court, responsible for a population of 21,000 there was not a single summons (on a Thursday before the New Year)

– a thing unknown since the Court was formed fourteen years previously and the ceremony of the white gloves was observed. In Cardiff the Mayor handed the chief constable a pair of white gloves in memory of there being no cases at all on the charge sheet on the last day of 1904.[11]

Whole football and rugby teams were converted and praying became more important than playing! Games were either cancelled or put off until a more convenient time, whilst other teams disbanded. Theatre attendance dropped, dance halls were deserted and pubs were emptied and closed; the landlords were furious! Talented actors and actresses failed to draw the crowds and those foolish enough to jest about the revival, indulged in by comedians, not only fell flat, but aroused indignation.

Under the inspiration of the Holy Spirit, many chapel soloists became inspired worship leaders carrying the heart of the nation in song, one in particular was Anne Davies, from Maesteg who often sung, 'Dyma Gariad' – 'Here is love, vast as the ocean.' This love song from the revival has been said to be the most popular, and like most of the revival hymns were best sung in the native Welsh language.

Choruses began to break through which were sung in English, especially Moody and Sankey's, which before the revival had been taboo in many Welsh speaking congregations. As the singer and minister, David Matthews' in his book, *I saw the Welsh Revival* wrote: 'I had never heard a single English chorus sung in our orthodox assemblies. To make such an attempt would have been rated almost "a sin against the Holy Ghost." Such a statement may seem strange, but it is nevertheless, strictly true (the exception being during singing competitions)…the singing of gospel choruses in another language was unthinkable…Revival makes a radical change in our prejudices.'

If the revival of 1904 had anything that might be called a slogan, it was this, 'Bend the church, and save the people.' The word 'bend' in Welsh conveys the meaning of submission to God, and the taking away of resistance to His will.

A circular issued by the Free Church Council of Carmarthen about the time of the great outburst in 1904 states, 'We cannot justly expect sinners to be saved, and our places of worship be filled by those from outside, until we ourselves get right with God; and this can only be done by an absolute surrender of our whole lives to Jesus Christ as King, and a faith acceptance of the Holy Spirit.' An awakened church creates the atmosphere in which decisions by the lost to accept the Saviour will be made easier.[12]

Jessie Penn-Lewis in her book, *The Awakening in Wales* wrote: 'We find all sections of the church affected by it [the revival], for the Holy Ghost is no respecter of denomination any more than persons, and He freely wrought in every place where He was welcomed when He began to work, and was given room.'

CHAPTER SIX
God is Gracious and Merciful (2 Chronicles 30:9)

God said, "For My thoughts are not your thoughts, nor are your ways My ways," says the Lord. "For as the heavens are higher than the earth, so are My ways higher than your ways, and My thoughts than your thoughts" Isaiah 55:8-9.

'Sing praises to the Lord, who dwells in Zion! Declare His deeds among the people…He does not forget the cry of the humble' Psalm 9:11-12.

China, Korea and Manchuria 1906-1909

Jonathan Goforth, a missionary of around thirteen years experience in China, in 1901, began to be restless and dissatisfied by the results of his work. From a human perspective his ministry in the city of Changte in the province of Honan (as part of the North Honan Mission) was very successful, but Goforth called it, "just touching the fringes" of the multitudes without Christ, as he longed to see in his ministry the "greater works" which Jesus had promised, (John 14:12-15).

Goforth received a master plan from the Lord of how to reach the multitudes, to which he informed his wife in May 1902 (who had just returned to the mission field with their five children). Every month they were to move to a new location, rent a native compound, preach the gospel in extensive evangelism, plant a church and move on. At first the Honan Presbytery (who he was in submission to) hampered and held back this plan until he told them they should allow him a three-year trial of this plan (which he would finance), which they eventually agreed to.

Jonathan Goforth, his family and other labourers began this ministry and were living in an out-centre when he received some pamphlets about the Welsh Revival of 1904 from an unknown source in England, which for a time arrived weekly. Then from India he received a little booklet called *A Great Awakening* which contained selections of Finney's *Lectures on Revival.* Finney emphasised that any company of Christians can have a revival if they will fulfil the necessary laws (250,000 people were saved under Finney's ministry). Finney wrote: 'I fully believe that could facts be known, it would be that when the appointed means have been rightly used, spiritual blessing have been obtained with greater uniformity than temporal ones.' Goforth said, "If Finney is right, and I believe he is then I am going to find out what these laws are and obey them, no matter what the cost may be." He requested from Canada various book and spent so much time in intensive study of the Holy Spirit, and prayer for revival that his wife was concerned for his mind. After all his study Goforth said, "Slowly the realisation began to dawn on me that I had tapped a mine of infinite possibility."

As part of this study he made notes in his two-inch wide margined Chinese Bible. Soon he began to preach on these notes to the locals and Christians alike. After eight or ten sermons the Christians came under deep conviction of sin (and were broken down, confessing their sins) while among the local heathen there was an increased results in conversions.

Early in February 1906, he was preaching at the time of great idolatrous fair in Hsunhsien (Hsun Hsien). Goforth said, "It was at this fair I began to see evidences of the first stirrings in the people's heart of the greater power. Convictions seemed to be written on every face. Finally, when I called for decisions, the whole audience stood up as one man crying, 'We want to follow this Jesus who died for us.' " As he turned he saw ten Chinese evangelists with awed looks. One whispered, "Brother, He for who we have prayed so long, was here in very deed tonight." This was the beginning of Goforth's revival ministry and at every centre (in Changte city and to the north which was his designated field of labour) for more than a year (until the spring of 1907) where the gospel was preached, *men came forward seeking salvation. *It was customary within Chinese meetings for men to preach to men and women to preach to women.

At this time there was a wonderful revival in Korea, (50,000 people were converted in 1907) and Dr. MacKay (foreign mission secretary) along with Goforth was invited to visit that country in the summer of 1907 for three weeks. Goforth said, "The Korean movement was of incalculable significance in my life, because it showed me at first hand the boundless possibilities of the revival method. Korea made me feel, as it did many others, that this was God's plan for setting the world aflame." On their return journey they returned to China via Manchuria (Manchuria used to straddle Russia, Mongolia and China but is now modern day Northeast China) and visited three mission stations, Mukden, Liaoyang and Peitaiho. Impromptu meetings were held where Goforth told of what they had witnessed and each station begged him to return for a ten day mission. The Korean Revival was preceded by months of prayer by the missionaries and as Goforth said, "Those missionaries seemed to carry us right up to the throne of God." After this Goforth told the story of the Korean Revival to missionaries in China.[1]

In Kikungshan a conference was held where those present resolved that they would 'pray every day (wherever they were) at four o'clock in the afternoon until the divine blessing fell upon the church in China.' In this way a prayer movement for revival was started which prepared the way for Goforth's revival ministry in China and Manchuria.[2]

In February 1908, after six months of negotiating with the Honan Presbytery they gave consent for one months leave (including travelling) to Manchuria. He held around forty meetings and taught on the Holy Spirit from his wide margined Bible, and the Holy Spirit came and dealt with the people! The first being an elder who came early one morning into Goforth's room, sobbing his heart out and confessing his sins and said, "After your message last night, I was searched as by fire. Last night I could not sleep a wink..."

Rev. James Webster (who worked under the Scotch Presbyterian Mission in Manchuria) accompanied Goforth to these three mission stations. He wrote: 'Mr Goforth's message [watchword] was 'Not by might, not by power, but by My Spirit.'...The cross burns like a living fire in the heart of every address.' Goforth would condemn idolatry and superstition in no uncertain terms being not fruit of the Spirit and also denounced those who have 'been baptised in the faith of Christ, but are living under the influence of hatred, jealousy, falsehood and dishonesty, pride, hypocrisy, worldliness and avarice, are living in that which is in active opposition to the Spirit of God.' Webster continued, 'What oppresses the thought of the penitent...the thoughts of their unfaithfulness, of ingratitude to the Lord who had redeemed them, of their heinous sins of trampling on His love...this it is which pricked them to the heart, moved them to the very depths of their moral being, and caused multitudes, being no longer able to contain themselves, to break out into a lamentable cry, "God be merciful to me a sinner." '

In the spring of 1908 Goforth was released by the Honan Presbytery from his mission station for the continuance of the revival, to carry the fire elsewhere. His wife and children had to return to Canada because the Presbytery would not allow her to continue at the mission station without the presence of her husband.

The revival missions were generally from seven to ten days in duration and held amongst different denominations; Episcopalians, Congregationalists, Baptists, Methodists, and Presbyterians etc. The first revival mission they had was at Chefoo, on the Shantung Peninsula, where one thousand people gathered. Goforth said, "From the first, there was deep conviction of sin. God was very present. Frequently there would be many praying at once and with deep emotion." Goforth's object was *not a revival amongst the heathen, but among the Christians, and all who could come to Changte Mission station were from the seven counties of the district. In October, Goforth was in Shansi, seven hundred were present, there was public confession of sin and spontaneous crying aloud for mercy, 'confessions that torture could not wring from men.' Dr. Murdock McKenzie, Goforth's honoured colleague of many years said, "There was no restraining it, and no attempting to do so…some were imploring the Holy Spirit not to leave them…that which weighed most heavily on the consciences of all was that we had so long been grieving the Holy Spirit by not giving Him His rightful place in our hearts and in our work. While believing in Him we had not trusted Him, to work in and through us…It was a time when we [missionaries and native converts] were all brought very close together…"[3]

*Inevitably, non-Christians attended (and those who were part of the mission compounds, especially, school children), came under the same intense conviction of sin and met the Saviour. Others upon entering a compound where Goforth was present would come under conviction; on other occasions, while another leader was taking the meeting (with Goforth in another room) the Spirit would also descend. Whilst there were confession of the sins, of theft, adultery and murder, most of the confessions from Christians were due to neglect of duty. Neglect of Bible reading and prayer or little or no concern for the lost.

Goforth and his evangelistic teams did encounter opposition, mostly from traditional missionaries who believed they knew their people better than God did. Many did not like the emotion which was displayed; while some leaders initially believed Goforth hypnotised the crowds; but within a few days they had publicly repented of their wild assumptions and doubt. At several of the mission stations the Spirit was hindered from moving in fullness until a leader(s) had publicly confessed his or her sin and where necessary made a wrong right, and or made restitution as applicable. On occasions demons were cast out from heathen and Christians alike and there were cases of deliverance and healings of opium addicts who were instantly set free and delivered from their cravings and addictions.

Two and a half decades later, Rev. Jonathan Goforth in the foreword to *The Revival We Need*, wrote: 'In Manchuria and China, when we did nothing else than give the address and let the people pray, and kept out of sight as a far as possible, we saw the mightiest manifestations of divine power.'[4]

Azusa Street Outpouring 1906-1909

The Azusa Street Outpouring, also known as the Azusa Street Revival, in Los Angeles, California, America was nurtured under the one-eyed black man, William Seymour, with 'help' from Evangelist/Journalist Frank Bartleman. It brought about a fresh touch of the Holy Spirit, bringing disciples the new awareness of the old truth of the baptism in the Holy Spirit. This blessing ushered in the worldwide twentieth century Pentecostal renewal. In 2006, the centenary of the Azusa Street Outpouring, it has been estimated that there are over 600 million Pentecostals worldwide.

Previous to the Azusa Street outpouring there were revivals in Houston, Texas and Kansas City where believers were being baptised in the Holy Spirit. Amongst the Christians, this led to a general excitement and hunger for the things of God, and prayer meetings were commenced for seeking the blessing in various quarters.

Seymour was invited to be a pastor of a Holiness Church, on Santa Fe Street in Los Angeles, but as soon as he started to preach on the baptism of the Holy Spirit, he was locked out of his church and his lodgings upstairs! He was taken in by some church members who agreed with his teaching and felt obligated to help him out. In his prayer closet he pressed in after the things of God. A prayer meeting was held at his new lodgings and he became known as a man of prayer.

In late February Seymour moved to new lodgings in North Bonnie Brae Street and was invited to hold meetings there, and with a small group they began to pray and fast. One man was healed instantly after being anointed with oil by Seymour and after a second prayer, the man began to speak in tongues, and people flocked to this house church. As the spiritual fire from heaven descended, many witnesses believed the house itself was literally on fire and the fire brigade was called out! It was not until April 1906 that Seymour began to speak in tongues.

In April, the house church found new premises on 312 Azusa Street. The building (formerly a Methodist church) was made of wood and had been previously used as a stable and store house for several years and was in quite a state of disrepair. People flocked to the building, where sawdust covered the floor.[5]

In the beginning in Azusa they had no musical instruments or hymn books, as they felt no need for them, all was spontaneous. Someone would give a testimony, sing or read some passages of Scripture and eventually someone would preach, regardless of age, colour or gender. All the well known hymns were sung from memory quickened by the Spirit of God and especially the song, 'The Comforter Has Come.'

Seymour sometimes preached behind a wooden box but as the move of God progressed, he was frequently found praying behind the box as the Holy Spirit did what He wanted to. The meetings became spontaneous. Services lasted for hours, half a day, or continued all night.

Eventually the meetings were held three times a day – morning, afternoon, and night. Tongues-speaking was the central blessing which attracted multitudes of curious people, but healing of the sick soon followed and the walls were soon covered with the crutches and canes of those who had been miraculously healed. The gift of tongues was soon followed by the gift of interpretation.[6]

Train loads of passengers from across the States came to experience this new move of God. People on route to the meeting would be prostrated; some would rise and speak in tongues. By the summer thousands were turning up and were being blessed by God.

In September 1906 a local newspaper reporter frowned on the events taking place and wrote that the Azusa Street mission was a 'disgraceful intermingling of the races...they cry and make howling noises all day and into the night. They run, jump, shake all over, shout to the top of their voice, spin around in circles, fall out on the sawdust blanketed floor jerking, kicking and rolling all over it. Some of them pass out and do not move for hours as though they were dead. These people appear to be mad, mentally deranged or under a spell. They claim to be filled with the Spirit. They have a one eyed, illiterate, Negro as their preacher who stays on his knees much of the time with his head hidden between the wooden milk crates. He doesn't talk very much but at times he can be heard shouting, 'Repent,' and he's supposed to be running the thing...They repeatedly sing the same song, 'The Comforter Has Come.' '[7]

On Friday June 15 1906, 'At Azusa the Spirit dropped the "heavenly chorus" into my soul...no one could understand this "gift of song" but those who had it. It was indeed a "new song" in the Spirit...the Lord has sovereignly bestowed it, with the outpouring of the "residue of oil" the latter rain baptism of the Spirit. It was exercised as the Spirit moved the possessors, either in solo fashion, or by the company. It was sometimes without words, other times in "tongues"...it brought about a heavenly atmosphere, as though the angels themselves were present and joining with us...this "new song" was altogether different, not of human composition. It cannot be successfully counterfeited. The crow cannot imitate the dove. But they finally began to despise this "gift" when the human spirit asserted itself again. They drove it out by hymn books, and selected songs by leaders. It was like murdering the Spirit, and most painful to some of us, but the tide was too strong against us.'[8]

Eventually things turned bad at Azusa, people accused Seymour of starting a new denomination. There were many misunderstandings and new ideas being thrown about which generally led to confusion and frustration, while others were working it up in the flesh. One of the misconceptions of tongues was that some who felt called to the mission field believed that they already had the ability to speak in another nation's language and were devastated on arrival at their mission field. Though at the meetings when some people spoke in tongues, others nationalities heard them speaking in their mother tongue and were converted because of this sign from heaven!

East Anglia Revival 1921-1922

This revival has been referred to as The Forgotten Revival as it has been widely overlooked within evangelical Church History. It is also known as the Lowestoft Revival.

In the first week of March 1921, the Rev. Douglas Brown, minister from Balham, London was invited to hold a five day evangelistic campaign in Lowestoft, East Anglia, England. There would be several meetings throughout the day, notably the prayer meeting in the morning in which prayer requests would be received, a Bible study in the afternoon and the evangelistic service in the evening. In the first week more than a hundred people got converted – Rev. Brown stayed for one month (returning home to his parish at weekends) and more than five hundred people were saved.

For two years prior to Rev. Brown's visit, the weekly prayer meeting at the London Road Baptist Church, under the Rev. Hugh Ferguson, was flourishing as the people prayed for revival and the Bible classes for men and women were also very well attended. The seating capacity of the Baptist church was seven hundred and fifty. During the service on Monday there was a spirit of expectancy. On Tuesday, the Holy Spirit's power was felt in the meeting. On Wednesday, the Rev. Brown, after he had finished preaching told the people that he was going into the vestry and that those who wanted help or desired to surrender themselves to Jesus Christ should follow – and they did!

During the first week and subsequent weeks, Rev. Brown preached at different churches within Lowestoft, the minister of various denominations working in unity, rejoicing together in the harvest. Christians got revived, drunks became sober, debts were paid and many saw their sin and met the Saviour for the first time. The fourth week of the campaign saw the largest attendances. In St. John's, the eleven hundred-seat church was not big enough, people sat in the isles, on the window sills and even on the pulpit steps!

Rev. Brown returned for another five day mission in the Whitsun week (Pentecost) and since his first visit, over a thousands people were converted in eleven weeks! He then held campaigns in other localities, Ipswich, Yarmouth, Norwich and *Cambridge (*with assistance from the evangelist and revivalist Gipsy Smith). God moved in all these localities and Rev. Brown returned to Lowestoft for a Convention in the third week of September. Rev. Brown at the convention was able to state that during the past months they had known the 'felt presence of the Lord.' While the President of the Baptist union in 1921 ignorantly (or possibly demonically) wrote an article in which he dismissed the work in East Anglia as an 'emotional wave' produced by a 'hypnotic preacher' yet addressed Rev. Brown as his 'beloved friend!'[9]

Jock Troup, a well built man and former barrel maker, turned evangelist was also used during the East Anglia Revival and the North-East of Scotland Revival of 1921-1922.

Jock arrived in Yarmouth in October 1921, in the midst of economic downturn when the herring industry was long passed its prime. He came under the auspices of the Baptist's and the Salvation Army. Jock preached on the third Saturday night of October, at the Plain Stone in the Market Place, where hundreds of people, notably fishermen and fisher-girls were milling around. His text was from Isaiah 63:1, speaking of the Messiah's judgment: 'Who is this that cometh from Edom, with dyed garments from Bozrah?' It was said that Jock's voice could carry 450 metres without amplification and after this sermon hundreds were slain to the ground under the sword of the word of God – convicted of sin and fearful of the wrath to come. Further meetings were held in different churches and fishermen out at sea were also converted as God came down!

The revival was exported by fishermen from Anglia to Scotland and vice versa as they plied their trade in pickled herrings back and forth as the boats followed the migratory fish beginning in spring at Lerwick, Shetland and moving down the east coast until they reached East Anglia by October and returned again.

After Jock left for Scotland a few weeks later the revival continued under the Rev. Brown who continued his visits from his parish. After receiving a vision from God, Jock visited Fraserburgh and preached in the open air until rain drove him and the people into a Baptist Church where the deacons were discussing about inviting Jock to hold meetings there! Religious as well as secular newspapers reported this religion of revival. In the villages of Inverallochy and Cairnbulg, in December, six hundred people were converted in two weeks out of a population of fifteen hundred!

In many of the towns, cinemas and public houses became empty and dancing halls shut due to lack of interest in worldly amusement. The Salvation Army soon taught the new convert's how to sing, whilst the leaders and lay members of the revival continued in earnest prayer for the Holy Spirit to come down. Jock would constantly make appeals for people to embrace the Saviour and later on in 1922, he was encouraged to study at Glasgow's Bible Training Institute, which he did for two years (on and off) in between preaching the gospel and went on, to have a powerful evangelistic ministry.[10]

Shanghai Revival 1925

In the last week of June, amidst anti-English and anti-foreign sentiments (as rioting swept across China), a revival broke out in Shanghai, China. It was fostered under the leadership of Dr. and Mrs Henry Woods, who were missionaries from the Southern Presbyterian Church.

On the 30 May 1925, students caused a riot in Shanghai. They were brought to trial and a missionary of long standing defended the actions of the police, which resulted in huge anti-English and anti-foreign sentiments being stirred up. This led to hatred and bitterness towards the Japanese and Americans. The slogan went forth, "Kill the foreign devils." Many mission stations across the country were closed down as they fled to Shanghai for safety.

In January some missionaries started planning to hold their annual conference in the summer. They wrote to Mr Pagnet Wilkes, to ask for his assistance in evangelism (during the conference season) along with the Rev. and Mrs Russell Howden of England, who were coming on invitation of the Stewart Evangelistic Committee. The British authorities advised against this project due to the riots and some of their friends withdrew their financial support. But as the missionaries prayed they had the assurance of the Spirit that what they were doing was right. The Lord showed them to use the Union Church which was entirely British constituency, which in the natural realm was the last place to hold these meetings under the anti-English sentiment. The room they used could hold one hundred and fifty and they expected about fifty to attend, but several hundred Chinese people came so they moved into a bigger room.

On the 7 July, a morning prayer meeting was held and great blessings were enjoyed. In those meetings, on the 11 July, a Chinese lady with tuberculosis was prayed for and healed immediately and started attending the meetings. People were drawn by the Spirit to attend the meetings.

A Mr Leland Wang, a Chinese evangelist (through a series of divine appointments in answer to prayer) was found and was used in the meetings. The 18 July, was an all-day meeting of prayer, fasting and praise and so many attended that the Union Church auditorium was commissioned, which held around seven hundred people. Illness struck Mr Wilkes and it took a week for him to recover, but a Mr Thornton, a missionary from Japan preached via translation and the attendance rose. At the parting of Mr Thornton, Mr Wilkes said, "Mrs Woods, this is not a conference. A conference is dependant upon the speaker. This is revival. I have never in all my experience seen anything like it…"

Wednesday the 5 of August was set aside as a day of prayer and fasting and continuous prayer went forth to the throne room of God. At 3 o'clock people were led of the Holy Spirit to confess their sin openly, which cost them dearly. Theft and covetousness were the two sins given greatest prominence and wrongs were righted as restitution prevailed, and others gloried in their new-found salvation.

When the evangelistic meetings were being held, two separate prayer meetings for men and women were also conducted – the power houses, so that as prayer went up, the Spirit came down. Souls were saved and around fifty yielded to Christian service.

Rev. Howden, deputy director of the China Inland Mission, spoke at the final meeting in September, the church was filled with all nationalities, more souls were saved, and from Shanghai other revivals broke out.[11]

CHAPTER SEVEN
A Rushing Mighty Wind (Acts 2:2)

'...For You, Lord, have not forsaken those who seek You' Psalm 9:10.

'For I will pour water on him who is thirsty, and floods on the dry ground; I will pour My Spirit on your descendants, and My blessing on your offspring; they will spring up among the grass like willows by the watercourses' Isaiah 44:3-4.

New Zealand, Ngaruawahia Easter Convention 1936

In 1936, J. Edwin Orr was in New Zealand as part of his world tour, promoting full surrender to the Lord Jesus Christ and encouraging prayer and participation for local and national revival. In the previous two years he had travelled round Britain, Europe, Canada and America and had seen localised revivals in several countries.

The Ngaruawahia Easter Convention in Auckland, North Island, was the "Keswick" of New Zealand and Orr was one of several notable speakers. It ran from Thursday the eighth till Monday the thirteenth of April; there were over 750 registered people and 1,200 people in the big tent meetings. On Tuesday the seventh, Orr and Jack Sherriff (who was also assisting Orr in this leg of his world tour) got together to pray that revival would sweep the Ngaruawahia Easter Convention on the Saturday.

Ngaruawahia is a little Maori town at the confluence of the Waikato and the Waipa River. Orr spoke at the Friday afternoon meeting, 'the meetings were pent up with expectancy, but no break occurred.' After the evening service a man who had been in the revival two days previously in Keith Rimmer's marquee, Mount

Eden district, Auckland, asked Orr to visit tent number twenty-nine. Inside he found men and women who were concerned about revival. Orr spoke about hindrances to revival and deep conviction prevailed. Orr challenged them, "Do you really believe that God will give us revival?" "Amen" they replied. "Do you really believe that He will start the revival here in this tent tonight?" After a silence one man said quietly, "If we pay the price." They got down on their knees and were about to pray when one of the men blurted out that he needed to confess the sin of criticism to another fellow (within the same tent), he asked the person's forgiveness. After a painful silence the other fellow gave his forgiveness and stated that he to, was guilty of the same sin. Prayer began to ascend, prayers of confession to God, secret sin, pride, unbelief and lust etc.

Orr wrote: '...Then the spirit of revival began to fall on us – it was an amazing meeting. We sang, we prayed, we rejoiced, we cried to God. Orr urged those present to go and get some other tents on fire for the Lord. They divided up into parties of three. Orr had gone to his hotel, but being unable to sleep had returned to the camp site. In one tent, he was informed that they were not well received, 'they said we must be crazy.' They wandered over to the big marquee at around 11pm as a prayer meeting was coming to a close. One of those from tent 29, a quiet fellow 'went to the front of the meeting and boldly interrupted the prayers' and challenged them, "Listen here, you fellows. What's the use of praying for other fellows sins? You ought to confess your own, and get a revival in your own heart first." They explained what had happened in 29, and 'in a twinkling of an eye' there was conviction as the Holy Spirit descended.

By this time Orr had gone back to his hotel (for the third time) to sleep (he was used to taking twenty meetings a week for months at a time, whilst travelling on average a thousand miles a week), only to find himself locked out. After thirty minutes of trying to get in he decided to return to the camp, where he heard noise coming from the big marquee. Orr wrote: 'Men were broken down, confessed sin, cried for mercy, sought forgiveness, asked for revival. And the prayer meeting in the big marquee went ablaze with spiritual power...the meeting was crying out for experienced leadership, so I quietly took charge.' More people confessed sins and whilst some were reconciled with each other, tears flowed. Praise swept over the group. Orr wrote: '...The scenes that night were the nearest thing to spiritual intoxication that I had ever seen.' One man started the electrical amplifying apparatus, his voiced boomed out into the sleeping tents, "Praise the Lord – revival has begun in the camp!" Soon, people started to turn up to the marquee in their pyjamas, but quickly returned with their overcoats! They sang praises into the midnight hour. Soon there were sixty persons present, more sin was confessed, and enemies were reconciled, whilst other souls received transforming power. At one in the morning, Orr tried to persuade the people to go to bed; he pronounced the benediction and the praise service started up all over again! Orr eventually slept on the camp site.

The next day, Saturday, there were complaints about the noise, Orr explained what had happened the previous night and the sixty testified to their revived state, most were satisfied. Orr preached in the evening, after the appeal, lots of people went to the front to confess sin and people began to break down throughout the tent. Before long there were five hundred people being dealt with. Various leaders dealt with different groups, 'there were seventeen after-meetings scattered throughout the camp...pastors and workers confessed backsliding and there were many conversions. Two Chinese men who could not understand English came under conviction of sin and were led to the Lord through an interpreter. By 10:30pm there were one thousand people in the tent again, an hour later the leaders persuaded them to go of to bed, but by midnight praises were still being sung by a few hundred people.[1]

Lewis Revival 1949-1952

The Lewis Revival is also known as the Lewis Awakening, the Hebridean Revival or the Lewis and Harris Revival. The Rev. Duncan Campbell, due to unexpected circumstances had been asked to preach in the Outer Hebrides, UK for ten days, but he stayed for over two years.

Before revival broke out, a declaration was read in every congregation of the Free Church on the Isle of Lewis, Outer Hebrides, exhorting its member to pray for God's awakening on their land. Some people took this declaration very seriously.

Two elderly sisters in their eighties, Peggy and Christine Smith, one being blind and the other being severely afflicted with arthritis, met at their home and travailed in prayer from 10pm into the early hours in their little cottage often until three in the morning. One night God gave one of the sisters a vision in which she saw their church crowded with young people and declared to her sister that she believed revival was coming. At this time not a single young person attended public worship in that community! The minister was called for and the sister explained what she saw and believed. The minister took this word as from the Lord and asked what should be done. "What" she said, "Give yourself to prayer!" For two nights a week for at least three months many church deacons and elders met; they prayed for revival and waited upon God in a barn amongst the straw at one end of the parish pleading one promise, "I will pour water on him who is thirsty and floods upon the dry ground" Isaiah 44:3, while the sisters prayed at the other end of the parish. One night a young deacon rose to his feet and in Gaelic (the native language), read part of Psalm 24, 'Who has clean hands and a pure heart...' The deacon said, "It seems to me just so much humbug, to be waiting as we are waiting and to be praying as we are praying, if we ourselves are not rightly related to God." He lifted his hands to heaven and cried, "Oh God tell me, are my hands clean? Is my heart pure?" He fell onto his knees as the others, and went into a trance. Something in the spirit realm broke and the awareness of God began to grip the community.

In the church at Barvas, on the Isle of Lewis, in late 1949, there was a great spirit of expectancy at Duncan Campbell's first meeting. At the end of the service, as the people dispersed, one of the church deacons declared, "God is hovering over; He is going to break-through. Do not be discouraged, He is coming. I hear already the rumbling of heavens chariots wheels." Then he suggested to the already travel weary Duncan that they and around thirty others go and seek God in prayer in a nearby cottage. Rev. Campbell later described what happened: 'God was beginning to move, the heavens were opening, and we were there on our faces before God. Three o'clock in the morning came, and God swept in. About a dozen men and women lay prostrate on the floor, speechless. Something had happened, we knew that the forces of darkness were going to be driven back, and men were going to be delivered. We left the cottage at 3am to discover men and women seeking God. I walked along a country road, and found three men on their faces, crying to God for mercy. There was a light in every home; no-one seemed to think of sleep.' He arrived home at 5am. When Duncan and his friends gathered at the church late in the morning, it was crowded as fourteen buses had come from all-over the small island to fill the building, one bus even came from the Isle of Harris. Revival was under way, some fell into trances, other swooned, and many wept and slumped to the floor.

Later in the day Rev. Campbell pronounced the benediction (close of the service) and the people started to leave. 'A young man began to pray and was so burdened for the soul of his friend that he continued for three-quarters of an hour. During this time people flocked back to the church and by the end there was as many outside the building as inside. People gathered from Stornaway and Ness and other parishes. It was 4am the following day that Campbell pronounced the benediction for the second time! As he was leaving he was told of many people who were in deep distress of soul, under the starlit sky were people [prostrated] by the peat stacks, on the road, by the cottages crying for mercy; revival had truly come.'

I visited the church at Barvas as a teenager nearly two decades ago when I was on a mission with my father, Michael, who has been greatly influenced (along with other family members) by the life and work of Rev. Duncan Campbell. In later life I came to appreciate how spectacular the speed at which the news of a revival spread amongst the remote communities, but sadly at the time of my visit revival had not burned deeply within my soul as it has now.

Rev. Campbell said, "Of the hundreds who found Jesus Christ at that time, seventy-five percent of them were gloriously saved before they came near a meeting, before they heard a single sermon from myself or from any other minister in the parish, the power of God was moving, the Spirit of God in operation, and the fear of God gripping the souls of men…"

God came down and met with the body of Christ and the unconverted and a good hand-full of these converts later became missionaries and ministers. People were drawn to church by an unseen hand, woken out of bed and drawn to church, or to fields where too many people assembled to fit into any of the buildings, while many fell where they were in agony of soul as they were won through to Christ and delivered from past bondages. Two bagpipe players who were to play at a local dance in Carloway were converted, but the dances continued without them until the minister arrived at 3.30am and asked the people to sing a Psalm, the people broke down as God's Spirit swept in.

In these church buildings and during services there were no musical instruments (as tradition said they were instruments of the devil). They sang Psalms and paraphrases of the Bible and even today many Scottish and Highland churches still hold to this point of view. God met with these people because their hearts were right before God. And that is the big lesson for all of us; "Is my heart right before God?"

Twice during the Lewis Revival preceding a mighty movement, heavenly music was heard. One night about twenty of them were walking along a country road around midnight when suddenly, heavenly music was heard above them; they fell on their faces in amongst the heather as some thought the end of the world had come![2]

The revival on the Isle of Lewis spread to the Isle of Harris (but did not sweep across the Hebrides as some reports at the time stated) and then was carried by Duncan Campbell who was drawn across the six mile body of water (as the crow flies) to the small island of Berneray (also known as Bernera) which had a population of just four hundred people. During the Easter of 1952, Duncan Campbell had been preaching at a conference in Bangor, (and was booked to preach the following night) but felt constrained by the Spirit to leave. From the pulpit he turned to the chairman and stated that he had to leave immediately for Harris, apologised, and went to pack his case. From Harris he took the boat to Berneray and within a few days every home on the island was affected by the Spirit of God.[3]

In 2005, whilst on a three week mission to Scotland and the Outer Hebrides, I visited the Island of Berneray (which is now linked to North Uist via a causeway) and was able to appreciate (to a small degree) the awe and majesty that must have prevailed when God came and visited the island. One elderly lady who I spoke to, who lived opposite the church at Berneray knew nothing about the revival and sadly did not want to know anything about God. Whilst on the other hand, a middle aged man (who did not attend church) invited me and my fellow labourers into his home for tea and biscuits, a welcome rest bite from the bitter piercing Hebridean winds.

Korean Revival 1950

The first Protestant missionary to Korea, the Rev. Robert Jermain Thomas arrived in the Hermit Kingdom in September 1865. Due to the death of his wife, he resigned from the London Missionary Society. Thomas then became an agent for the National Bible Society of Scotland and whilst in Korea he found employment as a translator aboard a French vessel. They left him behind at one port (as he was getting supplies) so he got a job on an armed American merchant-marine schooner as a translator. This small ship he used as his travelling base for evangelism and Bible distribution. Thomas was heavily disguised when he went ashore as those he sold Bibles to risked being decapitated if discovered. They sailed up the river to Pyongyang (which is now North Korea's capital) but were warned to leave as the Koreans did not want foreign trade, but the captain opened fire much to Thomas' horror. The chief of police boarded the vessel, and was kidnapped. The army was called out, who used cannons against the ship. By this time the ship floated onto a sandbank as the tide was going out. Fire rafts were sent out towards the ship. Thomas opened his case of Bibles and started to throw them to those who lined the shore whist shouting "Jesus, Jesus." Thomas with his clothes on fire leapt overboard with his few remaining Bibles and swam to the bank and frantically gave out the Bibles until he was captured and taken before the governor. All crew members, the owner of the ship and Thomas (aged 27) were executed. Thomas' executioner accepted the last red Bible from this martyr, and as Tertullan said, "The blood of the martyrs is the seed of the church." The executioner used the Bible as wallpaper and one day was converted as he read the decorative Scriptures. During the Korean Revival (1906-1907) an old man who attended a Presbyterian Church in Pyongyang, during a time of public confession went to the front and confessed that he had been the one who had killed Thomas, nearly forty years ago.[4] In 1907 during the Korean Revival 50,000 people were converted.

Bob Finely wrote, "When Bob Pierce, Gill Dodds and I were invited to Korea we discovered that our Lord had brought us into the midst of revival that might well have been lifted out of the pages of the book of Acts. I saw revival in Korea. I saw more than 25,000 persons profess to accept Christ as Saviour within six weeks. I saw more than four thousand persons daily at 5am prayer meetings. I saw hundreds continue all night in prayer for days on end. I saw crowds up to 75,000 come together to hear the gospel. In such a movement of the Holy Spirit, our part was incidental. These meetings in which we participated were only a small part of the great revival in Korea. All the while there were other great meetings being held by Korean pastors and evangelists. The revival is a demonstration of the awful reality of the person of the Holy Spirit.[5]

Over the past six decades, Korea has had a mega spiritual explosion where some churches have seven or even nine services a day. Still multitudes of believers meet for prayer at 5am, and many churches have tens of thousands of believers with multiple services on a Sunday.

Whilst at Bible College I studied with many Korean students and the majority were eager to go into full-time ministry. I asked one of the younger students, how many people attended her church. Casually she replied, "Thirty thousand." I was quite taken back having been used to preaching in churches across South Wales with congregations as low as five and no more than eighty. How many services do you have a day I asked? "Seven" she responded.

Today, Korea is the second largest mission sending country. Several years ago I was in Budapest, Hungary and met a coach load of Koreans who were travelling around, Europe, praying for the continent – Thank you.

Congo Revival 1953

The Congo Revival of 1953 shook the church in North-eastern, Belgian Congo (modern day Democratic Republic of Congo – formerly known as Zaire). This was the heart of Africa and the field that English Cricket legend, C.T. Studd entered into in 1913, and a year later with his son-in-law to be, Alfred Buxton under the name H.A.M. (Heart of Africa Mission) a supplementary of the W.E.C. (Worldwide Evangelisation Crusade). On many occasions they went on exploratory trips deep into the cannibal infested jungles. Within two years the heart of Africa had been surveyed and four strategic centres had been chosen.

The revival fires began in spring of 1953 when the missionaries and the natives decided to get right with God. There was much heart and soul searching, prayer and teaching on the Holy Spirit for months prior to the outbreak of revival fire.

At one station they thought a hurricane was coming as the wind of the Spirit blew through the building and came upon many. Numerous shy native ladies would shout praises, "Hallelujah!" at the top of the voices. Others shook all over and collapsed on the floor in groans and travail as intercession for souls was birthed in them. Other people in various mission stations saw holy light or bright light as part of a vision.

People were slain in the meetings and would tremble and jerk uncontrollably or perspire and fall off their seat and roll in the mud in agony of soul. At first the missionaries were not sure if these were godly manifestation or not, until many such people came through and testified of their sin in front of all, knowing that they had been pardoned by God. There were flaky people, one claimed to be the Holy Spirit and was sharply rebuked, but the people had a teachable spirit and were able to receive correction from those in leadership. Other mentally disturbed people were set free from demons, by the power of God, in the name of Jesus Christ.

The fires spread from one station to the next, as people travelled to tell of the wonders of God. Revival teams were also sent out carrying the fire with them to other missionary stations.

One missionary wrote: 'We are convinced that wherever there is a genuine desire for revival and a willingness to accept what God sends, without any heart reservations, God will not pass them by. Let us humbly, by prayer and heart searching, seek God's face continually and be ready to pay the price for revival.'[6]

Singing and prayer went on into the early hours as the brethren had such thankful spirits that they had been saved and forgiven. Some people hardened their hearts and refused to confess their sin and turn from their wicked ways. Some of these heathen held onto trees and posts to stop them from being thrown to the ground by the Holy Spirit – but He always got His way! People's hands and knees were fused together; others were stuck to the ground and would not be released until they had confessed their sin!

Several of the missionaries commented, that a lot of what they saw could have been straight out of John Wesley's journal. Even 'good living,' soul winning Christians came under the conviction of their secret sin, which had to be brought to light. Confessions of adultery, lust, robbery etc. were common place from the front of the church, those who had been there before used to encourage the confessor to confess all in the sight of God and his or her brethren (James 5:16).

In a missionary run girl's school, many were converted and then prayer went up for the boy's school until they too had been touched by the fire of the Holy Spirit. Some of the students had been unaffected and had hardened their hearts so groups of students fasted and prayed for hours on end to see them broken and humbled in the eyes of God.

The Holy Spirit had given life to that which had been dead and the church became alive, a living reality; healings took place, singing and praying in tongues resounded. The natives sung like never before and in several of the mission stations construction work which had carried on for months was completed in a matter of days. There was much restitution and things made right. Some of the natives, who owned orchards of special palm trees from which alcohol were obtained, upon conversion or under conviction of their use, cut them down at great financial loss to themselves.

At Ibambi mission station (where revival broke out in 1925 under C.T. Studd) the leader and his wife wrote: 'The Holy Ghost came down in mighty power. We have never seen anything like it before. Words fail to describe it, but we know something now of what it must have been like on the day of Pentecost. As one prayed, another began to pray, and another, and then the whole congregation together. Such a noise as they poured out their souls in prayer and praise to God. Men, women, boys and girls just drunk with the Spirit, many shaking beyond their control, others throwing themselves on the floor, some leaning, some standing…We just stood there amazed, but were not afraid, as we knew it was the Sprit working…It was impossible to makes oneself heard. If this had not been of God, it would have been terrible, as they were beyond all human control.

'Strange things have accompanied every true revival, but when the Spirit is allowed full sway He is able to take care of His own work. We need to be ready for any revelation He gives. As the enemy seeks to get in, we shall have discernment and be able to recognise his devices. We have certainly seen manifestations we never saw before, but we know the work is of the Spirit because of the outworking of it in a practical way in so many lives.

'The Holy Spirit leads the meeting, and we don't know what is going to happen next. We are so full of joy that God has visited us at last. He has no set way of working, and it seems to come differently in each place'.[7]

I was present at a Bible College meeting when the Rev. David Davies, a former student and missionary to the Congo, told of what he saw during the Congo Revival. Rev. David Davies stated that during the Congo Revival in the 1950s; the locals returned hundreds of stolen shovels to their foreman, as after each portion of construction work prior to this, they used to keep them for themselves.

At the end of the meeting there was opportunity to ask him questions, and there were many questions. The meeting lasted thirty minutes beyond the usual service length, and being there was thirteen meetings a week, it was one of the longest services on record. One person asked, "How do you justify people falling over [in the revival]?" "Well" he replied, "At first my brother and I was a bit sceptical about it, but knew that if we could get a precedent in Scripture then it would be safe to assume that it was from God. We found Revelation 6:17 '...who shall be able to stand [in His presence].' Well that was good enough for us!" I can still see the Rev. Davis behind the pulpit, stating what he had witnessed and what had happened to him nearly fifty years ago in the middle of Africa and it was still very vivid in his mind and evident in his close walk with the Lord.

Effects of Revival

During the Congo Revival there were six distinct signs or effects of the revival:

1. Conviction of sins, public confession of major sins by people and leaders alike and restitution of even the smallest items or debts.
2. Often those who were under deep conviction would shake, tremble, collapse on the floor or perspire until they had confessed their sins.
3. People had a really thankful spirit that they had been saved and forgiven.
4. The brethren who were involved had a teachable spirit and were able to receive correction from those in leadership, especially when they moved from the Spirit into the flesh or were trying to 'work up' the blessing of God.
5. The people would open up to singing whereas before they would hardly open their mouths.
6. The brethren had an eagerness to intercede for others so that they would pull through their deep conviction of sin and be brought to a saving knowledge of Jesus Christ.

CHAPTER EIGHT
Greater Works than These (John 14:12)

'Be exalted, O God, above the heavens; let Your glory be above all the earth' Psalm 57:5.

'Seek the Lord and His strength; seek His face evermore. Remember His marvellous works which He has done, His wonder and the judgment of His mouth' Psalm 105:4-5.

Revival in Argentina 1954

In 1954, American evangelist Tommy Hicks from Lancaster, California, held a healing and evangelism campaign in Argentina, which resulted in an eternal harvest of around twenty thousands people.

Of all the revivals I have researched and read about, the 1954 revival in Argentina has the most varying statistics of attendance, conversions and in the numbers of days the revival (crusade) lasted. Having looked at three main sources (and noted a fourth), the crusade was fifty-two, sixty, or sixty-two days long, but I believe *sixty days was the correct figure. Total attendance statistics for the duration of the crusade vary from two million, four million or six million, while conversion figures range from eighteen thousand, twenty thousand, half a million and up to three million, but around twenty thousand is the more accurate figure. One of J. Edwin Orr's students researched the official church membership statistics which revealed that more than eighteen thousand new member were taken into fellowship, which was the largest figure in the history of Argentina! Praise God. Edwin Orr retelling the facts stated that Tommy Hicks naively concluded that three million people made a confession of Christ (*100,000 people attended each day for sixty days and half the people {50,000} put up their hand). Edwin Orr stated that Latin American's will raise their hands for any invitation, 'do you want to love Jesus more' therefore three million conversions was not a realistic figure. Hicks also stated that 100,000 took decision cards, but as Edwin Orr explained, "If you're piling out of a stadium and someone is holding out cards, you'll take one"[1]

In early April 1950, little known Tommy Hicks was called of the Lord to go to Argentina to see a man called Peron. Peron he found out in 1954 en-route to Argentina was the President of Argentina. Three years prior to the campaign, Bible College students, just outside of Buenos Aires had prayed and interceded for a move of God in their land, alongside Dr. Edwards Miller, who soaked the land with tears.

In 1953, Hicks received an invitation from some Pentecostal leaders, the Christian Missionary Alliance and the Assemblies of God to go to Argentina to hold mass evangelistic meetings. Hicks was not their first choice. Hicks agreed and told them to hire a football stadium, to which they disagreed, initially the leaders had a hall that could hold five hundred, but Hicks believed 25,000 would turn up. Anyhow the President himself would have to authorise such a large gathering of people.

In 1954, Hicks asked the committee leaders who had invited him to come over, to arrange a meeting with the President, to which they said it could not be done. Hicks walked to the 'Rose House' where the President lived and asked to see the President. Hicks explained to the guard on duty that he wanted to lead an evangelistic healing crusade. The guard laughed as he did not believe in God's healing ability. Hicks caught hold of the guards hand, who had told him he was sick and under doctor's supervision. As Hicks prayed for the guard, the sickness disappeared. J. Edwin Orr states that Hick's got to see the Minister of Cults before he prayed for the guard (who was one of Peron's close bodyguards) and was healed of a swollen leg as Hick's kneeled, laid hands on him and prayed in Jesus' name. The guard (bodyguard) told him to return tomorrow for a meeting with the President! The next day, Hicks explained via his interpreter to President Juan Peron what he wanted to do and that he needed full media coverage. Peron asked if God could heal him, as he had an incurable and disfiguring skin condition. Hicks took him by the hand and prayed and he was instantly healed! Peron gave Hicks everything he needed to organise such a crusade.

In Buenos Aires, in mid April the crusade began in the 25,000-seat Atlantic football stadium, but this proved too small. They moved to the 180,000-seat Huracan bullfighting ring and upwards of 100,000 flocked in around the clock, with 200,000 on the final night. Around six million people attended and thousands were healed. Hicks for two months hardly slept or ate and the members of the local church who were ushers were rushed off their feet, working in twelve hour shifts.[2]

North Uist Revival 1957-1958

The Island of North Uist, Outer Hebrides, UK, is only seventeen miles long by twelve miles wide and was not touched during the Lewis Revival. It is important to note that the Spirit of Grace was grieved in South Uist, which was (and still is today) predominantly Roman Catholic. As the inhabitants got word of what was happening on the Isles of Lewis and Harris (1949-1952) they began to set up life-sized statues of Mary and baby Jesus on the roadside (which are still there today), resisting this 'Protestant' move of God. The closest island to North Uist (where revival came during the Lewis Revival) was the even smaller Island of Berneray, which today is joined by a causeway and like all of the Outer Hebrides is a very windswept land.

In November 1957, Miss Mary Morrison (now known as Mary Peckham) of the Faith Mission, Edinburgh travelled to the Island of North Uist with a small team of other 'girl evangelists' and landed in Lochmaddy.

In 1957, 'women's ministry' was greatly frowned upon and to much extent still is today amongst some of these small communities. The faithful pilgrims endured their persecution just as Duncan Campbell did, who was even called "a worker of the devil!" during the Lewis Revival.

In Lochmaddy the ministers had told the people not to assist these girls in lodgings; so they booked themselves into a poor house even though at this time seven other districts were pleading for their help, but they knew that this was where God had called them too. For two weeks they prayed and pleaded with God's promise to, 'pour water on the dry ground' until they knew revival was to come. They called for Rev. Duncan Campbell to assist them and organised a meeting and around forty people attended, as a minister was coming. They began preaching inside the poor house to those assembled inside this old rickety old hall. The Rev. Campbell was still suffering from the effects of a fourteen hour sea-sick crossing, due to an intense storm which greatly delayed the ferry. Rev. Campbell later said, "I had never been in such a meeting!" as one of the pilgrims spoke on the rich man and Lazarus for an hour often quoting John Bunyan, "Listen to the sighs from hell!" and from that moment the North Uist Revival broke out as someone let out a cry and people began to tremble. The speaker asked Rev. Campbell to end the meeting and they left the work to God. At midnight over thirty people came to their lodgings seeking the Saviour! The next morning the church was crowded and the minister could not understand because no one had arranged a meeting, but the fear of God swept the community.

The four young pretty girls (as some referred to them), all of whom were in their twenties, travelled across this particular island holding evangelistic campaigns in the various villages for several weeks, to a month at a time as the Spirit led. Sometimes they would work in pairs and at other times all four of them would be working together. Generally, the meetings were about two hours long, in both English and Gaelic and a prayer meeting was held afterwards in which seekers could call upon God in prayer and join with the believers. As people were drawn to Christ other ministers were called upon to assist in the work, including the Rev. Duncan Campbell, who frequented the island for several days or weeks at a time.

In mid January 1958, the young girls went to the school in the parish of Solas (which consists of four very small villages linked via a single track road, as is much of the island) and asked the headmaster if they could use the building to hold evening services. He replied, "You'll get no joy here" but nonetheless consented to their request. At the evening service many people gave their lives to the Lord and even the headmaster inquired about his own soul.

I visited the island of North Uist in 2005 whilst on a mission. The small school is still there today on the edge of Middle Quarter, Solas. The reason the numbers of attendees (or conversions) are small compared to the Welsh Revival or the Argentina Revival etc. is because the populations are so small in comparison. Like many of the communities in the Hebrides, you cannot truly appreciate how isolated some of the communities and houses are unless you visit such a place (and this is the mistake that several authors from other continents have made when writing of the 1949-1952 Lewis Revival). In the twenty-first century, car ownership is generally the norm, but fifty or sixty years ago most people had to catch the bus or travel on foot and the elements are unmerciful. I asked one brother who lived on the Isle of Benbecula (below North Uist) jesting about the weather, how long their summer was, "Three days" he replied, I laughed to which he responded "No, I'm not joking." This is not intended to put you off visiting such a magnificently beautiful land, but to try and portray the natural elements and landscape in the context of people being drawn to church or attending religious meetings, often in the bleakest of weather conditions.

The small team of ladies travelled around the island of North Uist from door to door, and the Holy Spirit gave blessing to their labours over the next several months. The Rev. Duncan Campbell, speaking a few years after the revival quoted from the local press: 'The drink trade in North Uist has been ruined!' One of the pilgrims in a letter wrote: 'Three prayer meetings are held every week in every parish!' The team left in May 1958, but did revisit the island to see how the new converts were doing nearer Christmas.[3]

Indonesian Revival 1964-1971

The Indonesian Revival is perhaps the most supernatural revival the world has ever seen – truly of biblical proportions with many personalities involved. Indonesia has over 13,000 islands, 3,000 of which are inhabited. Muslims were affected as were nominal Christians and the animists or heathen.

During the revival under the Indonesian 'umbrella' multitudes were converted and set free from demonic oppression and curses, sorcery was defeated. The blind saw, the deaf heard, the lame walked, the lepers were healed, the dead were raised, the waters were calmed, the rain was commanded to stop; all in the name of Jesus. People received visions and dreams, words of knowledge, prophecy and extraordinary discernment – knowing the secrets of men's hearts; whilst others received songs from God, a few were taught by angels (being illiterate) and Jesus even appeared Himself to others. Some of the missionary teams ate supernatural food (manna from heaven), another team had flames of fire over the churches where they preached at, others saw supernatural light, which guided their footsteps by night, one mission team was transported in the Spirit, others witnessed food multiplying, and food not going-over in the tropical heat. In one place the house shook as they prayed as in Acts 4 and one church saw water turning into communion wine (non-alcoholic) – which was the tastiest ever; this happened on at least ten occasions!

A Holy Spirit sent movement began on the Island of Rote, south of Timor (also known as, Roti) in 1964 as the word of the Lord was preached. Two men, Pak Elias and Pastor Gideon (who first met in 1966) were both figures at the forefront and natives of Rote. Prayer groups sprang up which became the backbone of the revival. As they preached the saving message of the cross, the locals became overwhelmed in their sins and called on the Saviour and within a year a thousand people had been converted.

On the island of Sumatra (a thousand miles away) God began a work amongst the Muslims 'poison mixers' on the southern tip when their tribal leader, Abram decided to tell his people about the story of Bethlehem (which he had heard through an open window of a church whilst a Christmas sermon was in progress, after he had finished attending a Communist educational course). Abram sent a letter to some Christians asking for help as his people wanted to hear more about the Christ-child. The help duly arrived and within five years, 1,500 were converted.

I spoke to someone who was ministering on the Island of Sumatra in late 2000 as part of a mission team. He told me that the island has large numbers of believers and the local pastors that he met still speak of revival with warm affection and some said that they were still in the midst of revival.

From October to December 1964 a 'Healing Campaign' was held on the Island of Timor (on the eastern extremity of the Indonesian archipelago) where several thousand people were healed, but sadly the message of repentance was not prominent. 450,000 inhabitants out of more than one million belonged to the former Dutch Reformed Church, but there were only 103 pastors, so the church was not in a healthy state. From 1963-1968 church communion attendance in Indonesia went up twenty-fold.

In July 1965, David Simeon arrived on Timor with an evangelistic team from the Bible School in East Java; they stayed for two months. The message was of repentance, rebirth and sanctification, and this became known as the official birthday of the revival. The Christians got cleaned up and on fire for God and the natives piled their fetishes high and publicly burned them.

Out of the revival, as people got right with God, they desired to spread the good news and missionary teams were formed, (the first being in September 1965, under Pastor Joseph, the superintendent of the Presbytery in Soe). On the 1 October 1965 the Communists tried to take over the country, but failed, this led to a bloody backlash by the Indonesian Muslims. In later years some of the converts became missionaries in other lands.

The evangelistic teams lived by faith and were guided by the Spirit, and saw supernatural events and results. Drunks got sober, natives destroyed their fetishes, and some tore down their temples; Muslims saw Jesus as the Son of God, wrongs were righted and many illiterate people (especially women) received visions and were called to go and preach, under the leading of the Holy Spirit. Sermons of five hours were common and could be as long as fifteen hours as the people were hungry for the word of the Lord, and the sense of time was lost in the presence of God. Crowds flocked to hear these preachers. Within a year 80,000 people were converted to Jesus Christ, half had formerly been Communist and the other half heathen and 72 evangelistic teams were formed and sent out. Within three years, 200,000 had been converted.

The Bible School in East Java played a significant role in the revival as converts were trained and then went forth with the good news in the power of the Spirit. In 1967, the wind of the Spirit swept through the School bringing deep repentance and reconciliation between staff and students who had previously been at odds with each other.

During an eighteen day missionary campaign in West Irian (modern day West Papua) nearly 3,000 people were converted and 250 young men dedicated themselves to full-time gospel work. The evangelising and revival did not go without its opposition and God's judgment was poured out on many a person who stood in His way, some died whilst others were afflicted by the hand of God.[4]

Argentinean Revival 1982-1997

Buenos Aires, in Argentina, had seen an awakening in 1954, under Tommy Hicks healing and evangelism campaign, which won to Christ around twenty thousand souls. The pastors knew that what God did then, He could do again, as long as the conditions were met – prayer, holiness, reconciliation and preaching of the gospel of the Lord Jesus Christ.

The years 1976-1983, were years of oppressive dictatorship under evil military rule. The Roman Catholic Church also had good sway over the people and many had intertwined Christianity and native occult practice which was rampant across the country. Daily witches, warlocks etc. were on national television. The "Dirty War" in which people were detained in the middle of the night by the army or police for no apparent reason had claimed up to 80,000 lives. The economy was a disaster; inflation was over 1000%! The loss of the Falkland War of 1982, over the Malvinas Islands between Argentina and Britain, shocked the proud nation who had been told by the military propaganda machine that they were winning. All these situations gave the people a reason to look forward for answers, something new, which the old order could not give, and Jesus Christ became that answer to millions.

Carlos Annacondia, a nut and bolts businessman was converted in 1979. When he had fully consecrated his life to Christ, he had a powerful desire to be an evangelist and his evangelistic campaigns began in 1981. He held the evangelistic campaigns in the provinces of Buenos Aires and hundreds started to come to Christ during different campaigns. He became the key figure of the revival, but others to name but a few; Pablo Bottarai, Claudio Freidzon and El Silvoso also held strategic positions.

In the early days of the Argentinean Revival, it was the poor and the destitute who filled the plots of land and later the stadiums which were brightly illuminated and pleasing to the eye, a crowd drawer. There were no seats which gave the people freedom to move around so that they did not become restless. As the years progressed, people from other social classes came to know the Lord in these mass evangelistic campaigns. Healings were common, signs and wonders the norm, creative miracles were not unknown, even raising the dead! Deliverance was essential for all new believers along with mass discipleship and being committed to a church of whatever denomination or style took the persons preference.

Many people had to be trained to organise the crowds, others had food stalls to satisfy the natural appetites of man. Months before any campaign commenced prayer would be going up to heaven in which local churches participated.

In some areas, years prior to an event spiritual mapping of an area would be done, various intercessions and obedience's and prayers to help dislodge or disengage a principality/territorial stronghold (e.g. unbelief) over a geographical area (which aided the people being able to respond to the gospel) as the veil had been taken away, and those who were blinded by the enemy were able to see the light of the truth. Old grievances were repented of between different leaders and denominations, which led to open confession and reconciliation which aided rapid church growth.

By 1984, in La Plata, Ensenda and Tolosa, 50,000 people came to Christ and later that year 83,000 souls were won in Mar del Plata under Annacondia's ministry. In some of these campaigns he would preach for two months every night and behind the platform would be a 150-foot tent with yellow and white stripes, which was the "Spiritual intensive care unit" where mass deliverance sessions would be held. Trained workers, "stretcher bearers" would be on the lookout for people manifesting (under the influences of evil spirits/demons) and carry them to the tent where they would pray for them to be delivered. As time went on mass deliverance sessions were commenced as the strong man was bound, Jesus' name invoked and curses were broke.

After the revival ten percent of the population were evangelical. Huge churches were birthed; Omar Cabrera, the 'dean of the revival,' Vision of the Future Church had over 150,000 members who met in various locations across the country.

A.O.G. Pastor Juan Zuccarelli and a prison warden in Olmos Prison, the largest and highest maximum security prison in Argentina saw revival, when three hundred prisoners came to a 'singing meeting' and were locked in! At the end of the preaching of evangelist, (Jose Luis Tessi, from Zuccarelli's church), the Holy Spirit swept in, guards and prisoners were slain on the floor and one hundred people gave their lives to Jesus. Both prisoners and guards received deliverance and a process of diligent discipleship begun. By the end of 1995 forty-five percent of the prisoners were converted (out of over three thousand prisoners) and began holding daily church services. Later the Christians had their own evangelical cell blocks, where formerly the various criminal elements were segregated – but are now one in Christ! The church at Olmos Prison loses members daily, not because they backslide, but because they are released or relocated to other prisons.[5]

Whilst I was at Bible College, prior to the new millennium I was talking to a new student who was the daughter of missionaries to Argentina. They had ministered in Argentina (where she had also lived) for many years. I asked her about the Argentinean Revival and how it was going. She replied, "What revival? There is no revival in Argentina!" This is the problem when you have a country that is three thousand miles long, with populous city centres and like all countries, isolated areas. Firstly, not everybody will get to hear of what is happening, especially if you live in an isolated environment or only move in certain circles. Secondly, a revival may be named after the specific country of origin, but it does not mean that the entire country, or even a quarter of it is affected. There can be many 'hot spots' in strategic areas from which revival flows out from. Just like the Welsh Revival 1904-1905, certain valleys were entirely unaffected as God passed them by, and there are numerous reasons for this.

CHAPTER NINE
Turned the World Upside Down (Acts 17:6)

'But you are a God ready to pardon, gracious and merciful, slow to anger abundant in kindness, and did not forsake them' Nehemiah 9:17.

'Through the Lord's mercies we are not consumed, because His compassions fail not. They are new every morning; great is Your faithfulness' Lamentations 3:22-23.

Claudio Freidzon, Buenos Aires, Argentina

In February 1986, Claudio Freidzon, held an evangelistic campaign in the public square of Plaza Noruega in the Belgrano district of Buenos Aires, Argentina. God moved mightily, there were testimonies of healings, especially those with flatfoot, others whose teeth had been supernaturally filled (who had needed treatment) and more importantly, one thousand people (Claudio's neighbours) surrendered their lives to Christ in just twenty days, and the The King of Kings Church was birthed![1]

By December 1992, what had started for Claudio as a personal thirst for more of the Holy Spirit began to impact large crowds. He rented the largest auditorium in Buenos Aires, with 12,000 seats. When the building was full there was still 25,000 waiting outside! The people waited for three hours for the second service. The Assemblies of God, foreign mission magazine, *Mountain Movers*, published an article which stated: '...Though the awakening began in Claudio's church, it extended to hundreds of pastors and churches...'[2]

In 2006 Joel News reported that in Presencia de Dios, a church in Buenos Aires has seen a powerful move of God. Described as being 'under a growth rhythm where figures do not stop.' There are 1,400 discipleship groups, over forty associate pastors and six daily services! Healings testimonies, economical miracles, conversions and baptisms number in thousands.[3]

Philippines and Argentina

In 1992 pastor Benny Hinn held a historic watershed crusade in Araneta Coliseum in the Philippines, where more than 500,000 people attended services.

In 1994 pastor Hinn held a crusade in the 100,000-seat Huracan Stadium in Buenos Aires, Argentina and had overflow crowds in each service.

Pensacola Revival 1995-2000

The Pensacola Revival is also known as the Brownsville Revival or the Father's Day Outpouring. The vast majority of the factual information below is an eye witness account of what I saw and what I heard, when I visited this revival in July 1997.

For over twenty years faithful members of the congregation had been praying for revival, but in the last two and a half years prior to the revival breaking out the Sunday night meeting was given over entirely to prayer, praise and worship.

In 1992 Dr. David Yonggi Cho (who in 2006 has a church membership of over 800,000) was ministering in Seattle, Washington and began praying for revival in America. As he prayed, he felt the Lord prompt him to get a map of America and to point his finger on the map. It landed on Pensacola, Florida. He sensed the Lord say, "I am going to send revival to the seaside city of Pensacola, and it will spread like fire until all of America has been consumed by it."

Pastor John Kilpatrick was fed up with his role at the large, successful Assembly of God church at Brownsville, Pensacola, Florida, America, and knew there was more. One night in the early hours, whilst alone, he went into the church, placed his keys on the platform, and cried out to God in desperation for His glory: "God, I want to see You move. If You are not going to send revival here, please send me to a place where You are. I don't care if it's a small congregation in the middle of nowhere with just twenty-five people. Just take me where You're going to move." He walked out and left his keys there. Every Saturday night he returned to pray and the Sunday morning sermon was frequently on the theme of revival.

Evangelist Steve Hill and former missionary to Argentina came to preach on the Sunday morning Father's Day service in June 1995 and proclaimed that God was going to do something special. At the end of the service, Steve Hill started to pray for people and God turned up; Pastor Kilpatrick was touched by God and fell to the floor and was in a wheel chair for the next few days, being unable to stand in the presence of God! When the people saw their pastor on the floor, then they knew that God was in the house, as this was so out-of-character. Steve who came with only five sermons was asked to preach in the evening service and eventually stayed for five years!

Steve Hill never stepped into the pulpit without the intercessory team praying over him first. By July 1997, over 300,000 people had responded to the call of salvation (and got right with God) and 1.7 million people from all sorts of social and economical backgrounds had visited from around the globe. They came to witness, to be a part of, to see the presence of God manifest and to get a fresh touch of fire. By the close of the millennium over 3.5 million people had visited Brownsville, and multitudes had taken fresh fire to their home churches and glowing reports of what had happened to them. I personally met a young man at a Christian camp who a year previously, as a backslider visited Pensacola, got right with God and was still on fire (for God).

Thousands of people would turn up for the Tuesday night prayer meeting as the sanctuary was spiritually cleansed for the new week's meetings which started on the Wednesday. Some people queued at 4:30am (yes, am!) for the 7pm service! Hundreds upon hundreds of people queued on the streets in temperatures above 35 degrees centigrade in the summer months. I personally saw crowds hundreds of metres long, two to four people thick in the mid afternoon summer heat. Security guards were employed to help assist in security and people management, so as not to cause chaos in the rundown community and there was a big car park to look after. Night after night as the doors were opened at 6pm (the service started at 7pm), people eager for God would cram into the two thousand seat auditorium, others would file into the other building which could seat around seven hundred (a larger building was later built); people were also in the choir room, other overflow rooms and even in the corridors as speakers were located throughout the complex of God's sanctuary, even in the toilets! The *Pensacola News Journal* for November 1997 reported that the Brownsville Church had 107 church employees and their wage bill exceeded one million dollars annually.

Lindell Cooley led the worship, which could last for two hours while heaven and earth met as people and angels sung glorious tribute to the Lamb that was slain.

Steve Hill, night after night (five nights a week) preached a hard core uncompromising message of holiness and repentance – get the sin out of your life, embrace the cross, look to Jesus and call upon Him. Hill would always use props in his sermons and it was different each night. Some of the more notable were a coffin, a tombstone, shackles, a bed of affliction and enlarged playing cards. One night he preached on the blind leading the blind and wore dark glasses, held a white stick and was tapping his way around the stage. On another night the lights were dimmed as a lady wearing a wedding dress marched to the front. One evening very late into the altar call, he felt prompted by God to ask one of the musicians to play a military tune, similar to a bugle call, to which military persons came to the front at the last stages of the altar call.

Every night hundreds of people ran to the mercy seat (and I mean ran!) as teenage Charity James sung the song, "Run to the Mercy Seat." Hill called the people forth, to call upon God to repent; many cried, wailed and moaned in deep repentance, remorse and grief, tears flowed copiously as both child and adult alike called upon the risen Saviour. For me it was the most eerie sound I have ever heard and have never before or since heard repentance like it. But, I know that when people repent like what I saw and heard, they got well and truly saved, as those who have been forgiven more, love more (Luke 7:47).

At the end of the service anybody could go forward for prayer. There were numerous helpers and some strong catchers as most people hit the deck after being prayed for within a few seconds. Many people shook whilst under the power of God, and were covered with modesty blankets, to keep people decent, both men and women. Frequently the leadership would address the issue of ladies dressing like prostitutes and that it was not helpful for anybody. They would also state that they were not talking to new Christians (as it does take time to buy a new wardrobe), but to those who should know better, being older in the faith. The scene was frequently like a close combat battle zone as hundreds and hundreds were touched by God, many appeared to be in a coma and lay on the floor motionless for hours (as issues were being dealt with by God), whilst others would twitch and their closed eyelids would move, some had visions and revelations and some had to be carried out in the early hours and driven to their hotels! The hotel staff in and around the locality got very used to these scenes and after a while quickly realised where their guests had been.

Billionaires attended, as did prostitutes, the homeless, murderers, backsliders, homosexuals, witches and warlocks; burnt-out discouraged Christians and many left changed persons. Others mocked this revival and said God was not in it – it was of the flesh. On at least one night at which I was present members from another church in the locality placed leaflets on those who had been slain in the Spirit, stating how foolish they looked. This was also addressed from the front, not to mock what God was doing.

Steve Hill often said, "Opinions are like trash cans [rubbish bins] everyone's got them, and most of them stink!" But the results of the fruit of these individuals' lives speak for themselves, the drug addicts were set free, backsliders left their ways of sin for holiness, marriages and broken relationships were restored, restitutions were made and several thousands of adults enrolled into the School of Ministry which they set up to train these new disciples, who have fanned throughout the world as witnesses for Jesus Christ and been fire-starters in their own churches. The *Pensacola News Journal* for November 1997 stated that there were 507 students attending the School of Ministry, 120 of which lived on campus.

Members of Brownsville Church during the revival held Awake America campaigns in different states of America; Steve Hill would preach and give an altar call, thousands of people responded, if not tens of thousands during these campaigns.

Before the revival only three out of the thirty-two schools in the area had Christian Unions, within two years, they all had them! Students in class would be touched by the Holy Spirit and collapse on the floor and many of the schools had separate rooms where these pupils could be placed. Countless testimonies of people poured in over the years and the healing power of God was very evident.

On the Sunday morning Pastor Kilpatrick would take the service. As in most churches an offering was taken (of which they had about twenty offering plates). They told the visitors not to put their tithe into this offering as it would in affect be a curse. They stated that all tithes should go to your home church [unless directed by God otherwise], but they would accept any offerings and stated that the revival was expensive to maintain.

The leadership frequently stated from the front, that many people had so called 'words from the Lord' for the church, and that if they did, they were to submit it in writing, with a covering letter from their pastor. Included in the letter had to be their commitment to their home church, references to their lifestyle and that they regularly tithed, otherwise the Brownsville leadership would not be able to take them seriously.

As in all revivals, many people spoke against this move of God, whilst other churches in the locality and beyond embraced it and saw the fire of God move in their church. About twenty-five members of the Brownsville church left, as it upset their weekly routine. One person from another country wrote a booklet describing why Pensacola was not of God after watching just one video, and having never visited! Members of another church denomination in the local area which I visited, also thought that the Brownsville move was not from God, and had nothing good to say about it – jealousy is a dangerous thing (Acts 13:44-45). Several people over the years have spoken to myself and in their opinion told me why the Pensacola Revival was not from God (and never in a polite manner) though they never visited the place or researched the facts themselves which I thought was very sad indeed. It was after my visit in July 1997 to the Pensacola Revival, that I received my call to Bible College and full-time ministry and if I had not been obedient to the divine call then this book would have never been written.[4]

China's Phenomenal Growth

In the latter part of the twentieth century the Church in China saw phenomenal growth, as the House Church movement was estimated to be growing by sixty thousand persons each day at one stage and that in the midst of terrible persecution. China's pastors, evangelists, house leaders and ordinary Christians are frequently taken into captivity, imprisoned and tortured (breaking bones, ripping flesh and even killing their prisoners by over zealous sadistic provincial officials or guards). One evangelist was imprisoned for forty years and for at least three decades was routinely beaten for refusing to renounce the Lord Jesus Christ, another was released after forty-five years in a labour camp.[5]

At the beginning of the twentieth century under the Boxer Revolution many of the missionaries in China fled for their lives as anti-Western sentiment swept the nation, hundreds were martyred along with thousands of indigenous believers. Further persecution arose under the Cultural Revolution of Chairman Mao and his disastrous reforms.[6]

Since this time there have been sporadic persecutions across China even though China itself claims: "Citizens of the Peoples Republic of China enjoy freedom of religious belief..." but as long as you register your church etc. and conform to the "administration organisation site autonomously." In other words, as a Christian church/organisation you are accountable to the atheist Communist regime (and they tell you what you can or cannot preach on or do, and who you can and cannot employ). It is the non-religious and godless, dictating to the righteous and godly.

On Sunday 20 November 2005, American President, George W. Bush, during his visit to China attended a state-run "patriotic" church (one of only five Protestant churches permitted in Beijing). It was an appeal for China to grant greater religious and political freedom to its citizens. He said prayers and wrote in the guest book: "May God bless the Christians of China." Outside the church President Bush said, "My hope is that the government of China will not fear Christians who gather to worship openly, a healthy society is a society that welcomes all faiths." Within a few days some of the leaders within the House Church movement were released from prison.

In the city of Wenzhou, this is known as "China's Jerusalem" there has been phenomenal growth. Out of a population of over seven million, there is believed to be nearly one million Christians (fourteen percent) and literally hundreds of churches in the city, some as tall as a five storey building. This amount of Christians in one area has led to a huge growth in private enterprise and a six hundred percent rise in Gross Domestic Produce (GDP) from 1980-1990. In this city the authorities generally turn a blind eye to the churches which though registered as "places of religious worship" are not associated with the government's legally registered Three Self Patriotic Movement (largely a puppet denomination of the Communist state), but there have been crackdowns in the past where churches and temples have been demolished by orders of the Religious Affairs Bureau.[7]

The House Church in China is now estimated to be over 120 million strong out of a population of 1.3 billion and has permeated all social levels of society, from the fields to the shops, from the universities and even into the government.

SECTION III

UNDERSTANDING REVIVALS AND AWAKENINGS

CHAPTER TEN
What are These? (Joshua 4:21)

'God came from Teman, the Holy One from Mount Paran. Selah. His glory covered the heavens, and the earth was full of His praise. His brightness was like the light; He had rays flashing from His hand...' Habakkuk 3:3-4.

Peter preached, "Repent therefore and be converted, that your sins may be blotted out, so that times of refreshing may come from the presence of the Lord" Acts 3:19.

Common Characteristics in Preparation for Revival
With all revivals, there are differences, but there are also common characteristics and features, regardless of the people involved, the decade or century, and in which country or continent the revival took place. If you were to read extensively about revivals and revivalists down the ages, then you will start to see some common threads woven through history. Some of these common characteristics are:

- Before a revival comes, there will always need to be preparation on behalf of the body of Christ. This frequently occurs when a minister starts preaching and teaching on the nature and conditions of revival, and out of this comes prayer.
- Revival always begins with a burden. It could be one person or more, who become(s) a watchman/woman or watchpersons who stand in the gap (intercession) on behalf of the land.
- Those with a burden would have long realised that personal revival always precedes a local or

national revival. They would have got their own lives sorted out before they can expect God to moves others enmasse.

- Genuine disciples of Jesus Christ will be grieved and burdened over the state of the Church, their community, city, or country, as sin and lawlessness abounds. They will be grieved that the name of God is blasphemed and derided on a daily basis.
- They desire Jesus' name to be lifted high and flown as a banner across their land. They wish all Christians could enter into a living relationship with the Holy Spirit, to know Him and His convicting and guiding power.
- Before a revival comes, things will often look there worst. God frequently steps in at the last minute, at the darkest hour (if God did not step in with His mercy, then He would have to step in with His judgment).
- Before a revival comes, faithful disciples of Jesus Christ will be praying and interceding for God to move His mighty hand and to pour out His Spirit from on high. They will plead the promises of God as contained within the Holy Bible. It has been said by many a preacher that preceding revival, the word O' is always used in passionate prayer and pleading. Many a revivalists will go through a period of agony in prayer until they get an assurance that God will move.
- These disciples will be earnestly trying to live righteous and holy lives. They will talk, read and study about past revivals and awakenings and encourage others to seek God for revival blessings.

Dr. Martyn Lloyd-Jones speaking in the context of how revivals begin in regards to persons present and places involved (cities to villages) said, "Those who try to lay down rules and regulations, and think because it happened once in this way it will happen again in the same way, are showing a complete misunderstanding of the laws of the spiritual realm. There are endless variations in the way in which it [revival] begins...and the variations in the type of men God uses in revival. Sometimes God uses very great men...but He doesn't always do that...[at other times] He uses simple, ignorant, unknown, most ordinary men."[1]

Common Characteristics of Revivals

Generally, Christians when referring to manifestations think of the demonic and the activity of the devil, the work of the anti-Christ. In this book, unless stated otherwise, the word manifestation(s) refer to physical phenomena, which come from the Spirit of God.

- When revival comes there will be a heightened awareness of God's presence. The Holy Spirit, as the third Person of the Trinity will be honoured. He will not be seen as a "thing" or "influence" but as a Person, who can convict of sin, show true righteousness, guide into all truth, give direction etc. and glorify Jesus.
- There is a deeper reality of the cross of Calvary, the blood of Jesus, and what He has done for mankind (Isaiah 53).
- God's Spirit is no respecter of persons. People of all ages, from different social backgrounds of varying educational levels get saved, including young children. Teenagers become radical for Christ. They may not dress like you, but they will press in for the deeper things of God and are not ashamed to shout Jesus from the rooftops! The majority of these converts will stay true to God and be trophies of grace, lasting fruit.

- There will be conviction of sin to a lesser or greater degree. Many non-Christians will writhe in agony of soul and be in deep torment until they bow the knee to Jesus Christ, or if they are already a Christian until they get specific sins out of their life. Some will fall out of the pew or the seat that they were sitting on or fall over if they were standing up!
- There are always sceptics because of the physical phenomena (manifestations) during revivals. These manifestations can be crying, screaming, shrieking, falling down, turning pale, being unable to walk, jerking, trembling or shaking – to name but a few. All of these manifestations can be from the finger of God, while some will be of the flesh or of demonic origin.
- It is not uncommon for people to fall on the ground under agonising conviction of sin. Some shake, tremble or jerk (not always under conviction of sin, but the Holy Spirit is doing a work), others appear to be in a coma or even dead! People will be converted inside and outside of the church building or wherever people meet, work or sleep. Some people will not even have had contact with another Christian, but the Holy Spirit will get them!
- Those who are under conviction of sin will be encouraged and urged by believers to repent of their sin and to turn to Jesus.
- Not all who are under conviction of sin (those who have been awakened) will come through to conversion and there are numerous reasons for this.[2]
- There will always be confession of sin, frequently in public meetings. These confessions are

prompted by the Holy Spirit and aid the joyous release of forgiveness.

- During revival, Christians will have a sharper conscience and will feel quick conviction for seemingly minor offences, (though in God's eyes, sin is sin).
- Praise and worship to God will become more real, regardless of the style of worship you are used to.
- Bible reading, prayer and Sabbath observances will be more strictly observed; not out of compulsion or coercion, but out of a desire to please the Master and to get to know Him and His ways more.
- Denominational and sectarian barriers are often broken down as God's people hunger and thirst after righteousness. For example, Pentecostals and Baptist, Wesleyan and Presbyterian, Anglican and Charismatic's come together. Those with Calvinistic and Armenian theology will also rejoice together in the harvest and promote the work of God. Sometimes the clergy of certain denominations will not embrace the move of God, but those within their churches will. Brethren will not be focussing on the minor issues of doctrine. They will realise that we are united by our faith in Jesus Christ and not our doctrine. They will focus on the more important task of glorifying Jesus, reaping the harvest and aiding discipleship.
- Many secular pursuits and hobbies, (though not sinful in themselves) are disregarded for the greater price of the heavenly things above.
- The press and frequently the secular papers will write articles about the move of God. Often they are open and honest, but some reporters will always denounce it as fanaticism, hypnotism,

emotional experience or some psychological trick, to pull in the masses. Good as well as bad reports will bring the unconverted closer to what is happening, as curiosity always gets the better of people.

- Leaders will have to lovingly rebuke Christians who act in the flesh (trying to imitate the things of God) and on occasions those who oppose the things of God.

Revival and the Community

- Crime will drop; the police and local magistrates will notice the effect, though not all in authority will acknowledge the decrease of crime as a work of God.
- Wrongs will be righted; restitution and reparation (where applicable) will be commenced.
- It is not uncommon to find whole families turning to God in times of revival.
- There will be a greater freedom to worship in public. Especially before the popular advent of motor cars, it was common during revivals, to hear passengers on trains and buses singing hymns as they were going to and from revival meetings.
- The sales of Bible's and other Christian literature always increase as Christians are revived and the young converts hunger for more biblical truth. Many will frequently advance from milk to meat in a short space of time, as if being fast-tracked by God.
- During revival, evangelism always takes on a new and important responsibility for every Christian. New converts become the newest (and often best) evangelists and desire their friends, family, work colleagues etc. to come and meet God for themselves. During revival, people love

to give their testimony and tell people what God has done for them, as a trophy of grace. Often visitors from another town who have tasted of the heavenly fire, upon giving their testimony in a place where revival has not yet started will become a fire-starter in that church or community. If they are asked to pray for believers (the laying on of hands) they will soon realise that they have received a level of anointing which has been transferred to them.

- When people hear of what God is doing in another town, this acts as an encouraging stimulus to pray for God's Spirit to come to their town.
- There is always a social impact, ministry of helps where those converted want to do more to reach and help their fellow man, (e.g. Temperance Societies, Missionary Societies, abolition of slavery, workers rights etc.) sometimes it is felt straightaway, at other times these ministries are birthed during a revival or after a revival.
- During revival, Christians always become more generous and liberal in their giving. The finances will in some shape and form frequently filter into the community. In many revivals this has included: employing new staff, social aid, paying off the church mortgage, being able to afford essential repairs to the church building, purchasing new(er) church vehicles and supporting budding evangelists and new missionaries etc.
- As people hear of a revival breaking out, many hungry Christians will visit the church or location. They will naturally spend their money on hotels, B&B's, food, petrol, spiritual resources etc., and the community benefits with new jobs being created.

Supernatural Events of Revival

Everything to do with revival is supernatural as it is an awesome move of the Spirit of God, but the items listed are just a taster of what God has done and can do in revival.

- Certain persons, (Christians and non-Christians) men, women and even children will have dreams and visions. Some people have visions of hell, the lost, of heaven or of the Saviour etc. Generally speaking, during revival Christians have had visions to give extra impetus to the work of evangelism, whereas non-Christians have had visions to either show them where they were going (hell, the judgment of God) or visions of the Saviour (the mercy of God).

- There will be prophecy. Often speaking about the nearness of the Second Coming and the call to get right with God, to be ready for Jesus Christ's return.

- To a lesser or greater degree, the supernatural hand of God will move. Anything from instant healings, instant deliverance from demonic powers, to angels appearing or hearing angels singing or supernatural light appearing. On occasions, Jesus Himself has appeared.

- It is not uncommon for non-Christians to fall, drop or sink to the ground under agonising conviction of sin (though some do appear peaceful), being stricken by God. Some shake, tremble or jerk; others appear to be unconscious, in a comma or even dead. And can stay in that state for hours or days, and have to be carried from the meeting or the field, depending on where God struck them.

- Some Christians will agonise in prayer for the lost, being burdened by the Holy Spirit. Those under such burdens may fall to the ground and groan in the Spirit.

- Some of the physical phenomena during revival can be that non-Christians lose their sight, hearing, ability to speak or the ability to walk for a period of time. Some Christian can become drunk in the Spirit and have to be carried from the meeting; others are incoherent for a time – intoxicated by the Spirit of God.
- Buildings have been shaken in past revivals as the Holy Spirit comes down. Others have felt the wind of the Spirit as He blows through a meeting.

Reoccurring Experiences in Revival

- Those who have been under deep agonising conviction of sin (many of whom appear to be in a coma or even dead) and who had led dreadfully evil lives get delivered from demonic spirits, as well as being converted. It appears that the longer they stay on the ground 'as stricken' by God, the deeper the work of grace and the greater the deliverance that they receive.
- The Holy Spirit through the ages has descended on schools; bringing children, teenagers and teachers alike into a saving knowledge of Jesus. Often it is like a ripple effect, moving from one classroom or floor to another. On occasions this effect had travelled outside of the school gates and into the community.
- There are always some believers whose faces shine or radiate with the glory of the Lord. This could be a revivalist, coming out of their prayer closet, or a new convert, rejoicing in his or her newfound salvation. This glowing or radiance can last for hours or a few days.
- In past revivals down the centuries there have been several cases where businesses (shops

and *factories) have had to close for a period of time. The workers being dismissed because of God's Spirit falling on the work force. Firstly, the saving of people souls is more important than profit. Secondly, *it can be unsafe to work in such situations. Thirdly, the workers minds are occupied with something of a far greater importance (eternal issues) than manual work.

- The consumption of alcohol always drops. Pubs in small communities or even larger towns will go out of business and the drinking trade will take a steep decline. Landlords and brewery owners will be furious. Sometimes Christians do become drunk in the Holy Spirit and are unable to stand or become incoherent in their speech.

- In the presence of the Lord time does not exist; five hours in the presence of the Lord can seem like ten minutes. This is why revival meetings are so protracted and frequently go through the night, until sunrise. If a revival persists for some time, the leader will usually try to end a meeting in the early hours, so as to allow those present to get some rest, ready for the next day. Worship as well as preaching (if there is any) can go on for hours and hours, without people getting restless.

- God's grace always reaches down to the worst of sinners. Even those who openly mock God (mock the revival and defy His laws) have been stricken by the Holy Spirit. Some get stricken with the grace of God, whilst others become stricken with His judgment. The latter leads to death and an eternity in hell. Sometimes these God mockers are struck dead instantly, at other times within hours or weeks, often suffering in a most miserable way. Some even take their own life.

- There are always a good number of those who were once mockers of the things of God (especially those who spoke badly of the revival and publicly maligned the leaders); upon conversion will be led to come and apologise to the leaders of the revival.
- Sometimes the leaders of certain denominations will not embrace a revival but those within their churches will. Roman Catholics have frequently disdained revivals (often believing them to be Protestant). Some openly mock the Protestant 'excitement' yet still some get converted.
- Many of those who have been in revival or converted in times of revival will be led into the ministry and some will become missionaries.
- Ladies and young women have been used in revivals, as revivalists, evangelists, or singers, helpers or intercessors who accompany a revivalist as part of a team.
- In many revivals there have been instances of heavenly music, as if the angels themselves are singing in the heavens above and can be heard on earth. These events have happened inside and outside of the church, even in the open fields.
- Fishermen or sailors (who have been aboard their ship upon coming near port where there is a revival), have been struck by the Spirit of God whilst others have been converted on the open seas, having had no contact with the revival!

Physical Dangers with Revivals
- Extensive and prolonged revivals (those that go on for months or years, and the longer the better!) are exhausting. Evening meetings can continue until the sun rises, but it is unwise to rise up early and to go to bed late. There is a big

danger in being so excited about the things of God (spiritual hyperactivity) that people neglect to rest, sleep and eat at sensible times. This can lead to burn-out or a physical breakdown.

- Daily life still goes on, children have to go to school and most adults have a job to hold down. Do not neglect the necessities of life. We dishonour God by doing shoddy workmanship when we have the ability to do better.

- A church or small village could be overrun with visitors, seeking to have an encounter with God – this is a good thing, but your church could get swamped with people, having protracted meetings, day in, day out and this will take its toll on the church building and property. You could also have car parking problems. People will be queuing to get inside church (praise God!), but the neighbours may not appreciate it, and in more modern day revivals, security guards and nursery carers have been employed to assist in people management (and these cost money to employ).

- Revival often precedes a time of judgment or persecution. This is to prepare the Church for the hardships to come; this was clearly seen twelve years after the revival in the Belgian Congo of 1953 when civil war tore the country apart. At other times amidst persecution revival can break out. This is most clearly seen in the Indonesian revival of 1964 and the revival in China from the twentieth century onwards, where the church has seen phenomenal growth.

Demonic Dangers with Revivals

- There will always be opposition to revivals and new moves of God. There are always a minority who resist change. It is not uncommon for some of those who have prayed for revival to reject it when it comes, as it did not line up with their preconceived ideas.

- When God moves, the devil likes to rear his head and causes opposition. Christians, who may be unspotted from the world, can still come under the influence of the evil one. If those who have received God's grace can cause problems, how much more the graceless!

- Even within a revival there will be those who prophesy, but not of the Spirit of God, it could be demonic or of the flesh. It is the leader's responsibility to address the situation and the person concerned, to rebuke the devil and to protect the flock.

- Depending on your country, during revival there will be witches, warlocks, satanists or witchdoctors turning up at the meetings to do spiritual battle. It may be chanting, incantations, casting spells, cursing or placing accursed objects etc. in and around the church building. They should be challenged in the name of the Lord. Intercessors remember, 'we do not fight against flesh and blood, but against principalities and powers…' (Ephesians 6:12). Some of these children of the devil will get converted, some will not.

- Leaders of the revival will suffer persecution and possible attempted assignations. Most attempted assignations have only been in the hearts of the perpetrators who have turned up at a meeting with a sword, knife or gun etc., but have been struck by the mercy of the Spirit of grace and supplication. On one occasion a gun was put to a revivalists head, the trigger was pulled but it failed to fire. One revivalist was attacked in his lodgings by a 'seeking' gentleman wielding a sword, the revivalist cried, "Murder, murder!" and people came to his rescue! Open-air preachers will get objects thrown at them. Someone once said that you cannot have a true [open-air] revival without a riot! The apostle Paul would agree with that statement. Some modern day high profile men of God, who have been used in revivals, do have bodyguards. This is wisdom, and so is wearing a stab/bullet proof vest. Within certain denominations they have a space in front of the pulpit called the "Big Seat" where the elders sit and face the congregation. This was birthed from the occasions where people would try to mount the pulpit and assault the preacher. '...There is nothing new under the sun' (Ecclesiastes 1:9b).

A True Revival

Some theologians claim that a true revival will have three characteristics (though I say four) and if these three things are not evident, they say, then it cannot be described as a revival in the true sense of the word.

1. A palpable sense of God's presence.
2. A deep desire to be rid of all sin.
3. A powerful impact on the outside community.

A fourth point is that when people are changed, there will always be a practical outworking of manifest fruit in a persons daily life. Frequently there will be restitution (where possible) for various sins committed prior to conversion, e.g. returning stolen goods, making bad debts good etc., or reparation, e.g. returning a bribe etc.

During the 1904-1905 Welsh Revival (and other revivals) bad debts were paid and many a child who had been neglected due to his or her father's drinking habits, upon conversion was loved immensely and was clothed properly.

CHAPTER ELEVEN
A Fountain Shall be Opened (Zechariah 13:1)

'Who is this who comes from Edom, with dyed garments from Bozrah, this One who is glorious in His apparel, travelling in the greatness of His strength? – "I who speak in righteousness, mighty to save" ' Isaiah 63:1.

Jesus said, "...I will build My church, and the gates of Hades shall not prevail against it" Matthew 16:18.

Why Revival is Needed

Revival is needed because God said, "By those who come near Me, I must be regarded as holy; and before all the people I must be glorified" (Leviticus 10:3). Revival is therefore primarily for the glory of God and for the honour of His name. God sends revival to the body of Christ, "that all the people of the earth may know the hand of the Lord, that it is mighty, that you might fear the Lord your God forever" (Joshua 4:24). Revival is a vindication of Himself and asserting His own power and glory so that the people of the earth "shall know that the living God is among you..." (Joshua 3:10). Revival reminds us that God dwells in the Church (Ephesians 2:21-22) and that 'the gospel of Christ is the power of God to salvation' (Romans 1:16).

Revival is not an option; revival is a MUST. God will not stand to be mocked by popular society without either sending His judgment or revival. I MUST BE GLORIFIED are His words and only in times of revival will nations turn and truly glorify the Lord.

In a time and place where Jesus' name is used as a cuss word, when Christians are lukewarm, when materialist mindsets have become more important than reaching-out to the lost, then revival is needed.

When church attendance and religion is down, yet binge drinking and crime is up; alongside vandalism, a lack of the fear of God and low morality, where lawlessness abounds, and where there is total disrespect for those in authority, then revival is needed.

Jesus Christ needs to be lifted high as a banner across our land. For those who do not put their faith in the Lord Jesus Christ for their eternal redemption, they will be doomed in hell for all eternity, because the Judge of all the earth will do that which is right (Genesis 18:25).

- Andrew Bonar, writing on revival said, "The rousing up and reviving of believers is not a small matter; it concerns the glory of God. If the lamps do not shine, it does not speak well for the oil, nor for the care of the keeper. And if the children of God do not testify for Him, it does not speak well for their High Priest in heaven, nor for the Holy Spirit within them."[1]
- Rev. Duncan Campbell (used in the Lewis Revival 1949-1952) said, "Revival is not churches filled with people, but people filled with God. Revival is God going among His people. In revival, the church, the roadside, the hillside – become places made sacred by the presence of God and the cry of the repentant."

Charles Finney, nineteenth century revivalist stated nine reasons for when a revival is needed:

1. When there is an absence of love, confidence, and unity among Christians. It is vain to call upon them to love one another while they are sunk in stupidity and coldness.
2. When there are jealousies, dissensions, bitterness, and evil speaking among Christians.

3. When the Church becomes worldly in dress, parties, amusements, reading novels and worldly books.
4. When professing Christians fall into gross and scandalous sins.
5. When a spirit of controversy prevails among Christians.
6. When the wicked triumph over, and mock and scoff at the Church.
7. When sinners are careless and stupid (going down to hell unconcerned). The duty of Christians is to awake them, like that of a fireman in the case of a fire. Their guilt is similar to that of firemen who will sleep on when the city is ablaze.
8. Without a revival sinners will grow harder and harder under preaching.
9. There is no other way in which a church can be sanctified, grow in grace and be ready for heaven. Hearing sermons week after week is not enough and every week it is more difficult to rouse the believer to do his duty.[2]

Evangelist and teacher Leonard Ravenhill wrote: 'Why does revival tarry? The answer is simple enough – because evangelism is so highly commercialised. The tithes of widows and of the poor are spent in luxury-living by many evangelists. Revival tarries because of cheapening the gospel. The platform has become a shop window to display our gifts, and the "visiting team" look like a mannequin parade. Revival tarries because of carelessness. At the altar, too little time is spent with those souls who come to do eternal business. The evangelist is happy seeing his friends; and while sinners groan at the altar, he is drinking in the rich cream of men's praises. Revival tarries because of fear. As evangelists, we are tight-lipped about the spurious religions of the day as if there were more than one name whereby men must be saved. But Acts 4:12 is still in the Scriptures. Revival tarries because we lack urgency in prayer. The biggest single factor contributing to delayed Holy Ghost revival is the omission of soul travail. We are substituting propaganda for propagation. How insane! Finally, revival tarries because we steal the glory that belongs to God. Away with all fleshly backslapping and platform flattery! Judgment must begin with us preachers!'[3]

Oswald J. Smith wrote: 'The greatest need of the world and the Church today is a mighty manifestation of the Spirit of God. Before the days of Finney revivals there were only 200,000 church members in the United States. When Finney ended his ministry, over three million had joined the churches. The greatest days of the Church have been the days of revival. Nothing can take its place. The best that man can do does not meet the need. Only as God comes upon the scene in revival power are the problems solved.'[4]

Dr. Martyn Lloyd-Jones, spoke in 1959 (the centenary of the 1859 revival), from Joshua 4:21-24; the twelve memorial stones that the Israelites set up to remind the children of God of the past miracle (when the Jordan River dried up and the Israelites crossed over into the land of Canaan). Dr. Martyn Lloyd-Jones said, "The need of the hour is revival in the Church...man is impotent to deal with it [the state of the nation]. There is no more important subject for the Christian Church at this present hour than this very question, of the need of revival. I say there is nothing more important than this, it is second to none. And the greatest need of the hour [See Appendix C] is that the thoughts and the minds and the prayers of Christian people, everywhere throughout the world should be channelled and directed into this matter, of the urgent need of revival...the greatest problem confronting us in the Church today is that the vast majority of professing Christians are not convinced of the reality and the desirableness of revivals."[5]

- Politicians can make good laws, but they cannot make good people. The Holy Spirit not only shows people how they ought to live but can give them a new heart to enable them to obey Him (Ezekiel 36:25-27).[6]
- Bishop Ryle (from the nineteenth century) said, "If it were only a little mending, a little patching, a little turning over a new leaf, then man might do this. But when it is a translation, [a complete transformation] a creation, a resurrection, God must do it."
- An eye-witness from Bicester during the 1860 revival in England said, "It is not asserting too much to say that a greater number of sinners have been converted to God in Bicester, and within eight miles of it, during the last ten months than have made an open profession of religion during the last two hundred years!"[7]

Thomas Jones in October 1859, gave a typical statement of the nature of the work accomplished during the Welsh Revival of 1859. '1. The additions to the churches amount to many thousands, far greater than has ever been known in Wales within the same period of time. 2. I have gathered from inquiry that not one person in every fifty of those who have assumed a profession of religion within the last four to six months, has relapsed into the world. 3. The people generally have been solemnised and brought to think of religious things. I asked an individual near Machynlleth whether the morals of the people had improved; he replied, 'Oh, dear, yes, entirely', and then turned to his wife for a confirmation of his statement. 'Yes,' she said, 'they are; every day is a Sunday now.' 4. A missionary spirit has taken possession of the churches. There is no limit to their desire to save the whole world. 5. The ministers and preachers are anointed with fresh zeal, and are animated with a new spirit. The churches and their office bearers are filled with ardour of their 'first love'. 6. There is a great increase of brotherly love amongst professing Christians, and more cordial co-operation amongst the various denominations in their efforts to do good, and to oppose the common enemy. These are undoubted facts; and I am sure they have not been produced by satan; nor could they be effected by men without aid from above.'[8]

Colin C. Kerr in a broadcast for the British Broadcasting Corporation (BBC) from St. Paul's Church, London in October 1942 said, "When there have been these great movements of the Holy Spirit, then there's invariably been a tremendous sense of sin, and that had led to emotion. How could men suddenly come face to face with their lost condition, with un-forgiven sin, and with the realities of death and judgment and still be without emotion? The point is that when God visits a land in this way...the emotion is that of sincere repentant soul crying to God for mercy and newness of life. That sort of emotion leads to something [a changed life]. That is why the great revivals have immediately begun the great moral revolutions. When God saves a man's soul He begins to purge his character."[9]

Revival is needed because there lays vast sways of ripe harvest which at any time could go over and be spoiled for ever. Without Jesus Christ no man can get to heaven and without holiness no man can see the Lord. When the Holy Spirit comes in revival power He can move vast multitudes of people to see their unholy state before a holy God and cause them to cry unto God most high. This is not mans persuasion to compel them to come in, but God's arm of love drawing them to Himself in convicting power of sin; the goodness of God leads to repentance, enabling a realisation that forgiveness is only found at the cross of Christ in faith and repentance in the Lord Jesus Christ.

Not everything that Glitters is Gold

There is a common saying which originated from the days of the gold rush, 'Not everything that glitters is gold.' There is real gold and there is fools gold. Fools gold is counterfeit; it still comes from the ground and looks like the real thing, but after testing (or examination by a well trained eye), it can be seen for what it is – fake and worthless.

It has just gone five in the morning and I have awoken much earlier than I usually do, especially as the day before was an eighteen hour day which was exceptional long by my standards. This past month of March 2006 there has been a pastor on Christian television claming that his church is experiencing revival and has done so for many months. Naturally, as someone who is writing a book on revival and who desires to know all about historical revivals that there are, I was excited and curious to see this move of God from my armchair in another part of the world. At first I did wonder whether it would be an evangelistic campaign as since the 1930s many North Americans refer to revival as such; as J. Edwin Orr, in reference to a man telling him of a failed 'revival' (which was in reality an evangelistic campaign) where no one got converted said, "For many it is the only place where a meeting can be a non-starter." Edwin Orr then went on to explain to the man how he did not have revival.

I watched the thirty minute show and came away disappointed. It was not an evangelistic campaign so there were no misperceptions of the word in that context. But what I saw shocked and grieved me, I saw a lot of hype and people being worked up in the flesh (though I do not doubt that God was touching some people), there was no mention of God being glorified (or Jesus being lifted up, praised and worshipped), no mention of repentance, the cross, the blood, sin, of people getting right with God or souls being saved. But within this thirty minute show there were five appeals for your money   (that's one every six minutes!), one of which stated, 'if you want a part of this revival then the only way is to partner with us.' This really disgusted me, linking a 'so called blessing' from God with finances to 'me and my ministry' (as the pastor said who was presenting the show) – who's kingdom was he building? I would suggest his own. This was not revival. This was fleshly manipulation, hype and I-want-to-build-my-own-kingdom mentality.

It is wrong to pass judgment on just one hearing so I tuned in again a week later. Once again there were talks about this revival, more talks from the pastor and more appeals for finances. By now I was feeling quite an aversion to this choreographed charismatic hype and appeals to fleece God's people of their hard-earned cash all in the name of revival, in the name of God Himself – this bordered on blasphemy! Another week passed, the pastor came on air and claimed that the revival had started eighteen months earlier to what he had stated previously – when he gave a so called 'prophecy.' This prophecy was shown, but it was not of God's Spirit, he was prophesying from his own imagination (or from the pit of hell), parts of which were not even Scriptural; it was as if this was another gospel of which the apostle Paul warned off. I visited this ministries website to confirm what had been spoken on TV the night before and watched their thirty minute web broadcast. There were eight appeals for finances, one of which was approximately two minutes long; 'sow your very best seed' was a constant theme. Some of these appeals were linking anointing with finances, whereas anointing is linked to sacrifice, taking up ones cross daily and denying self and abiding in the vine (see, John 15:1-11 and Romans 12:1-2). Part of the self-appointed prophecy included "…the five-fold ministry of the evangelist…" Implying that the evangelists has a five-fold ministry, that's not Scriptural (see, Ephesians 4:11-14) and God does not make mistakes! But even if the pastor went from the Spirit into the flesh (and I do not think that he was ever in the Spirit, but we will give him the benefit of the doubt, as we all make mistakes). When they were advertising their pastor's conference they said, "…we will be anointing this revival into your life." Is that Scriptural? 'To the Law and to the Testimony' I say. Revival is a sovereign work of God. On the final part of the broadcast there was an advertisement to visit the church (an opportunity to sow your very best seed!) and the commentator said, "…Miraculous move of God in every service, the atmosphere is charged with signs and wonder…" he continued, "As revival continues at (name) church…join us at (name) for revival as God shines the spotlight of His favour on you."

Two weeks later I tuned in again, but the entire thirty minute show was about money and you were still encouraged to 'sow your very best seed.' The pastor repetitively said, "Try an experiment and send your best gift, a month's wage, or a week; however you get paid…if you do sow into my ministry a spirit of revival will be released into your life, into your church!" This is not revival. It was pure lies, hype and manipulation – that's witchcraft. You cannot buy God's favour or blessing. May God have mercy on their souls and may God grant us the grace that we never fall into the same trap.

Real Gold or Fools Gold?

Whilst in every revival there will inevitably be mistakes made from within the leadership (and if there is no repentance then the revival will cease), but the basic fundamental truths of any revival have to remain and where they are not present then it cannot be revival. God will not share His glory with another, He will not play second fiddle to another and He will not be mocked, because what a man sows, He shall reap and if we sow to the wind, we shall reap the whirlwind of His wrath. But in His wrath He can still show mercy because He does not treat us as our sins deserve.

As I have already stated I was disturbed by what I had seen and heard but had to base my conclusions not on my emotions, but on the word of God, the Holy Bible. Also, we must all beware of having preconceived prejudices (nationalistic, racial, personal, theological or denominational) which can distort biblical doctrine and sound unbiased judgment. I also compared the alleged revival from accounts from revival Church History. Whilst God can do what He wants, how He wants, when He wants, He will not contradict Himself as revealed in the written word. Throughout Church History there are always common characteristics and features in every revival (see, chapter ten) which reappear regardless of the denomination, personalities involved, country, culture, continent, or century in which the revival took place. But what was present in this alleged revival?

What Could be Seen?

1. God was not being glorified, given honour, worshipped, praised or adored for the alleged revival which was taking place. It was about a personality, a church and a ministry and not about God.
2. There was no mention of Jesus, the cross or the blood. There was no mention about His life, His work or His sacrifice for fallen mankind.

- 146 -

3. There was no mention of the Holy Spirit (also known as the Holy Ghost, God's Spirit or the Spirit of God) who comes in power to convict of sin, to guide into all truth, who manifests His presence (which brings about revival) to glorify God, to revive those who are spiritually stale and to give life to the spiritually dead.

4. There was no mention of sin, of people getting right with God, forsaking sin, confession of sins, living holy or taking up ones cross and daily following Jesus.

5. There was no mention of Christians having being revived (getting right with God and each other, humbling themselves) or souls being saved.

6. The word of God, the Holy Bible was not being honoured, that is, it was not being used to give, to build up, to challenge or to convict, but to get – to get your financial support.

7. There was no mention of any ethical results, such as restitution and reparation; marriages and relationships having been restored, sinful habits having been abandoned or bad debts being repaid etc.

What was There?

1. There was great emphasis about the pastor, the church and the ministry involved. There was also no humility displayed by the leadership team.

2. There was a lot of repetitive talk about money, and that it should be sent to those involved.

3. Some of these financial appeals were linking anointing with finances, it was also stated that the revival could happen in our church or imparted into our lives if we gave financially and this was the only way! This is not Scriptural.

4. There was a contradiction on the start date of the revival by eighteen months. If you cannot get the basics facts right then there is little hope for the deeper things.

5. There was a self-appointed prophecy in which one part was not even Scriptural.

6. There was a lot of hype, Scriptural manipulation, and false promises because they were not based on the word of God – you cannot buy God's favour, blessing or anointing.

There are many who give lip-service to God having wrong motives and those who have no substance. We must also be on our guard against those who are preaching another Jesus and a different gospel with another spirit (2 Corinthians 11:4). The word of God warns about the last days, false prophets, apostles and teachers etc. and warns of those people who will set up teachers to teach them what they want to hear, they are sugar coated preachers with smooth talking tongues. God will tell them on the Judgment Day, "I never knew you," and they will reply, "But Lord, we did all this in Your name, we prophesied, cast out demons and did many wonders" and God will reply, "I never knew you, depart from Me, you who practice lawlessness." Why? Because they did not do the will of our heavenly Father, see Matthew 7:21-23.

Why is revival needed? So that God can be glorified, so that His name can be vindicated amongst the people, so that the Church can get right with God and become revived, so that multitudes of souls can be saved and drawn by the Spirit of God into a saving knowledge of Jesus Christ. Once you have seen revival in person, (or read extensively {not one or two selected books} about revival and awakenings) it makes it a whole lot easier to discern the wheat from the chaff, but we should be able to make wise judgments on everything by its fruit, (or lack of it), see, Matthew 7:15-20; we have the Scriptures as our absolute reference. Revival is needed so that we can be aided in our discernment between the true and the false – "The crow cannot imitate the dove," said Frank Bartleman from the Azusa Street Outpouring.

CHAPTER TWELVE
Arise, Call on your God (Jonah 1:6)

The Lord said: "If My people who are called by My name will humble themselves, and pray and seek My face, and turn from their wicked ways, then I will hear from heaven, and will forgive their sin and heal their land" 2 Chronicles 7:14.

'...Waters shall burst forth in the wilderness, and streams in the desert. The parched ground shall become a pool, and the thirsty land springs of water...' Isaiah 35:6-7.

How to see Revival

To fully understand revivals and awakenings – the pouring out of God's Spirit, we must understand the sovereignty of God. The fact that He is in control of all things, and that all things are under His control. God can use whomever He wills as His instrument(s), wherever, and whenever He wills – because He is sovereign. God chooses the place and time of revival, though man has a part to play, as whenever we do not fail to abide by God's conditions then He will not fail to fulfil His. But we must remember that God's ways are not like our ways and His timing is very different than ours.

Whilst disciples of the Lord Jesus Christ, can prepare themselves as a holy bride, waiting for the Bridegroom, pleading the promises of God, abiding in Him, getting on with the Great Commission, loving our neighbours as ourselves and seeking God with all our strength, heart, mind and soul; we must never forget that 'the wind blows where it wishes.'

Revivals and awakenings are not man made – it is totally, utterly and unequivocally the Spirit of grace being poured out from on high – God coming down and moving the hearts and minds of men, calling them to repentance, faith in Jesus Christ and holiness; as 'without holiness no man can see the Lord.'

Whilst some evangelistic meetings are advertised as 'revival' meetings – this is an incorrect concept of the biblical and historical word 'revive' meaning to bring back to life that which was dead. Therefore, primarily, revival is for Christians, to raise them from the grave, a call out, like Lazarus, "Come forth." Out of this, evangelistic zeal is raised, commitment to God (and each other, John 13:34-35) is deepened, which can affect a whole community as God comes down, as 'the hills melt like wax before the presence of the Lord.'

Dr. Martyn Lloyd-Jones speaking in the context of can a revival be manufactured? said, "A revival is a miracle, it is a miraculous exceptional phenomenon, it is the hand of the Lord and it is mighty...a revival is something that can only be explained by the direct action and intervention of God...these events belong to the order of things that men cannot produce. Men cannot produce them. Men can produce evangelistic campaigns, men cannot and never have produced a revival, oh, they tried too many times...a revival by definition is a mighty act of God, and it is a sovereign act of God, it is as independent as that. Men can do nothing, God and God alone does it!...if you can explain what is happening in a church, then it is not revival...if you can explain a thing then it isn't a miracle. A miracle is the direct sovereign, immediate supernatural action of God and it cannot be explained and that is the essential truth about a revival...there are no methods used in a revival. If methods are used, you can understand the results; if you do certain things you will get your results."[1]

- Rev. Duncan Campbell, at a conference for ministers said, "God is not obliged to send revival because we pray. But He's bound by covenant promise, to send revival when we humble ourselves and pray; when we humble ourselves [in] brokenness of spirit."
- Evangelist and revivalist, Dwight L Moody said, "Move the arm that moves the world" and "The Christian who kneels more, stands better."
- Evangelist and revivalist, Steve Hill said, "Nothing will happen in our nation or in our churches unless we get rid of the sin in our lives."
- Rev. Duncan Campbell said, "A God sent revival must be related to heart purity, a God sent revival must be related to heart holiness...are my hands pure? Is my heart clean? If I'm not prepared for that, then my talk about revival, my praying for revival are just a laughing stock of devils; sincerity, honesty; if our hearts condemn us not, then have we confidence towards God."
- Billy Sunday, evangelist from the Mid-West was converted in 1887. He later saw 40,000 'hit the sawdust trail' (who were truly converted during one month in Philadelphia). He often said, "The carpet in front of the mirrors of some of you people is worn threadbare, while at the side of your bed where you should kneel in prayer is as good as the day you put it down."[2]

Steps Towards Revival

Charles Finney, stated that before revival can come, there needs to be a necessity of union (Matthew 18:19). Obstacles of disunity that hinder the coming of revival and other factors are:

1. Rotten members of the church (so called 'mature members') need to be removed if they refuse to repent and change whilst in gross sin. Sometimes when an attempt is made to cast them from the church, a division will arise, causing a bad spirit, an uneasy atmosphere to prevail – away with all the dross! Deliberate wilful sinning needs to be punished as a little yeast will work through the whole batch of dough. Correct young converts and help train them, teach them and don't beat them, be tender and faithfully watch over them.

2. Whenever wrong has been done to any, there should be a full confession.

3. Unforgiveness is a great obstruction to revival which can lead to a revengeful and unforgiving spirit towards those who have injured them.

4. What is your motive for revival? For the denomination, for the church or for the glory of God? An increase in attendees and more money for the church? Sometimes ministers want revival because their church is going through difficulties which the minister needs to deal with and address, but is afraid to face the issue. At other times another denomination is being blessed more than them and the minister or congregation members wants to even the score.

5. Parents who pray for their child's conversion need to realise that their children are rebels against God, obstinate in their rebellion against Him; a sinner through and through, having a depraved heart who is deserving of the fires of hell; but is in desperate need of the Holy Spirit's quickening. The same is true of believers who pray for non-believers who feel that the sinner is not to blame for his or her actions! The sinner is

to blame for his or her actions and will stand before God on Judgment Day to give an account!

Confession, Repentance and Restoration

If we want to see revival, then each of us needs to be revived. But before we can be revived we need to repent of all known sin and deal with the past, because 'he who covers his sin will not prosper, but whoever confesses and forsakes will find mercy' (Proverbs 28:13).

It is the job of the Holy Spirit to bring conviction of sin to our lives, but our confession is our response to it. Once we have repented of specific sins, then we can express outwardly what has been revealed inwardly – the forgiveness and cleansing in Christ Jesus (Isaiah 1:18 and 1 John 1:9).

We have all sinned against God by breaking His laws, and sinned against each other by personal sin or personal failure (by our wrong actions, reactions, attitudes or decisions that we have made). We may have also sinned against our own body by being sexual immoral, see 1 Corinthians 6:18. Specific sins need to be specifically repented of and confessed by name, 'when he is guilty in any of these matters, that he shall confess that he has sinned *in that thing*' (Leviticus 5:5), author's emphasis. We cannot generalise sin and pray, "Lord forgive me for all I have done wrong" or deny sin and pray, "Lord if I have done anything wrong, please forgive me" for all have sinned and if we say we have no sin, we deceive ourselves (Romans 3:23 and 1 John 1:8). We must repent of specific sins and pray, "Lord please forgive me for being lustful, for stealing, for lying, for being bitter, for being critical, for being angry etc. If we are not sure about certain situations (or habits) whether we have sinned or not then we can pray the prayer of the Psalmist, "Search me, O God, and know my heart: try me, and know my thoughts: and see if there be any wicked way in me" (Psalm 139:23-24, AV).

Within the Christian Church there is a place for private confession to another brother or sister whom we have wronged (Matthew 5:23-24 and 1 John 1:3-7) and at times, a place for public confession so that our brothers or sisters can pray for us to be healed and delivered (James 5:16). If we have sincerely confessed our sin before God then we have received His forgiveness; therefore there is no reason to keep the confession alive because God has forgiven and forgotten (Psalm 103:12 and Micah 7:19). The apostle Paul was the chief of sinners but did not retell the event. Too often those who give testimony, glory more on the past than in God's saving grace. If we need to publicly confess sin, we must specify the sin, but not necessarily go into the details of it. The body of Christ does not need to hear about our lurid fantasies about sister or brother so-and-so or the details of the gory fight we got into because of our binge drinking. To say that we have struggled with fantasy or lust, lashed out at another due to alcohol abuse is adequate. If we are married, we should also ask ourselves what will be the response of our spouse if we decided to publicly confess the sin of adultery without their prior knowledge. With some sins and in certain situations it is not appropriate to confess publicly only to cause another to sin because of what we have confessed, (you confess adultery, unbeknown to your spouse, who is now publicly broken-hearted, humiliated and grieved and they may want to divorce or kill you there and then!) though during times of revival lurid sins are frequently confessed, especially adultery, theft and murder (of the heart and flesh).

J. Edwin Orr who travelled the world, preaching and teaching on personal and national revival, in his book, *This Is The Victory* wrote: 'If you sin secretly, confess secretly, admitting publicly that you need the victory, but keeping the details to yourself. If you sin openly, confess openly to remove stumbling-blocks from those whom you have hindered. If you have sinned spiritually (praylessness, lovelessness, and unbelief as well as their offspring, criticism, etc.) then confess to the church that you have been a hindrance. The devil is ever ready to take advantage of distress of heart, but the Holy Spirit can give the last word in wisdom.'

Those of us who are in leadership are prone to make decisions, which though appeared correct at the time, in hindsight we realise we have not made the wisest of choices, which has since alienated and hurt many from within the congregation. We all make mistake and we can all learn from them, but we still have to face up to our responsibilities, set an example to humble ourselves, apologise and make amends or restitution where appropriate. Revival Church History records that if the leadership within a church (mission compound or Bible College etc.) are not right with God or with other people, especially members from the congregation or community, then they are a hindrance to revival and will entirely block or plug up the channels of divine blessing.

In dealing with an offended party, the longer we delay our responsibility and put it off, the harder it will be. This was vividly illustrated when Jacob returned to be reconciled to his brother Esau whom he had wronged nearly two decades previously. Jacob truly feared for his life, but when Esau saw him, they embraced and wept (Genesis 32:3-12 and Genesis 33:1-4). As long as we fulfil our responsibility and try to be reconciled to our brother or sister then we cannot be held responsible for their decision if they choose to respond in a negative manner.

If we are truly sorry for slanderously spreading malicious rumours about another, then it is our responsibility upon repenting of the sins, to ask forgiveness to the one we have wronged and to counteract our previous statements to those we have gossiped to. As a general rule, the circle of apology only needs to extend to those within the circle of offence.

During the 1859 revival in Wales, unity was manifested amongst several denominations, particularly the non-conformists bodies. 'This unity arose from two main sources; the one, an agreement as to the basic truths of the gospel, and the other, a common, fervent desire for a visitation of the Holy Spirit to glorify Christ as Saviour and Lord. Inasmuch as each denomination based its faith and practice at that time upon God's revealed truth, as found in Holy Scripture, their unity did not involve the violation of any of their distinctive principles, nor the surrender of any essential belief, as these were all common to all. Consequently, their prayer meetings and joint services were eminently useful in furthering the work of the revival, being soundly based on essential, divinely-revealed truth.'[3]

Evangelist Steve Hill, speaking on the revival in Brownsville Assembly of God, Pensacola, said, "I liken revival to war. A soldier trains for war, but when war breaks out the training is over. It's time to fight. I'll fight until the battle is over each night. Like war, revival takes its toll. Revival is expensive – financially, physically, emotionally, and spiritually. You must have a real hunger for God to move."[4]

Pastor John Kilpatrick of Brownsville A.O.G. said, "Revival is work – *major* work. Whenever a church or pastor says, 'Let's make a little room for revival,' they're going to have to amend their whole lifestyle to accommodate a move of God."[5]

Conditions for Revival

Evan Roberts stated that there were four conditions for revival:

1. Is there any sin in your past with which you have not honestly dealt with, or not confessed to God? On your knees at once. Your past must be put away and cleansed.
2. Is there anything in your life that is doubtful – anything which you cannot decide is good or evil? Away with it. There must not be a trace of a cloud between you and God. Have you forgiven everybody, EVERYBODY? If not, don't expect forgiveness for your sins. Better to offend ten thousand friends than grieve the Spirit of God, or quench Him.
3. Do what the Holy Spirit prompts without hesitation or fear. Obedience: prompt, implicit, unquestioning obedience at whatever cost.
4. Make a public confession of Christ as personal Saviour. Profession and confession are vastly different. Multitudes are guilty of long and loud profession. Confession of Christ as Lord has to do with His workings in your life TODAY!

When Revival can be Expected

Charles Finney stated that revival can be expected when:
1. Christians have a spirit of prayer for revival – they feel anxious for souls, he or she thinks of it day and night and dreams of it by night. (Pressing into God and pleading His promises until the blessing comes).
2. When this feeling of, 'My little children, of whom I travail in birth' (Galatians 4:19, as said the apostle Paul), prevails in a church, then there will infallibly be a revival of Christians generally and will involve conversion of sinners to God.
3. Christians confess their sin one to another (Proverbs 28:13 and James 5:16).

4. Whenever Christians are found willing to make sacrifices necessary to carry it on – their feelings, business, time, work etc. The minister must be prepared if it be the will of God, to be driven away from the place and leave the entire event with God!

How to Keep Revival

During the Great Awakening in eighteenth century America, Jonathan Edwards and his people were so fearful of losing the blessing of the Holy Spirit through division that they made a community resolution, a covenant which is dated the 16 March 1742.

1. In all our conversations, concerns and dealings with our neighbours we will be honest, just and upright.
2. If we wrong others in any way, we will not rest until we have made restitution.
3. We promise that we will not permit ourselves to indulge in any kind of backbiting.
4. We will be careful not to do anything to others out of a spirit of revenge.
5. When there is a difference of opinion concerning another's rights, we will not allow private interests to influence us.
6. We will not tolerate the exercise of enmity or ill will or revenge in our hearts.
7. If we find that we have a secret grudge against another we will not gratify it, but root it out.
8. We will not allow over-familiarity in our talk with others, or anything that might stir up licentious behaviour.
9. We resolve to examine ourselves on a regular basis, knowing that the heart is very deceitful.
10. We will run with perseverance the race that is set before us, working out our salvation with fear and trembling.[6]

CHAPTER THIRTEEN
Ask and it Will be Given (Luke 11:9)

Jesus said, "Abide in Me, and I in you. As the branch cannot bear fruit of itself, unless it abides in the vine, neither can you, unless you abide in Me. I am the vine, you are the branches. He who abides in Me, and I in him, bears much fruit; for without Me you can do nothing.

"If you abide in me, and My words abide in you, you will ask what you desire, and it shall be done for you. By this My Father is glorified, that you bear much fruit; so you will be My disciples" John 15:4-5, 7-8.

Prayer and Revival

Most Christians accept the statement that prayer is vital for the life of the believer, and still acknowledge their inadequacy in prayer. Perhaps it's because we think that we have more important things to do. On the other hand there are numerous distractions lurking around every corner – the lusts of the flesh which would consume our precious time and distract us from the more important issues in life.

All revivalists were praying people – being burdened for souls and the state of the society that they lived amongst. They put their faith into action, prayed, interceded and soul travailed; whilst getting on with their daily lives and understanding the more important issues of life – life and death, heaven and hell, and proclaimed the wonderful riches of Jesus Christ.

Jesus frequently got up before dawn, or went away into a solitary place to have communion with the Father. Jesus set the bench mark for prayer and we have to strive towards that goal. The Spirit is willing, but the flesh is weak (Mark 14:38).

We all need to crucify the flesh and take up our cross daily and follow the Master. How much time do we spend doing 'things' which are of non-eternal value? The object therefore is to get our priorities in orders and to glorify the Master.

Those who profess to name the name of Jesus Christ and who choose not to pray for revival are in affect saying, "Who cares about the others? I'm saved, that's their problem not mine!" Is there a Scriptural basis to disregard our neighbours in spite of our knowledge? I think not! This same attitude is also prevalent in those who choose not to witness for Christ. Should we not be concerned about our great cities (Jonah 4:11), our town, our villages, our streets, our neighbours, my neighbours, your neighbours?

Edwin Orr wrote: 'I have little sympathy with the type of Christian who declares that a revival is impossible before the Lord comes. Not only has he no Scriptural warrant for such a statement, but he is making a poor excuse for his own lack of spiritual progress. As a matter of fact, I will say that the man who is not praying for revival is not right with God. It is quite true that Scripture predicts apostasy in the last days…many shall fall away…there will be little faith left on the earth when the Lord comes. But what has that to do with the believer himself, or his relationship with the Master? If revival is possible in one's heart today, it is possible in every heart belonging to God. Revival comes from God the Holy Ghost. He is still able and willing to give refreshing so that the name of Christ might be magnified. The study of the past convinces me that every period of apostasy has been paralleled by a period of intense witness. The purpose of revival today is to prepare Christians for the witness which must be given to this dying world. The Lord is coming soon…but is the Church – the Body which will soon be united to the Head – ready for His coming? Is our present diseased state a credit to us? Never. We ought to be ashamed to think that Christ may come and find us so bankrupt of spiritual life. The truest preparation for the coming of Christ is a quickening in the Body of Christ. The believer who is not earnestly praying for such a revival ought to, and will be, ashamed of himself.'[1]

Andrew Murray wrote: 'Jesus Christ taught us that the answer to prayer depended on certain conditions. He spoke of faith, of perseverance, of praying in His name, of praying in the will of God. But all these conditions were summed up in the one central one: "If ye abide in Me, ask whatever ye will and it shall be done unto you."

'It is only by a full surrender to the life of abiding, by the yielding to the fullness of the Spirit's leading and quickening, that the prayer-life can be restored to a truly healthy state. In intercession our King upon the throne finds His highest glory; in it we shall find our highest glory too.

'The faith in God's word can nowhere be so exercised and perfected as in the intercession that asks and expects and looks for an answer.'[2]

Leonard Ravenhill wrote: 'Revival tarries because we lack urgency in prayer…The biggest single factor contributing to delayed Holy Ghost revival is the omission of soul travail. We are substituting propaganda for propagation. How insane! The only power that God yields to is that of prayer…Who will storm hells stronghold? Who will say the devil nay? Who will deny himself good food or good company or good rest that hell may gaze upon him wrestling embarrassing demons, liberating captives, depopulating hell, and leaving, in answer to his travail, a stream of blood-washed souls?'

Ravenhill continued, 'The secret of praying is praying in secret. Books on prayer are good, but not enough...We must learn to pray, and we must pray to learn...One may read about prayer, marvel at the endurance of Moses or stagger at the weeping, groaning Jeremiah, and yet not be able to stammer the ABC's of intercessory prayer. As the bullet unspent bags no game, so the prayer-heart unburdened gathers no spoil...At the judgment seat the most embarrassing thing the believer will face will be the smallness of his praying.'[3]

Charles Finney said, "The reason why so few Christian's know anything about the spirit of prayer is because they never would take the pains to examine themselves properly, and so never knew what it was to have their hearts all broken up in this way."

Revival Scriptures to Pray and Plead
- 2 Chronicles 7:14 'If My people who are called by My name will humble themselves, and pray and seek My face, and turn from their wicked ways, then I will hear from heaven, and will forgive their sin and heal their land.'
- Nehemiah 9:17 '...But You are a God, ready to pardon, gracious and merciful, slow to anger, abundant in kindness...'
- Numbers 14:21 The Lord said: "But truly, as I live, all the earth shall be filled with the glory of the Lord."
- Habakkuk 2:14 'For the earth will be filled with the knowledge of the glory of the Lord, as the waters cover the sea.'
- Psalm 139:23-24 'Search me, O God, and know my heart; try me, and know my anxieties; and see if there is any wicked way in me, and lead me in the way everlasting.'

- Isaiah 44:3 Thus says the Lord: "For I will pour water on him who is thirsty, and floods on the dry ground; I will pour out My Spirit on your descendants, and My blessing on your offspring."
- Isaiah 45:8 Thus says the Lord: "Rain down, you heavens, from above, and let the skies pour down righteousness; let the earth be open, let them bring forth salvation, and let righteousness spring up together. I the Lord, have created it."
- Jeremiah 14:7 'O Lord though our iniquities testify against us, do it for Your name's sake; for our backslidings are many, we have sinned against You.'
- Joel 2:28-29 Thus says the Lord: "And it shall come to pass afterward that I will pour out My Spirit on all flesh; your sons and your daughters shall prophesy, your old men shall dream dreams, your young men shall see visions; and also on My menservants and maidservants I will pour out My Spirit in those days."
- Matthew 5:6 Jesus said: "Blessed are those who hunger and thirst for righteousness for they shall be filled."

Intercession and Revival

The Rev. Dr. Colin N. Peckham of the Faith Mission Edinburgh, whose wife Mary Morrison (maiden name) saw revival in North Uist, Outer Hebrides, UK (1957-1958), in the foreword, *When God Came Down* edited by John Ferguson, wrote: 'God uses those who are available and useable. He uses those who are cleansed and filled with His Holy Spirit. He uses those who are prepared to pay the price of soul-travail. Burdened, broken, bold praying is the nerve-centre of revival…Intercession costs…true intercession is sacrifice. Because of the demands and price of intercessory prayer, many do not enter its portals and consequently do not gain its benefits…'[4]

Colin Urquhart, in the foreword to *Great Revivals* by Colin Whittaker, wrote: 'Revivals begin as God's response to the heart-cries of His people, not only praying for the lost, but facing their own need of spiritual revival…prevailing prayer can be costly…the cost is not only in prayer. It is the fervent prayers of the righteous that avail much before God. During times of revival there is a real concern among the Christians for righteousness and holiness; to be more Christ-like…[Christians] can only seek God for such times of blessings while being prepared to let the work begin in their own hearts and lives. So there is little point in praying for revival unless we are prepared for God to meet with us, to bring our lives into closer conformity to His will and purpose.'[5]

The Rev. Duncan Campbell said that long before the revival in Barvas, Isle of Lewis commenced (1949-1952), "Several groups of men and women in the parish church at Barvas were spending hours in prayer for an outpouring of the Spirit of God; indeed so great was their burden, and so intense their intercession that the small hours of the morning frequently found them on their faces before God." On another occasion Rev. Campbell said, "Revival did not come through the Faith Mission [which he was a part of], it didn't come because Duncan Campbell went to the Hebrides…revival came because God got His hand on choice men. Men of courage, men that He could depend upon, an enticing place, a place where He would meet them, and they were there to meet Him, come wind, come hail, come storm they were there to meet their covenant keeping God, and they would keep their covenant with Him; Oh where are such men today!?"

Andrew Murray wrote in regards to the coming revival:

1. Revive Thy work, O Lord! Revival is God's work; He alone can give it; it must come from above. 'O Lord, revive Thy work in the midst of the years' Habakkuk 3:2.

2. The revival that God is to give will be given in answer to prayer. It must be asked and received direct from God Himself. Those who know anything of the history of revivals will remember how often this has been proved – both larger and more local revivals have been distinctly traced to special prayer. An extraordinary spirit of prayer, urging believers to much secret and united prayer, pressing them to 'labour fervently' in their supplications, will be one of the surest signs of approaching showers and floods of blessing.

3. It is to the humble and contrite that the revival is promised (Isaiah 57:7). We want the revival to come upon the proud and self-satisfied, to break them down and save them. God will give this, but only on the condition that those who see and feel the sin of others take the burden of confession and bear it, and that all who pray for and claim in faith God's reviving power for His Church, shall humble themselves with the confession of its sin...Humiliation and contrition have ever been the conditions of revival. In all intercession confession of man's sin and God's righteous judgment is an ever essential element...If there be no humiliation and forsaking of sin there can be no revival or deliverance...Every deep revival among God's people must have its roots in a deep sense and confession of sin.

4. There is a last thought suggested by the text from Hosea 6:1-2 'Come and let us return to the Lord: for He hath torn, and He will heal us, He will revive us, and we shall live in His sight.' As

we return to the Lord, revival will come; for if we had not wandered from Him, His life would be among us in power.'[6]

Charles H. Spurgeon (who saw revival in his church in London during the 1850s) prayed: 'O God, send us the Holy Ghost! Give us both the breadth of spiritual life and the fire of unquenchable zeal. O Thou art our God, answer us by fire, we pray Thee! Answer us both by wind and fire, and then we shall see Thee to be God indeed. The kingdom comes not, and the work is flagging. Oh, that Thou would send the wind and the fire! Thou wilt do this when we are all of one accord, all believing, all expecting, all prepared by prayer.

'Lord, bring us to this waiting state! God, send us a season of glorious disorder. Oh, for a sweep of the wind that will set the seas in motion, and make our ironclad brethren, now lying so quietly at anchor, to roll from stern to stern!

'Oh, for the fire to fall again – fire which shall affect the most stolid! Oh, that such fire might first sit upon the disciples, and then fall on all around! O God, Thou art ready to work with us, today even as Thou didst then. Stay not, we beseech Thee, but work at once.

'Break down every barrier that hinders the incoming of Thy might! Give us now both hearts of flame and tongues of fire to preach Thy reconciling word, for Jesus' sake! Amen!'[7]

The Rev. Jonathan Goforth (who saw revival in China and Manchuria 1906-1909) wrote: 'If we all had faith to wait upon God in intense believing prayer there would be genuine Holy Ghost revival, and the living God would get all the glory.[8]

During the Welsh Revival in 1905, when it was in its full swing, Evan Roberts prayed the following prayer in a packed meeting where, thirteen hundred new converts were rejoicing in their new-found faith, "Lord Jesus, help us now, through the Holy Spirit to come face to face with the cross. Whatever the hindrances may be, we commit the service to Thee. Put us all under the blood, Oh Lord, place the blood on all our past up to this moment. We thank Thee for the blood. In the name of Jesus Christ, bind the devil this moment. We point to the cross of Christ. Oh, open the heavens. Descend upon us now. We shall give all the glory to Thy name. No one else has the right to the glory but Thee. Take it Lord, glorify Thy Son in this meeting. Oh, Holy Spirit, do Thy work through us and in us now. Speak Thy word in power for Thy name's sake. Amen and Amen."[9]

Marriage and Prayer

Jack Serra, in his book, *Market Place Marriage & Revival* wrote: 'God expects you to treat your wife in a certain manner – and if you don't, your prayers for the marketplace could be hindered (1 Peter 3:7).' Serra continued, 'The spouse we choose will be critical to every aspect of our lives. One of the most important keys to reaching your city through the marketplace is your marriage [if you are called to marriage]. You can't expect to fulfil Paul's instructions in Philippians 2:1-5 corporately if you aren't fulfilling them in the most basic of relationships, marriage. Paul exhorts us to be likeminded, having the same love and being one in spirit and purpose…to do nothing out of selfish ambition or vain conceit, but in humility, to consider others better than ourselves. We're also commanded to look to the interests of others…if we are doubled-minded about the necessity of a sound marriage, we cannot fully reach the marketplace for Christ, let alone a whole city…a strong and holy marriage is a prerequisite for fulfilling one's God-given destiny in the marketplace, and thereby, creating a foundation for revival and a great movement of God in our day.'[10]

It is interesting to note that John Wesley (who was used during the British Great Awakening 1739-1791) got married later on in life, after his revival ministry had been under way for twelve years. His wife was nothing but a complete nuisance to him, and a hindrance to the furtherance of the gospel. John Wesley married Mrs Vazeille in 1751 and for the first four years she travelled with him, but 'her absurd jealousy acted like fuel to her violent temper.' She would frequently intercept the letters of her husband and 'give them into the hands of his enemies; interpolating words to make them bear a bad construction, and publish them in the papers!' In 1758, she left her husband vowing never to see him no more, sadly she negated on her promise and John suffered more. 'In her fits of jealousy, Mrs Wesley would order a chaise and drive a hundred miles to see who was with her husband in his carriage when he entered town.' On one occasion, one of Wesley's preachers recounted this: 'John Hampton, told his son that he once went into a room in the north of Ireland where he found Mrs Wesley foaming with rage. Her husband was on the floor. She had been dragging him about by his hair, and still held in her hand some of the locks that she had pulled out of his head in fury!' More than once she laid violent hands upon him and tore those venerable locks which had suffered sufficiently from the ravages of time.'[11]

CHAPTER FOURTEEN
Mighty to Save (Isaiah 63:1)

Jesus said, "Remember the word that I said to you, 'A servant is not greater than his master.' If they persecuted Me, they will also persecute you...If I had not done among them the works which no one else did, they would have no sin; but now they have seen and also hated both Me and My Father. But this happened that the word might be fulfilled which is written in their law, 'they hated Me without a cause' " John 15:20, 24-25.

Revivals and Revivalists are Spoken Against

All revivals, awakenings and any move of God have been criticised, from all sides, from those within and outside the Church – Christians (some being tares) and non-Christians. There can be many reason and factors involved, as to why revivals and moves of the Spirit are spoken against – misunderstandings, traditions, jealousy, ignorance of the Scriptures, ignorance of Church History or demonic influences to name but a few. '...[they] speak evil of the things they do not understand...' (2 Peter 2:12).

Jesus had His share of critics, from the Pharisees to the Sadducees, but the common people heard Him gladly. The religious leaders knew the Law and what was written about the promised Messiah, but still they found fault with the work that He did in the name of the Father, even attributing the casting out of demons to Beelzebub, the ruler of demons and denouncing the lame being healed because it was performed on the Sabbath.

Well meaning people frequently get the wrong end of the stick (especially during revival) and will cause (you and others) nothing but agro. Often these people are sincere and eager to protect the name of God, yet they are sincerely wrong, as the move is from God! If something is from God, you cannot overthrow it – lest you even be found to fight against God! (Acts 5:38-39).

Whilst it is comparatively easy to ignore the negative comments from those outside the Church, and to bless those who persecute us, it is more difficult to accept criticism and derogatory comments from your own familiar friend [your Judas] in whom you trusted, who ate your bread and then turned against you (Psalm 41:9). Though Jesus, as He was being crucified was able to say, "Father forgive them, for they know not what they do" (Luke 23:34).

Gwen Shaw in her book, *It's Time For Revival*, wrote: 'All through the centuries, God's greatest revivalists have been rejected, hated and persecuted. Some were even put to death. It can be said of many of God's great servants, "...He was wounded in the house of his friends" (Zechariah 13:6). There will always be those uncommitted ones who become satan's plant to sow seed of divisions and strife...satan hates the true messenger of the Holy Spirit because he knows how powerful anointed preaching is and how much harm it does to his kingdom. That is why the true revivalist (see Appendix D) is on the devil's "hit-list."[1]

Dr. Martyn Lloyd-Jones preaching on revival, from Acts 2:14-18 in reference to physical phenomena (manifestations) said, "Let us always remember this, that whenever the Spirit of God is working in mighty power, the devil always seeks his opportunity. If he can discredit it, he will and he has always tried to do so, he's tried to bring in his counterfeits, he's trying to drive people to excesses and he has often succeeded with particular individuals. That is why you see, you have so much in the Bible about testing the spirits and proving the spirits, we mustn't be misled, there are test's which are given and it is our business always to employ them...Is there anything which is so foolish or ridiculous as to dismiss the whole because of the character of a very, very small proportion? If you begin to do that you'll have to dismiss the whole of the New Testament. Because here we are told that the other forces are ever trying to come in and we must realise the true and understand it, and withstand the other. The New Testament teaches us to expect this and to be on guard against the false and the spurious...these phenomena as the whole revival is as the apostle Peter says, the result of an outpouring of the Spirit of God. We mustn't seek phenomena and strange experiences, what we must seek is the manifestation of God's glory, and His power and His might, what we must seek is reviving; an outpouring of the Spirit of God upon us. And when that comes it will be so amazing that strange and unusual things may happen. But we shall always know that it is God moving amongst us and we shall be ready to identify the false, the spurious; that which indeed even belongs to the evil spirit and restrains it...We mustn't be concerned about these things. We must keep our eyes on the glory of God and the outpouring of the Spirit."[2]

George Whitefield (who was mightily used in the British and American Great Awakening's) was not amused over the physical manifestations which accompanied John Wesley's preaching. Wesley, in his *Journal* wrote: 'I found his objections were chiefly grounded on gross misrepresentations of matter of fact. But the next day he had opportunity of informing himself better: for no sooner had he begun [preaching] to invite all sinners to believe in Christ, than four person sunk down close to him, almost in the same moment. From this time on I trust, we shall all suffer God to carry on His work in the way that pleaseth Him.'[3]

Wesley continued in his *Journal* that a young gentleman upon reading *Whitefield's Journal* approached Wesley by stating that it was 'enthusiasm from end to end' to which Wesley replied after plying a few questions, 'Whatever is spoke of the religion of the heart, and of the inward workings of the Spirit of God, must appear enthusiasm to those who have not felt them; that is, they take upon them to judge of things which they know not.[4]

Evan Phillips who was present at a revival meeting led by Rev. David Morgan in Aberaeron, Wales, UK in early February 1859, wrote his reminiscence of the meetings to the 'Goleuad' of the 5 May 1905. 'The group acknowledged as leaders [Aberaeron presbytery] in the monthly meetings were antagonistic, and even menacing. It seems that they had come there with fists clenched and teeth set, and their new ropes ready to bind the half-crazy preacher, as they esteemed him. They thought they were doing God service.'[5]

Evangelist and teacher Leonard Ravenhill wrote: 'Wesley saw the doors of the English churches closed against Him, and Rowland Hill says of him, "He and his lay-lubbers – his ragged legion of preaching tinkers, scavengers, draymen, and chimney sweepers etc. – go forth to poison the minds of men." What scurrilous language! But Wesley feared neither men nor devils. Whitefield was burlesqued on the English stage in the basest way, and in the New Testament, Christian were stoned and suffered every ignominy. We can have riots without revival. But in the light of the Bible and Church History, where can we have revival without riots?'[6]

Steve Hill wrote: '…Many others at our revival services [Brownsville, A.O.G., Pensacola Revival] almost missed God because they listened to the opinions of others…Remember, there will always be a wave of opposition against us when we begin to enter the deeper things of God. If we desire revival in our churches or in our personal lives, we must get ready to face the persecution.'[7]

John Wesley stated in his *Journal* for June 1745 that a Methodist lay preacher, Mr Maxfield had been taken into custody as one who "disturbs the peace of the parish" and being without visible means of support. Wesley wrote: 'A word to the wise…the Methodist preacher; who "disturbs the peace of the parish" [is] like one who tells all drunkards, whoremongers, and common swearers, "You are in the high road to hell"? Maxfield was sentenced to serve in the king's army as a soldier. He was shipped to Penzance, Cornwall where he spent a few days in a dungeon, before an officer took charge of him.[8]

Thomas Phillips a reluctant historian for the 1859 Welsh Revival, in his book, *The Welsh Revival* which was published in the spring of 1860 wrote: 'Revivals, like everything else, will be freely canvassed by the friends and foes of religion; nor should we be surprised to find, that while some are "glad, and rejoice, and give honour to God," there are those who hesitate and doubt and perhaps a few who dare to go so far as to condemn the whole movement.'

Rev. Duncan Campbell spoke to a gathering of ministers on the theme of revival and what he had witnessed years previously on the Isle of Lewis during the Lewis Revival. One person stood up and said, "Brethren we want revival, but God save us from that!"[9]

- Rev. Duncan Campbell said, "It is not a true revival unless it is spoken against!"

- Charles H. Spurgeon once prayed, "Lord, send us a season of glorious disorder!"
- A senior missionary during the 1950s Congo Revival wrote: 'Grieve not the Spirit. Criticism, or attributing to the flesh that which is of the Spirit, can hinder revival tremendously; let us not be guilty of either.'[10]

In the Flesh or in the Spirit?

- Count Zinzendorf, founder of the eighteenth century Moravian community and missionary movement, speaking on revival said, "Let every minister rest assured that if he desires to enjoy ease, and have all things go on smoothly in his congregation, revivals and conversions dare not take place. For as soon as these occur, the devil is loose, no matter how decently and in order everything may be conducted."[11]
- David Matthews, in his book, *I saw the Welsh Revival* wrote: 'Is there any human being in existence anywhere who would foolishly deny the possibility of unpleasant occurrences during revival time? Such periods represent the abnormal in the experiences of the church of God.'
- John Wesley wrote: 'Be not alarmed that satan sows tares among the wheat of Christ. It has ever been so, especially on any remarkable outpouring of the Spirit; and ever will be, until the devil is chained for a thousand years. Till then he will always ape, and endeavour to counteract the work of the Spirit of Christ.'
- Kurt Koch, in his book, *The Revival in Indonesia* wrote: 'It is a well-known fact that where the Holy Spirit is at work, the devil is not far away. This is the danger threatening every

revival that the demonic and the divine stand so close together.'

- Steve Hill, speaking at the Pensacola Revival in the context of fleshly manifestations said, "Bright lights attract bugs, and these people are probably from your church!"
- Rev. Duncan Campbell, quoting L. E. Maxwell of Prairie Bible Institute, Canada said, "Unless the church senses her divine resources, unseen, untapped, unlimited, she is tempted to resort to any means fair, fleshly or foul to command attention. We need to remember that heresy of method can be as deadly as heresy of message."
- J. Edwin Orr, lecturing on revival said, "There will always be opportunists trying to have their own way."

Steve Hill said, "Revivals will have its problems. You can go to any meeting anywhere and see flesh, if that's what you're looking for. I don't go to these meetings looking for flesh; I go looking for God." By Steve Hill's estimate, 95 percent of what happened during the Brownsville Revival meetings is part of a sovereign move of God. "Am I going to concentrate on 5 percent? No. You deal with the important situations, but you let God control the revival."[12]

Andrew A. Woolsey, in his Biography of Rev. Duncan Campbell noted the revivalist's view of physical phenomena, specifically visions and trances which occurred during revival and wrote: 'This was an aspect of the work which Duncan did not attempt to encourage or explain, but he recognised it was of God and refused to interfere with it, warning those who would associate it with satanic activity, that they were coming perilously near to committing the unpardonable sin.'[13]

Thomas Phillips who documented the 1859 Welsh Revival, in his rebuttal to the objections that the new converts will backslide, betray religion and bring disgrace on the whole movement wrote: 'Suppose this would be found true in part, where would be the marvel? Is not the kingdom of heaven compared to ten virgins, of whom five were foolish? And to a net cast into the sea, which gathered of every kind? And is not the Christian Church a field in which wheat and tares grow together until harvest? We must be prepared for disappointments – a Judas will appear here – a Demas there – Simon the sorcerer, Diotrephes, and men of kindred spirit will "arise" again. It has been so in former revivals and have we right to expect that the present will be an exception!?'

Rev. Duncan Campbell told the following story: In a church evangelistic meeting the preacher had to stop due to the noise of the young people who were shouting for revival to come. Afterwards an elderly man who attended the meeting prayed at home with some others: "Lord I would like to thank You for the young folk at West Benhar, I like to thank You for their enthusiasm, but Lord it must have grieved Your heart, to have seen so much of the steam which ought to have gone to the piston blowing out through the whistle." A prayer of Willy Lesley, from Paisley, as quoted by Rev. Duncan Campbell who went on to say, "There is so much steam [noise and flesh] today in our efforts, just being blown out through the whistle and nothing going to the piston [to the throne room in prayer]. Young folk see to it that the steam goes to the piston and not out through the whistle."

Minister, Dr. J. Cynddylan Jones, in the introduction to *The Awakening in Wales* by Jessie Penn-Lewis, wrote: 'Is enthusiasm permissible in every department of life, but forbidden in Church life? A thousand times, no. How speaks the apostle [Paul]? "Fervent in spirit, serving the Lord." Fervent, literally boiling. "Boiling in spirit." Let none be ashamed of "boiling" in the service of the Saviour. At all events I prefer the congregation that boil over to the congregation that will not boil at all.'

During the Congo Revival of the 1950s, sometimes people within the meetings would try to imitate the manifestations of the Spirit as seen upon other persons. Whether by shaking, jerking or just getting over-excited in the flesh, trying to 'work up' the blessing. The elders, missionaries etc. rebuked such people and instructed accordingly as there is a difference between hindering the Spirit and working with the Spirit. Those within positions of authority who negate their responsibility which has been entrusted to them, to exhort and to correct in the spirit of meekness and humility, thereby sin and grieve the Holy Spirit.

Hindrances to Revival
Charles Finney knew that the way to help promote revival was to 'Break up your [ones] fallow ground: for it is time to seek the Lord, till He comes and rains righteousness on you' Hosea 10:12. These hindrances to revival are:
- Ingratitude, want of love towards God, neglect of the Bible, unbelief, neglect of prayer, neglect of the means of grace (silly and futile excuses as to why you cannot attend religious meetings).
- Performing Christian duties, such as prayer and Bible reading in a worldly frame of mind, in such carelessness that you can not remember what you prayed or read.
- A lack of love for fellow believers and no concern for the unconverted.

- Neglect of family duties, (setting a bad example before them, not reading the Bible to your children, or praying with and for them).
- Neglect of watchfulness over your own life, sinning before the world and before the church and before God!
- Neglect to watch over your brother in the Lord, unconcerned for their state of soul, not reproving them in love over their lukewarm attitude or blatant sin.
- Neglect of self denial in any areas especially in regards to serving the Lord.
- Worldly mindedness, pride, slander, envy, censoriousness (a bitter spirit), levity (lack of respect for God). *Lying, cheating, hypocrisy or bad temper. Finney's definition of lying was: *any calculated deceit; if you try to convey an impression contrary to the truth, you lie.
- Robbing God, in time, money (tithes and offerings), misapplying your talents and power of mind, wasting your precious resources or smoking.
- Hindering others from being useful, wasting their time (especially the minister), destroying fellow believers confidence, playing into satan's hand – repent and confess immediately.
- Taking sides against another Christian when a non-believer bad mouths him or her for whatever reason.
- Neglecting the claims of world mission; being focussed only on their own field of labour, their own church, their own circle of ministry.
- A dishonouring of the Sabbath and or fighting against the Temperance Reformation (a group who were against alcohol consumption).[14]

Pastor John Kilpatrick talking to *Charisma* about the move of God in his church, (Brownsville A.O.G., Pensacola, America) said, "If we stopped the prayer meetings, I know this move of God would grind to a halt."

Evangelist Steve Hill said, "One thing that could stop this revival dead in its tracks is exhaustion. Charles Finney recognised this as well. You can work yourself to death, and it doesn't glorify God. Revival will rearrange your schedule, but after you have become acclimatised to it, you've got to see how you can function."

Speaking about his family Steve Hill said, "I don't want to win the world and lose my own family [wife and three young children]."

Steve Hill saw his submission to Kilpatrick as one of the keys to the continuance of the Brownsville Revival. Kilpatrick stated that he would not do anything that would disturb his [Steve Hill's] authority. "We discuss everything, and we make a lot of decisions together."

Steve Hill said, "We try to stay out of the picture as much as possible, the revival is about Jesus. It's not about man…It's the defects of revival that often result in the revival being quenched – not by problems they create but by control-oriented leaders who try to act as God's deputies."[15]

Prayer Verses Persecution

During the Lewis Revival (1949-1952), Duncan Campbell and fellow ministers came under persecution from sections of the Christian church in Arnol who gave bitter opposition; accusing the Rev. Campbell of denying the confession of faith and saying that he was not sound in his theology, as he stressed the baptism of the Holy Ghost (Spirit) as a distinct and definite experience subsequent to conversion. Nonetheless the church was still filled by people coming from other parishes but very few, a mere handful attended from within the parish community at the church which he or the other ministers took part in. A prayer meeting was held in a house where five ministers and others attended. The praying was heavy and the forces of hell had been unleashed until an elder was asked to pray. He rose to his feet and prayed for around thirty minutes, paused for a little while, lifted his right hand towards heaven and prayed, "God, do you know that Your honour is at stake? You made a promise to pour water on the thirsty and floods upon the dry ground and God You're not doing it! Your honour is at stake. There are five ministers in this meeting including Mr Campbell and I don't know where any one of them stands in Your presence, but if I know anything at all about my own heart then I think I can say this, that I am thirsty for a manifestation of Your power and You promised to pour water on the thirsty and floods upon the dry ground and You're not doing it." After a pause again he raised his hand and said, "God Your honour is at stake! And I now challenge You to fulfil Your covenant engagement, to pour water on the thirsty and floods upon the dry ground" and at that moment the granite built house shook like a leaf! Rev. Campbell pronounced the benediction and they went outside at two in the morning to find the people of this village ablaze with conviction of sin as the Spirit of Grace came down. The drinking house of that village was closed forever and fourteen of the regulars were soundly converted later on. During that weekend the road was black with people walking the two miles to church, prior to that movement only four people left the village for the church.[16]

CHAPTER FIFTEEN
To Make Ready a People (Luke 1:17)

The apostle Paul wrote: 'Because of the grace given to me by God, that I might be a minister of Jesus Christ to the Gentiles, ministering the gospel of God, that the offering of the Gentiles might be acceptable, sanctified by the Holy Spirit. Therefore I have reason to glory in Christ Jesus in the things which pertain to God. For I will not dare to speak of any of those things which Christ has not accomplished through me, in word and deed, to make the Gentiles obedient – in mighty signs and wonders, by the power of the Spirit of God...' Romans 15:15b-19a.

A Revival Will Cease When
The most probable reason why any revival will cease is when those involved become complacent and prideful in action and attitude. You can be so caught up in the things of God that apathy sets in, and the wrong mindset comes over you, "no need to pray, God is here and will stay." But to keep a revival fire burning, it must continually be fed and stoked by prayer, abiding fellowship and the following of the commandments of God. But if you are foolish enough to boast and brag about the sparks that you have kindled, and walk in the light of your own fire (Isaiah 50:11), and neglect the One who is a consuming fire then the work of God will soon fizzle out, because the Spirit will be grieved. Never trust in your own works rather than the Spirit of grace and supplication.

There is also a big danger of being led of your emotions rather than of the Spirit of God. Revivals and any move of God are time consuming events – time just flies, but there is a danger in neglecting essential aspects of the human body, such as food and rest.

Though man can not live on bread alone (but by every word of God, Luke 4:4), without it, he will surely suffer.

Most people even in the midst of revival will have family to care for and jobs to hold down; don't become so spiritual that you become of no earthly good. A tired man is an unhappy man and it is difficult to be a light in the world when you stay up all night. Learn to pace yourself, whilst running the race so that you will be able to obtain the prize and enjoy it.

Diluting the precious word of God will also stop a revival; sin needs to be called sin and truth needs to be thundered from the pulpit as well as the streets.

A Christ-less, cross-less, blood-less message will result in spine-less, defence-less and power-less church goers with the nickname Christian, because a fast food gospel message will result in biodegradable believers.

John Wesley stated that he used to preach the Law (to bring awareness of sin) and then sprinkle it with grace.

- Charles Finney said, "Away with your milk and water preaching of the love of Christ that has no holiness or moral discrimination in it, away with the preaching a Christ not crucified for sin."[1]
- Andrew Murray wrote: 'It is comparatively easy to win people to a cross, but to a cross that leaves them un-crucified.'[2]
- Rev. Duncan Campbell said, "Oh beware, beware, of the cross that leaves you un-crucified; we sometimes say that in the natural world we 'live to die,' but in the spiritual world we die to live, that's the answer, that's the secret."

Richard Weaver of Scotland would hold captive hundreds and sometimes thousands of listeners night after night as he explained the plan of redemption so clearly and yet so simply; and told story after story and anecdote after anecdote with great zeal and power which would brings tears to peoples eyes and make them feel the force of their sin. The writer of *The Revival* paper 1868, in regards to this man of God, an open-air preacher wrote: 'Learned gentlemen would do well to sit at his feet and learn how to preach the simple truths of the gospel' the writer continued – 'We believe the present state of the Christian Church demands that the truth should be openly known, that such preaching – preaching simply the old story – Christ crucified, from a heart renewed by the Holy Spirit, and fired with a zeal for the conversion of souls, is what is needed; not grand essays; not fine spun sermons preached to a congregation as if they were all right for eternity. No, but the simple gospel pressed home upon the hearts and the consciences of unconverted men and women with an earnestness that ought to posses the hearts of men saved by grace, on behalf of lost souls.[3]

Duncan Campbell was preaching about never compromising [the truth of God's word] to accommodate the devil. He said, "Here you have the apostle Paul proclaiming a message that was profoundly disturbing [preaching to Felix and Drusilla who began to be afraid, Acts 24:24-25]. We are afraid of disturbing people today. You must not have their emotions stirred, you must not have people weeping in a meeting, you must not have people rolling on the floor under conviction of sin; keep things orderly. May God help us, may God have mercy on us. Who are we to dictate to Almighty God as to how He is going to work? If God chooses to move in that way, if God chooses to so convict men and women of their sin that they will be about to lose their reason, I say, God move on until we can see again what was witnessed in the Edwards

Revival, in the Finney Revival, in the Welsh Revival, and praise God, today in the Hebrides Revival [Lewis Revival] – God moving in supernatural reality…I would to God [desire] that a wave of real godly fear gripped our land."[4]

Charles Finney stated that there were many reasons why a revival would cease:

1. When the church thinks it will cease, it will. It does not matter what enemies say or believe, but if the church loses its faith, it will lose the revival.
2. When Christians consent that it will cease, it will. But if they see the danger, which drives them to their knees in agony and concern, it can be avoided.
3. When the church stops to speculate and argue about abstract doctrines that have no bearing upon practice.
4. When anything distracts the attention of the church, even the appearance of an angel.
5. The church taking wrong ground on some great moral question such as slavery [homosexuality, abortion etc. – authors note].
6. Ecclesiastical difficulties, the revivalist is called away from the work [or not permitted to return] to answer charges before his [or her] superiors regarding the use of new methods etc.[5]
7. When Christians become proud of their 'great revival' in what they have done!
8. When Christians begin to proselytise to their denomination, stirring up sectarian difficulties, promoting this or that denomination.
9. The Spirit may be grieved by boasting of the revival, to puff up the church; the pastor foolishly writing to the local newspapers [or emailing everyone! – authors note].

10. Some, under pretence of publishing things to the glory of God, have (often unknowingly) exalted themselves or their denomination.
11. When Christians lack brotherly and sisterly love, one for another.
12. Christians of all denominations should lay aside all prejudices. Prejudices hinder the person so that he or she cannot come to a correct understanding on the subject and are unable to correctly pray in this state of mind.
13. A protracted meeting should be conducted throughout by the same minister (or evangelist) if possible. Sometimes through courtesy visiting ministers are invited to speak and there has been no blessing as they did not come in a state of mind which was right for such a work.
14. When Christians become mechanical in their attempts to promote revival and prayer begins to wane, praying without emotion as before.
15. When the minister does not pour out fire (arousing passionate preaching) upon the hearers, when he is behind the pulpit.
16. When the church becomes exhausted by the labour, neglect to eat and sleep at the proper hours and let the excitement runaway with them so that they become exhausted and their bodies or mind give way and breakdown. [This is what happened to Evan Roberts].
17. When Christians do not feel their dependence on the Holy Spirit, believing they can do the work in their own strength, or promoting themselves or their ministry instead of the Lord.
18. A revival will decline and cease, unless Christians are frequently revived – frequently convicted and humbled and broken down before God.

19. Revivals can be put down by the continued opposition of the old school, combined with a bad spirit in the new school. When those who are for or against a revival battle it out, with a bad spirit, printing articles and rebuttals in the papers, for public viewing. Those who are engaged in revival should keep to the work [Nehemiah 6:3] and mind their own business when they or the work is slandered, as it is God who vindicates.[6]

Evan Roberts was invited to speak at a very successful Congregational Chapel in Dowlais, South Wales, UK, a few months after the 1904-1905 Welsh Revival broke out. Within thirty minutes of his arrival, he announced that someone in that service was blocking the way of revival by criticism of the revival and, more especially criticism of the revivalist. He declared that unless the spirit was expunged he would be compelled to leave. He would not remain or take part in mock worship where the Holy Spirit was grieved. He soon departed, leaving the service to the opposition.[7]

Persecution, criticism, slander, condemnation and accusations will all be levied against those who desire to do God's will and especially those who are involved in revival. But as the book of Proverbs informs us: 'If you faint in the day of adversity your strength is small' (Proverbs 14:10).

God said, "If you have run with the footmen, and they have wearied you, then how can you contend with horses? And if in the land of peace, in which you trusted, they wearied you, then how will you do in the flooding of Jordan?" (Jeremiah 12:5).

Edwin Orr, in 1936 as part of his American tour, which took in all forty-eight states was instrumental in several localised revivals wrote: 'I regretted to learn that I had made enemies...through speaking the simple truth, but one must expect a minority of people everywhere who get no blessing from the ministry because of the hardness of their hearts, and who are thus compelled to defend their position by slandering the messenger of the Lord...they do not choose to believe because it would follow that they must apply some of the things he asks *us* about.'[8]

Edwin Orr, in 1936 was preaching in Johannesburg as part of his South African Campaign. Orr was told by a friend that people were criticising the meeting that he had held at the university in which souls were saved. Orr said, "I did not expect my denunciation of sin to please impenitent sinners. And I did not expect my enunciation of the remedy – the cleansing of the blood of Christ to please those who prefer psychological reformation. It is a good sign that there has been criticism."[9]

Ministers, pastors, evangelists, missionaries and leaders are on the devil's number one hit list, they are his number one spiritual enemies. He knows that if he can take out the shepherd or the leader then the sheep are more easily scattered.

It is the responsibility of every Christian to pray for his or her minister and to lift them up before the throne of grace on a regular basis. If you feel that the pastor is not doing a good job, don't criticise him or her – pray for them and pray blessing upon their life, family and ministry. It's the easiest thing in the world to sit back and pick faults; we've all done it. But it must stop. Let your mouth be full of spring water and not salt water, stop cursing and start blessing.

It is imperative that each minister, pastor, evangelist, missionary and leader, allows the Holy Spirit to work in their midst, to do what He wants to do. The work is of

God and not mans – we may have good ideas, but is it God's blue print? Is this what God has called you to do? Each work must be God ordained and must have His seal of approval on it; otherwise it comes from the flesh. Many people will say on the Judgment Day, "Lord, Lord, did not we do great things in Your name" But He will reply, "Get away from Me, I never knew you" (Matthew 7:21-23).

Whose kingdom are you building and maintaining?

The devil's Five Deadly D's

John Kilpatrick, in his book, *Feast of Fire, the remarkable story of the revival in Pensacola* wrote: 'We must learn to pastor a revival or else run the risk of wandering away from the river...A flock needs a shepherd all the time, so a pastor cannot retreat from his duties just because God's Spirit has taken over. He needs to be aware of what it means to pastor a revival.

Kilpatrick continued: 'During the initial outpouring of the Spirit there are certain things Christian leaders must be prepared to come up against immediately in order to protect the flock and insure the work of God. I call them the 'devil's Five Deadly D's,' because if they are not understood, confronted, and dealt with up front they can dry up the outpouring of the river of life.

1. The first 'D' stands for doubt. Suspicion, doubt and scepticism are all inevitable responses whenever the Holy Spirit moves in a congregation in a new or unaccustomed way.

2. Distractions. When the Holy Spirit begins to fall on a church in a mighty way, there will be two kinds of distractions. First of all, there will be people who yield to bad distractions, such as watching an individual in a meeting who is drawing attention to himself or simply mimicking manifestations of the Spirit...The other type of

distractions might be those normal, natural things which happen in our daily living. For instance, when we really love revival and want to be enjoying the presence of the Lord, satan will allow distractions in our homes or businesses that are legitimate, but they take away our time and emphasis from revival.

3. The third deadly 'D' is disappointment. When we are excited and exhilarated by what the Lord is doing both in our personal and corporate lives, we want everyone to get in on it. We want others to enjoy what we are enjoying. That's why we begin to realise a feeling of great disappointment when others reject what we are experiencing. When our children, spouse, family or fellow church member do not dive in as quickly to the river of life, we can easily become disappointed. Worse yet, if they remove themselves entirely from the revival.

4. Discouragement. It is always a dangerous thing when people choose to wallow in disappointment. It can lead to discouragement. Discouragement leaves people depressed, cast down and suffering from a bad case of the blues...I know very few people who are even-tempered. Most of us spend our time in either really high places or really low places...We simply need to guard against staying in the lows.

5. Finally, pastoring a revival is sure to bring on defamation...I knew people were bound to talk, mock and accuse as a result of the revival. Could I live with the fact that other Christians were questioning my spiritual integrity and leadership?'[10]

Attacks on the Leadership
John Kilpatrick also stated that during revival those involved in revival can encounter difficulties, natural and supernatural as satan not only blinds the minds of unbelievers, but tries to distort and destroy God's work in the hearts of sincere followers.

1. After the Red Sea exodus came the golden calf. Get outside the perimeter of the Word of God and you get outside of the perimeter of the blood. Even Aaron was deceived when he made the golden calf and encouraged the Israelites to worship it (Exodus 32:1-8).

2. After the bread in the wilderness came Dathan and Abiram. Even in the midst of revival, rebellion rose up, in the form of Korah, Dathan and Abiram and two hundred and fifty leaders of the congregation, who contended with Moses (Numbers 16:8-17).

3. After David's kingdom was established came adultery. King David committed adultery with Bathsheba, the wife of Uriah the Hittite which led to murder (2 Samuel 11). In the midst of a great move when feelings are running high, be careful. Keep your passions harnessed. Exercise self-control.

4. After Elijah's fire came the attack of Jezebel. After the victory on Mount Carmel when Elijah ordered all the false prophets to be executed, Jezebel promised to kill Elijah. This led to intimidation and fear, so he ran for his life (1 Kings chapters 18-19). Beware of discouragement, disheartenment and disparagement.

5. After Nehemiah builds the walls, Tobiah gains position. While the people worked rebuilding the walls of Jerusalem, vicious men taunted them (Nehemiah 2:19-20). During revival, evil

persons will try to manipulate, distract and confuse (Nehemiah 6:1-4). Tobiah worked his way past the walls and gained a home in the temple, but was finally ousted (Nehemiah 13:4-9).

6. After Gideon's victory, man's ministry is worshipped. Beware of man worship. The people wanted to promote Gideon to a place of prominence after his military victory but he did not allow them (Judges 6:11-8:23).

7. After the miracles of Elisha, Gehazi covets silver. Covetousness made Gehazi a leper because he wanted the rewards which his master, Elisha, had refused from Naaman the Syrian after Naaman was healed from leprosy (2 Kings chapter 5).

8. After Gedaliah's passivity, Ishmael murdered the saint. Gedaliah, the governor over Judah was murdered because he did not heed the warning that an assassin was out to get him, and even believed the warning to be a lie (2 Kings 25:22-26 and Jeremiah 40:13-41:3). Just because the Spirit is moving does not make us immune to attacks from our enemies. Listen to godly counsel and resist the pride of a know-it-all spirit.[11]

SECTION IV

OUR RESPONSIBILITY

CHAPTER SIXTEEN
Yield Yourselves to the Lord (2 Chronicles 30:8)

'Sow for yourselves righteousness; reap in mercy; break up your fallow ground, for it is time to seek the Lord, till He comes and rains righteousness on you' Hosea 10:12.

'I acknowledged my sin to You, and my iniquity I have not hidden. I said, "I will confess my transgression to the Lord," and You forgave the iniquity of my sin. Selah. For this cause everyone who is godly will pray to You' Psalm 32:5-6a.

Live Holy Lives

Evangelist Steve Hill, preaching at the Pensacola Revival, (1995-2000) spoke with authority, of the love and the wrath of God, of His compassion, the cross, the blood and full-on repentance. He did not mince his words and told it how it was, under God's power and anointing. Below is a summary of some the main points of Steve Hill's, Christ embracing and holiness preaching during the Pensacola Revival.[1]

As Christians we are called to be holy (1 Peter 1:16, set apart for God), so let us get the sin out of our lives and the rubbish out of our homes. Destroy all videos, CD's, posters, magazines etc. which are anti-God in morals and principles, any swearing, cuss words or blasphemy. Don't forget the rubbish you watch on television. Quit it now! Get the junk out of your house and lives, the lucky charms, articles of affection that you know God is not happy with, the cursed ornaments, the devil's trinkets, any foreign gods, the fantasy novels, the men's girly magazines. Guy's get those earrings out![2] Ladies dress modestly.

We are in the world, but not of the world. We are called to be set apart and different, a holy people. Stop going to immoral places where satan's followers hang out (evangelise yes, socialise no). You're dancing with the devil and two-timing Jesus! You are crucifying Jesus again (Hebrews 6:6). His blood was shed for you! Don't be a God mocker. You mock Him with your lifestyle. Either you live like a Christian or you'd better change your name.   Quit the smoking, the drugs, the sleeping around, pornography, lustful thoughts, masturbation, attention seeking, arrogance and prideful snobbery glances; stop the judgmental thoughts, criticism, the back stabbing, the slander and the gossip. You are tearing the body of Christ apart. Stop loving your denomination more than Jesus, and put Him first.

Stop following the Christianity of Christ and follow the Christ of Christianity. God wants you to become a disciple, not merely a person with the nickname Christian. Religion is hanging around the cross; Christianity is getting on the cross! (Galatians 2:20). God wants total surrender in your life.[3]

As Christians let us walk worthy of our most holy calling in true assurance of our faith, being built up and grounded upon the word of God, looking to the Author and Finisher of our faith; Jesus being our Rock of hope and Chief Cornerstone in whom we can depend upon.

Duncan Campbell said, "I sometimes say, at the risk of being misunderstood, that we do not pray for revival in order that souls may be saved, [the primary reason for revival is that God may be glorified, Leviticus 10:3, see chapter eleven] but souls are saved in their thousands when we have revival, when the thirsty are satisfied, then the floods on the dry ground. If you want revival, get right with God. If you are not prepared to bring the "last piece," [of your entire consecration to God's altar] for God's sake stop talking about revival; your talking and praying is but the laughing-stock of devils. It is about time that we got into the grips of reality."[4]

Questions to Answer:
- Would Jesus watch what you watch?
- Would Jesus listen to what you listen to?
- Would Jesus join in that conversation?
- Would Jesus read that magazine or book?
- Would Jesus wear what I wear? Am I dressing to emphasis my beauty (and style) or to flaunt my sexuality?
- Would Jesus be proud of me?
- Would Jesus be welcomed in that establishment?
- Would He join in or tell them to repent!?
- If Jesus would not be welcome there, why take the Holy Spirit in with you?
- Would Jesus be allowed at that party or would He wait outside weeping and waiting for you?

If the answer to any of these is no, then should you? If it is questionable, then wisdom says, "Err on the side of caution."

- 'Adulterers and adulterous! Do you not know that friendship with the world is enmity with God? Whoever therefore wants to be a friend of the world makes himself an enemy of God. Or do you think that the Scripture says in vain, "The Spirit who dwells in us yearns jealously"?' James 4:4-5.
- 'Submit to God. Resist the devil and he will flee from you. Draw near to God and He will draw near to you. Cleanse your hands, you sinners; and purify your hearts, you double-minded. Lament and mourn and weep! Let your laughter be turned to mourning and your joy to gloom.

Humble yourselves in the sight of the Lord and He will lift you up' James 4:7-10.

- 'Confess your sins to each other and pray for each other so that you may be healed. The prayer of a righteous man is powerful and effective' James 5:16, NIV.

As disciples of the Lord Jesus Christ we are not allowed to pick and choose the bits of Scripture we want to obey, because that is disobedience and compromise. They're the paths that lead to destruction to the eternal fires of hell, where there will be weeping and gnashing of teeth, where the worm dieth not. As Jonathan Edward, in his most famous sermon, *Sinners in the Hands of an Angry God* said, "He is angrier with many who are now in the congregations of our churches, many who seem to be at ease, than He is with many of those who are now in the flames of hell."[5]

Holiness is the foundation for revival building. Prayer and fasting (humbling oneself) are the supporting walls. No roof is needed, the heavens will be open and God will pour in His Spirit! Can we declare, "Yes Lord, we will be faithful because You are faithful?"

Charles Spurgeon said, "Holiness is not mere morality, not the outward keeping of divine precepts out of a strong sense of duty, while those commandments in themselves are not our delight. Holiness is our complete being fully consecrated to the Lord and moulded to His will. This is the thing which God's Church must have, but it can never have it apart from the Sanctifier, for there not a grain of holiness beneath the sky, but what is of the work of the Holy Spirit. And, brethren, if a church is destitute of holiness what effect can it have on the world? An unholy church makes Christ to say that He cannot do many mighty works there because of its iniquity."[6]

Firebrands and Fire-starters

The more on-fire and holier the congregation are within a local church (the church being a body of believers) then the closer to revival you will be. If God places a deeper burden upon our hearts for lost souls, for the outcasts of society, then we know revival is closer.

Some Christians are fed up with all this talk of revival, but let me tell you, God is fed up and broken-hearted that many don't want it. Many foolishly say that it is not for today and is part of a bygone era. The Scriptures, Church History and the revivalist's all disprove this. What Bible did Jonathan Edwards have? Or the Wesley's, George Whitefield, Howell Harris and Moody and Sankey? What Bible did Smith Wigglesworth, Jonathan Goforth, Evan Roberts and Duncan Campbell have? I would say that they had the same Bible as we have today; they lived up to God's standards and knew how to plead the promises contained within and saw the heavenly fire fall!

An eye-witness from Bicester, during the 1860 revival in England said, "It is not asserting too much to say that a greater number of sinners have been converted to God in Bicester, and within eight miles of it, during the last ten months than have made an open profession of religion during the last two hundred years."[7]

When more souls are saved in one year of revival, than fifty years without one, why do many not want revival? God is fed up with our stale, hypocritical, going through-the-motions religion, He's fed up and grieved with the luke-warmness and backsliding within His Church. He's fed up and saddened that the young people in droves are leaving the Church in search of 'a spiritual reality' because the Church in all its religious rituals and trappings has lost the meaning of spiritual reality. If people do not see it in Christianity, they will look for it elsewhere and often that is in the occult. If people do not see the love of the brethren, they will look for love in all the wrong places.

God is fed up and grieved with all the murders, the rapes, the crimes, He's fed up and broken-hearted, with divorce, sexual abuse, theft, adultery, fraud, deception, white collar crime. He's fed up and grieved with the churches murmurings, backbiting and jealousies; the injustices and our unwillingness to get holy, and get praying for revival, living in humility and sincerity. Next time you sit in front of your television or flick through the paper and hear of the terrible crimes against humanity, remember how much God is fed up without revival, without His people standing in the gap and interceding on behalf of the land, see Ezekiel 22:30.

Friends, fellow labourers and brothers and sisters in Christ, wake up out of your spiritual slumber and rise from the dead, our world is in a desperate state, an abomination of sin and filth as lewdness lies and manifests itself in every town, in every capital in every country. Will you humble yourself and pray? You were called to stand in the gap; you have come into the kingdom for such a time as this!

Each generation is responsible for their generation and the following generation, because what we sow today, our children will reap tomorrow (Exodus 20:5). You will be held accountable for what you did (or did not do) for the least of these. You will also be held accountable for what you know, what you have been entrusted with and what you have done with it, 'He who has ears let him hear!' 'For many are called, but few are chosen.' Will it be, "Lord, Lord did we not do this and that in Your name," "Get away from Me I never knew you" or will it be, "Well done My good and faithful servant, enter into the joy of the Lord?" You who have been faithful in little, will be faithful in much, but cast out that worthless servant from My eyes. The axe is laid at the root of the tree, will it bear fruit worthy of repentance? If not, cut it down and throw it into the fire!

God said, "Son of man, I have made you a watchman for the house of Israel [your country or town]; therefore hear a word from My mouth, and give them warning from Me: "When I say to the wicked, 'You shall surely die,' and you give him no warning, nor speak to warn the wicked from his wicked way, to save his life, that same wicked man shall die in his iniquity; but his blood I will require at your hand. Yet, if you warn the wicked, and he does not turn from his wickedness, nor from his wicked way, he shall die in his iniquity; but you have delivered your soul" Ezekiel 3:17-19.

Cry out to God

It was said that John Knox (sixteenth century Scottish reformer), cried out in passionate prayer for his people, "Give me Scotland or I'll die!" Will you be prepared to cry out for the lost? Will you cry out to God day and night and ask Him to send showers of blessing on this dry and barren land; has He not promised to give water to him who thirsts? But the conditions of clean hands and a pure heart need to be applied. As long as we do our part, then God will not fail to do His.

'He who goes out weeping, carrying seeds to sow, will return with songs of joy, carrying sheaves with him' Psalm 126:6, NIV.

God has no pleasure in the death of the wicked, but that he or she would turn from his or her wicked ways – For God so loved the world that He gave…What will you give for this world? God gave His all, His only begotten Son. God wanted people so badly to be drawn unto Him that He allowed, He permitted His Son to be smitten, to be beaten, to be mocked, to be whipped, to be humiliated and hung on a cross for all to see and jeer at. That's how much God wants people to turn to Him and be saved from the damnation of hell. When Jesus is lifted up, He will draw all men to Himself. God paid the ultimate price for revival, for a vast ingathering of people, so that He would be glorified.

In the mid seventeenth century, George Fox, upon Pendle Hill in Lancashire, England saw his vision of 'a great ingathering of people' and founded the Society for Friends, 'Quakers' (the Quakers used to be evangelical). Pendle Hill stands high above the surrounding area and on my visit I could see for tens of miles, of fields upon fields reaching out in all directions. Maybe George Fox was reminded of the words of Jesus, "The fields are white unto harvest..." Anyhow, he got on with the job of preaching Scriptural truths and more than fifty thousand were converted back to the pure faith in forty years; 'Bid ye tremble at the word of the Lord' was their watchword. Today we have to ask, do we have the fear of God inside of us? Do you? The fear of the Lord is the beginning of wisdom. The fear of the Lord is the beginning of understanding. The fear of the Lord is to hate evil.

At the Pensacola Revival, (as in every revival) there were intercessors that identified with the pain that God feels over those who reject the forgiveness that is found in Jesus Christ. We need more intercessors and prayer warriors that will pay the price, and cry out their hearts for the lost, pleading for mercy and redemption upon the lost sheep. Evangelist Steve Hill would often be preaching and weeping at the same time (like the prophet Jeremiah), falling to his knees and pleading with the people to get right with God. He did not just give a sermon, he gave it his all. This was true of John Wesley, who would ride through knee-high snow and driving sleet to preach to one sinner or a great gathering. Both Moses and the apostle Paul were prepared to be damned for all eternity, if only their brethren may be saved!

If you want Jesus to be lifted high as a banner across the land then cry out to God, "In wrath remember mercy," pray that the bowl of mercy will outweigh judgment (Revelation 8:1-5). "Though our sins testify against us O Lord, do something for the sake of Your name."

'I have set watchmen on your walls, O Jerusalem, who shall never hold their peace day or night. You who make mention of the Lord, do not keep silent, and give Him no rest till He establishes and till He makes Jerusalem a praise in the earth' Isaiah 62:6-7.

Dr. Martyn Lloyd-Jones preaching on Isaiah 62:6-7 (prayer – watchmen on your walls) said, "If you go back and read (and as I exhort and beseech you to do) the history of any revival that you can find an account of anywhere, you will find that is always how revival has begun. God has thus put this burden upon someone, one man, a number of men, it does not matter what the number is, that's how it always begins. If you like a man becomes a sort of mono-maniac about this. Always talking about it, 'I will take no rest, I will not hold my peace,' speaking about it, telling people about it, exhorting people to consider it, thus I say God begins to move. That was true about the prophet Isaiah, course there were many people who thought he had gone mad, they thought the same about Jeremiah."[8]

Soldiers of the cross, let's put on the armour of God and march out for Jesus. This is spiritual warfare. God is on the move, the kingdom of God is forcefully advancing and forceful men will lay hold of it (Matthew 11:12). We are on the winning side and we have all authority in the name of Jesus Christ of Nazareth.

SECTION V

REVELATIONS FOR THE UNITED KINGDOM, EUROPE AND BEYOND

Chapter Seventeen
You Will Live Also (John 14:19)

'Surely the Lord God does nothing, unless He reveals His secret to His servants the prophets' Amos 3:7.

'By the mouth of two or three witnesses every word shall be established' 2 Corinthians 13:1.

Smith Wigglesworth's Prophecy 1947

Smith Wigglesworth from Bradford, England was known as the "apostle of faith." He moved in mighty signs and wonders and even raised people from the dead in Jesus' mighty name. Shortly before he passed into glory he prophesied:

"During the next few decades there will be two distinct moves of the Holy Spirit across the Church in Great Britain. The first move will affect every church that is open to receive it, and will be characterised by the restoration of the baptism and gifts of the Holy Spirit.

"The second move of the Holy Spirit will result in people leaving historic churches and planting new churches. In the duration of each of these moves, the people who are involved will say, 'This is a great revival.' But the Lord says, 'No, neither is this the great revival but both are steps towards it.'

"When the new church phase is on the wane, there will be evidence in the churches of something that has not been seen before: a coming together of those with an emphasis on the word and those with an emphasis on the Spirit. When the word and the Spirit come together, there will be the biggest move of the Holy Spirit that the nation, and indeed, the world have ever seen. It will mark the beginning of a revival that will eclipse anything that has been witnessed within these shores, even the Wesleyan and Welsh Revivals of former years. The outpouring of God's Spirit will flow over from the United Kingdom to mainland Europe, and from there, will begin a missionary move to the ends of the earth."[1]

Tommy Hicks Vision 1961

In 1961, healing evangelist, Tommy Hicks from Lancaster, California, received an end-time vision.

On the 25 July 1961, in the early hours of the morning, Tommy Hicks received and end-time vision and revelation which he received three times. The following is a brief summary of that vision: In this vision Hicks was above the earth looking down upon all the nations and people groups of the earth. Lightning flashed over the face of the earth. He saw a sleeping giant, covered by debris that was covering the earth. The giant gradually rose to life and stood up into the clouds, hands outstretched. Drops of liquid light rained down upon the earth and the giant began to melt into the earth itself and the earth became flooded with liquid light which turned out to be millions of people praising God. A roar from heaven came and Jesus Himself appeared glistening in glorious white. He pointed forth His hand and liquid light flowed from Him to those of the nations. Many people accepted this anointing and went forth in Jesus' name whilst others rejected it. Multitudes of people were healed as the power of God went forth to conquer. Sometimes this liquid light would fall on congregations who would burst forth into praise for vast periods of time. After this period of blessing destruction came from the north as God's judgment was poured forth across the earth.[2]

Jean Darnall's Vision 1967

During 1967, American evangelist Jean Darnall (from the Four Square Gospel Church) on her first trip to England en-route to Hong Kong, had the last of three reoccurring visions in different places. The third time she had the vision she was staying in the manse at St. Mary's Church in Poole, Dorset, England and knew that God was trying to get her attention. In these visions she was looking down upon the United Kingdom, having a birds-eye view of the British Isles. It is interesting to note that this church is next to Poole Hospital, a place of help with an accident and emergency department. Hospitals are a symbol of love, care and hope, a place to go to when you are in desperate physical need. The church also should have the same characteristics, (which caters for a persons spiritual need); our hope is in Jesus and when revival comes, multitudes will flock to a place of worship, whether in a traditional church building like St. Mary's, a modern one or a home church etc., and in these places people will find peace and rest and be able to be healed from their infirmities of the past as they look to Jesus Christ for the salvation of their souls.

The British Isles were covered in mist, a green haze, and Jean saw lots of pinpoints of light piercing through. As she moved closer, they turned out to be fires breaking out all over the nation, from Scotland in the north, to Lands End in the south. As these God-lit fires were joined together, they burned brighter. As she continued to pray (not fully understanding what she had seen), she saw lightning and explosions of fire and then rivers of fire flowing from north to south, from Scotland, Ireland, Wales into England. Some of the streams of fire crossed the channel into Europe, whilst others stopped. These fires were pockets of people who had been made intensely hungry for the word of God and New Testament Christianity, those who read the book of Acts and wondered where is this happy church? Where is this love? These people would come together to pray and extra meetings would have to be laid on to accommodate them all. Groups would be formed, prayer groups, Bible study groups, some would meet in churches others would be in homes, some converted other unconverted who would be searching and seeking.

In Britain, the method God would use is renewal in the churches. This would then spread outside the Church into the masses amongst the public, resulting in a public awakening. Jean went on to reveal how the Lord has promised her that He would raise up highly anointed preaching voices with signs following, who would be a gift to Britain.

Jean asked the Lord about the vision and had the distinct impression that there would be two moves of God. The first would be the renewal of Christian faith and fullness of the Holy Spirit within the Church. The second would be a national awakening. The awakening was the lighting that came down and strikes the earth when preaching voices [those with an anointing] will be sent out from these islands [of Britain] to the other nations. This move of God being a national spiritual awakening would move into every level of the nation's life; on the campuses, universities, colleges, schools etc., into the media, in the government. The word 'communicators' was strongly laid upon Jean's heart, and back then, was a word that was not trendy, like in the twenty-first century.[3]

Jean continued, as the rivers of fire moved, it would produce powerfully gifted communicators who would address the nation through the media. Through the arts, through journalism, the radio, television, actors, singers, teachers, powerful communicators who have an extra anointing working through the media who will be the new warriors that the Lord is raising up for His army [the younger generation] to reach the heart of the people on the Continent. There would be so many conversions that it would actually change the character of the nation and determine the future move of God in Europe. Jean continued that there would not be a part of the nation's life that will not feel the impact of the spiritual awakening when God releases it to the country.

These communicators will be excellent in all that they do and will go into Europe and meet those of like quality, in training and abilities and together they will work to release God's word speedily into Europe, which results in another wave of a spiritual awakening into Europe. Jean went on to say that the media ministry will be over the heads [not negative] of those who are involved in ministries of mercy [helping the poor etc.] on the ground. There would be communicators in government and within the educational system and wherever people are speaking [up] for others.

The vision of 1967 came at the time of the early Charismatic Renewal. Because of this reoccurring vision she stayed in Britain for over two decades along with her husband to help nurture the fires that God lit. Jean Darnall at the time of writing lives in Hawaii and works with Youth With A Mission (YWAM). She still anticipates the impending mass awakening of Great Britain and beyond as revealed in her visions.[4]

Michael Backholer's Vision 1989

In June 1989, a dedicated Christian of but five years was on his first short-term mission to Scotland. Michael Backholer was at North Queensferry, very early one morning, having been wakened by the Lord. He walked down near the water and was looking up at the majestic Forth Bridge, when the Lord said, "I had these bridges [one is for trains and the other for vehicles] built for the same reason the Roman roads were built – for the spread of My gospel." Suddenly as Michael looked up, he saw flames of fire appearing hundreds of feet high, flowing across the bridge from north to south. In astonishment he said, "What is it Lord?" having never received a vision before. "It's flames of revival, I'm going to send revival and it will start in the north and flow south" replied the Lord. "When will it come?" asked Michael, "Very soon," said the Lord.

Michael Backholer shares this vision of revival, on Christian television, which was recreated by ByFaith Media and first aired on UCB (SKY) ByFaith 'A Journey of Discipleship,' episode 2, Revival in Britain.[5]

"God is not a man, that He should lie, nor a son of man that He should repent. Has He not said, and will He not do it? Or has He spoken, and will He not make it good?" Numbers 23:19.

Understanding Prophecy and Visions

We live in a 24/7 age where people get bored waiting for the microwave to hurry up and finish! The Church, set into this culture can find itself with this 'instant' attitude. We are often in danger of forgetting the visions and prophecies of the past, because they did not come to pass in our 'suitable' time frame. We do forget that Malachi prophesied that the Lord was coming soon, and four hundred years later He did come! Now, no-one believes we have to wait that long for these words to be fulfilled, but maybe God is waiting for us to take Him at His word and seek Him today, for the fulfilment of the promises that He has been making for decades!? God started to talk about revival decades ago and He is still talking about the same coming revival today. 'He who has ears to hear, let him hear.'

Some Christians gave up on prophecy for revival because it did not happen in five years. It is a good job that Abraham believed God that Isaac would be born (though he did try to make it work on his own, and along came Ishmael who was not the son of the promise). What about the prophecies in your church? Have you forgotten them? Did God change His mind and move on, or is He waiting for you?[6]

CHAPTER EIGHTEEN
Life more Abundantly (John 10:10)

"Sing and rejoice, O daughter of Zion! For behold, I am coming and I will dwell in your midst," says the Lord, Zechariah 2:10.

'This is the word of the Lord to Zerubbabel: "Not by might nor by power, but by My Spirit, says the Lord of hosts" ' Zechariah 4:6.

The Call to Change Destinies – Prophecy

Prophecy is an important part of the body of Christ and must not be despised (1 Corinthians 14:1 and 1 Thessalonians 5:19-20). Prophecy is not something to be despised, disregarded or neglected but to be heeded (1 Thessalonians 5:20). All prophecy needs to be weighed, judged, prayed through and tested because many false prophets are in the world, trying to deceive and beguile who they can (1 Thessalonians 5:21 and 1 John 4:1). A prophecy can be from God, from the flesh or from the evil one (Job 26:4), or a combination, as some people can start in the Spirit, but wander into the flesh as they prophesy beyond their faith (Romans 12:6 and Job 26:4). But, by the mouth of two or three witnesses every word shall be confirmed (2 Corinthians 13:1).

Prophecy is often conditional and we have to fulfil our obligations in the eyes of a covenant keeping God. In 2 Chronicles 7:14 it states that 'If My people who are called by My name will humble themselves and pray and seek My face and turn from their wicked ways, then I will hear from heaven, and will forgive their sin and heal their land,' author's emphasis. If we have not done our part, then we cannot expect God to do His. God is a covenant keeping God.

The prophecy from Revelation 1:3 in regards to the Holy Bible needs to be read, heard and kept, and blessed is the person who does this. James stated that we should be doers of the word, and not hearers only, otherwise we deceive ourselves (James 1:22).

'We also have the prophetic word made sure, which you do well to heed as a light that shines in a dark place, until the day dawns and the morning star rises in your hearts, knowing this first, that no prophecy of Scripture is of private interpretation, for prophecy never came by the will of man, but holy men of God spoke as they were moved by the Holy Spirit' 2 Peter 1:19-21.

Understanding God's Revelations

- 'Surely the Lord God does nothing, unless He reveals His secret to His servants the prophets' Amos 3:7.
- Hanani the seer said, "For the eyes of the Lord run to and fro throughout the whole earth, to show Himself strong on behalf of those whose heart is loyal to Him..." 2 Chronicles 16:9.
- '...Those who seek the Lord shall not lack any good thing' Psalm 34:10b.
- 'Delight yourself in the Lord and He shall give you the desires of your heart' Psalm 37:4.
- 'As the eyes of servants look to the hand of their masters, as the eyes of a maid to the hand of her mistress, so our eyes look to the Lord our God until He has mercy on us' Psalm 123:2.
- 'I love those who love me, and those who seek me diligently will find me' Proverbs 8:17.
- '...Those who seek the Lord understand all' Proverbs 28:5.
- God said, "For I will pour water on him who is thirsty, and floods on the dry ground; I will pour

My Spirit on your descendants, and My blessing on your offspring" Isaiah 44:3.

- Thus says the Lord, the Holy One of Israel, and His Maker: "Ask Me of things to come concerning My sons; and concerning the works of My hands..." Isaiah 45:11.
- Jesus said, "Seek first the kingdom of God and His righteousness..." Matthew 6:33.

Words for the United Kingdom

Jean Darnall's Prophecy 1996

Jean Darnall was speaking in Birmingham, England, at a *Revival Now! Birmingham Ablaze* conference (hosted by Ken and Lois Gott who were blessed with the Sunderland Outpouring at their church). Jean Darnall towards the close of her meeting was talking about the coming revival (at an earlier session she had shared her vision of revival) and she began to mention that the gifts of mercy would be greatly used to affect the nation. More so than the work done by the Salvation Army (under General Booth). Jean then broke into prayer and within a few minutes began to prophesy:

"Ye, the Lord would say to you, that as you extend your hand towards the suffering and the weak, and defend those who cannot defend themselves, and speak for those who cannot speak for themselves, and bring healing to those who cannot heal themselves, and cleanse their wounds, and bind up that which is broken. As you do this, ye, as I heal them and restore them, I will raise them up. I will raise them up and they themselves, the weak will become the strong. And out of that strength will come leadership that will touch this nation. I will take the humble and the broken, and through your ministry of restoration and mercy, I will raise them up and make them national leaders, that shall lead this nation in righteousness."

"Hallelujah! Glory to God."

Great Britain's Prophecy 2004

On Monday the 22 March 2004, a prophecy was given to Michael Backholer, which was proclaimed in June 2004 at the heart of the nation, Dunsop Bridge, in Lancashire, (near Lancaster) England. This small village is the exact centre of the United Kingdom and its four hundred and one associated Islands as designated by The Ordinance Survey.

This is what the Sovereign Lord says: "For generations the devil has blinded the eyes of the believer and the unbeliever in this nation, to My full sovereign will and the true power of the cross and the blood of Jesus, My written word, My commandments and the Living Bread that came down from heaven; all this has been hidden from the people of this nation, but this is what the Sovereign Lord says, this is about to change, for in My goodness and My mercy, I shall send a visitation of My power, the power of the Holy Spirit, to turn the hearts of the people away from sin to My Son.

"Millions, yes millions will be saved and swept into My kingdom, for My glory and I shall empower them in these last days and they shall fan out as an army of witnesses, sharing the good news, all over this nation, including the islands offshore and I shall confirm My word with signs and wonders following them.

"There will be miracles and healings in abundance, and out of this visitation I shall form a chain of grace, that will reach across the Channel into Europe, and to the nations of the world, and there will be a great harvest, an end-time harvest in preparation for Jesus' second coming."

This prophecy was aired on Christian television, UCB (SKY) on ByFaith 'A Journey of Discipleship,' episode 2, Revival in Britain.[1]

Great Britain's Revelation of Revival

A revelation from God was given to Michael Backholer on Pentecost Sunday, 5 May 2005. "The blessing of a heaven-sent revival and end time outpouring of God's Spirit is backing up like a wall of water offshore. The devil has raised a barrier of unbelief over and around this nation. When the revival prophecy is released, My people will be encouraged by My Spirit and believe and pray for it to come to pass, and as their faith level rises, so will the sluice gates of unbelief and God's Spirit will flood in with a wave of blessing. This will be followed by wave after wave of liquid love from the throne of God. Melting the hearts and the minds of the people in all walks of life, from politicians to the homeless, from the elderly to the young and in the fullness of time the very character of the nation will be changed."[2]

'From the west, men will fear the name of the Lord, and from the rising of the sun, they will revere His glory. For He will come like a pent-up flood that the breath of the Lord drives along' Isaiah 59:19, NIV.

The initial floods and huge rivers which is the initial touch of God will be followed by liquid love to affect the masses over a period of time, perhaps a decade or more, which will change the character of the nation.

Prophecy for Ireland

This what the Sovereign Lord says to all of Ireland: "I have loved you with an everlasting love; I have drawn you with loving-kindness. I have watched over you through troubled times, but now, even now, I am calling you back to My Son. It is He, and He alone that you should put your faith in. He is the one that can truly deliver you and it was He who died for you, yes all of you; both north and south. And now in these last days I am calling you back to Myself, come, come I say and drink of that which can truly quench your thirst; not in semi-darkness, but in the true light. Yes, come all of you, enter into and receive the true Light of the World. Do not look to your traditions, look to My Son, Jesus Christ." Michael Backholer, Saturday 12 November 2005.[3]

Prophecy for Wales

This is what the Sovereign Lord says to Wales: "Land of valley and song, I say to you again prepare, prepare for a visitation of My Spirit. I have not forgotten or overlooked you. Once again the breath of God will be felt as My Spirit bloweth through you; a mighty wind, a powerful wind, a wind of change that will blow the shame from your towns and city centres. Though My back was turned for a time, now is the time for My people to call upon Me in the day of your shame and I shall turn and deliver you as I have in past generations. And again voices will be heard all over the valleys as I breathe a new breath of life into My people and add greatly to their numbers." Michael Backholer, Wednesday 16 November 2005.

Prophecy for Scotland

This is what the Sovereign Lord says to Scotland and its Islands: "O Land of the Covenanters, listen to Me, can you not hear My still small voice calling to you from the mountain tops, down the glens and across the lochs? Have you forgotten already when My Spirit came down on the Islands in the last generation? Even now, some of My people still cherish in their hearts that time of special visitation, but I give you notice of an even greater visitation that will thunder down from the mountain tops, through the glens and across the lochs. Get ready I say, get ready, this will be a time not to be forgotten; a time of extraordinary blessing.

"If you are to receive all that I have for you at this time – now is the time to make ready; turn from your sin and see My salvation come to the multitudes. Oh yes, I am about to do something so great in your day, that other nations will sit up and take notice. Prepare you hearts and minds to receive all that I shall pour out." Michael Backholer, Thursday 17 November 2005.

Prophecy for England

This is what the Sovereign Lord says to England: "In the darkness of your darkest hours you turned to Me, and cried out with one voice, you humbled yourselves and acknowledged your need of Me and I heard and answered you. When you were in deep despair you looked to Me, to turn the tide and deliver you, and you overcame your enemies.

"You were delivered for a purpose, and yet once again you took your freedom and went your own way. But now, I am calling you back to finish the work we began together. Your forefathers understood and so must you, there is a kingdom to be built, one that will last, and I shall call it into being and you shall rise up again and go forth into My harvest field and proclaim the good news to all the world. Get ready, be prepared, I am about to empower you for My purposes." Michael Backholer, Friday 18 November 2005.

Prophecy for Great Britain

This is what the Sovereign Lord says: "Yes, there is to be a harvest, yes a harvest of souls like no other harvest that this nation has ever experienced. For this harvest is a seed harvest, a harvest that will produce strong healthy seed that can be sent to other nations that in turn will produce another harvest, and in turn shall be sown again and again. And the wind of My Spirit shall blow the seed all over the earth in every direction. And it shall germinate and grow and spread forth its fruit, and there will be fields with sheaves in every nation. And that which was foretold from the beginning shall come to pass, and the sower and the reaper shall work hand in hand and be led by My Spirit to the most fertile places on this earth, as well as the dry and arid places. Yes, this will be a harvest to end all harvests. The Spirit of the Lord has spoken and it shall come to pass." Michael Backholer, Monday 16 January 2006.

Prophecy for Great Britain and Other Nations

This is what the Sovereign Lord says: "My sword will again pass through this land and you shall see a distinct separation between that which is righteous and that which is not. And indeed My word which is My sword will pass not only through this land, but through many other nations as well. And you shall see it pass through people groups and families as well as My Body, the Body of Christ. And you shall see a separation and understand that which is written in My word, that on that day, many, yes, many who profess Me as Lord shall say, 'Lord, Lord, did we not do all this in Your name?' And I shall tell them plainly, I know you not. So keep watch because all that is written shall come to pass and I shall return for a spotless pure and holy Bride. The voice of the Lord has spoken. Keep watch I say, keep watch, for the days are indeed dark, but I am the Light of the World and I shall shine for all to see and those who truly walk in My light shall be saved and those who refuse My light shall perish." Michael Backholer, Tuesday 24 January 2006.

A Word for the Body of Christ

This is what the Sovereign Lord says: "To those who are truly alert, watching and waiting at the door, you will have noticed that many of the spiritual fathers of your generation have departed from among you. Be encouraged I say, for I am raising up new fathers that the hearts and minds of My children will turn to. They have already gone ahead of you to prepare the way like

John did for Me. When you hear their voices, listen to them for they have seen the pitfalls and the dangers that lie ahead, but also they have experienced them and will warn you of the same. Yes, indeed you are a most privileged generation, but there is a cost and a cross to bear daily; be of good cheer for I have overcome and so shall you. Draw near to Me and I shall draw near to you.

"Test all things in this hour against My word for I have said, 'you shall know them by their fruit.' Look for the fruit and you need not be deceived; for there will be false prophets and tares among you, and in places you did not expect to find them, so be on your guard at all times." Michael Backholer, Wednesday 25 January 2006.

The prophecies, visions and revelations that have been set before you in this chapter (and the previous) need to be believed and prayed into being whilst the conditions as laid down within God's precious word are adhered too. If you believe these prophecies and visions to be from God, and they witness with your spirit; we ask you for the sake of the nation and the nations to pray them into being (as faith without works is dead), so that they will be fulfilled according to God's perfect timing and pleasing will.* We pray for God's mercy, (see chapter nineteen for God's guidelines for prayer) and that His will, shall be done here on earth as it is in heaven. We desire that the name of Jesus be lifted high as a banner across the nations so that we can all participate of the fruit of His righteousness and the splendour of His Spirit as the dove comes to rest and fans His wings, causing the wind of God to blow.

*Most of the prophecies found in this chapter can be read online at **www.revivalnow.co.uk** or **www.prophecynow.co.uk**. No prophecy or Scripture is of private interpretation (2 Peter 1:20), therefore we encourage you to visit these sites and inform other Christians to do the same, so that the prophecies can become widely known; to edify the body of Christ and to stir us to pray for the nation of Britain and the nations.

In 1954 Winston Churchill, the man of destiny who led Britain to victory during its darkest hour, World War II, spoke to the renowned evangelist Billy Graham and said, "I do not see much hope for the future unless it is the hope you are talking about, young man. We must have a return to God."[4]

Prayer for Restoration

Daniel was a godly man of understanding and the Spirit of God was with him. He searched the Scriptures, found out what they said about Israel's seventy years banishment and the desolation of Jerusalem. Daniel then prayed and made requests through prayer and supplication, with fasting, acts of humility and repentance for the past; his personal sins and for the sins of his forefathers (Daniel 9:1-19). Daniel pleaded with God based on His great mercies (not because of his righteous living) and pleaded for His great name's sake (Daniel 9:18). Daniel was only doing what King Solomon had laid down at the dedication of the temple in Jerusalem. When a nation goes away from God and is attacked by her enemies or suffers famine and pestilence, then its citizens needs to acknowledge and confess their sin (and the sin of the nation), return with all their heart and call upon God to intervene (2 Chronicles 6:24-40).

This is the model for genuine prayer for revival:
- Make sure that you are living a godly lifestyle, walking in holiness (1 Peter 1:16) and abiding in God's presence (John 15:1-11).

- What does Scripture have to say about people and nations? God wants us to ask for the nations as He desires all men to be saved (Psalm 2:8, Ezekiel 18:23 and 1 Timothy 1:4).
- Confessions of ones sins, the sins of our forefathers and our nation's sins are paramount to make sure that we are right before God (Exodus 20:5-6, Judges 2:6-19 and 1 John 1:9).[5]
- Plead with God because of His name's sake and for His glory (Leviticus 10:3 and Lamentations 3:22-25).

'O Lord though our iniquities testify against us, do it for Your name's sake; for our backslidings are many, we have sinned against You' Jeremiah 14:7.

'Remember the former things of old, for I am God and there is no other; I am God, and there is none like Me, declaring the end from the beginning, and from ancient times things that are not yet done, saying, 'My counsel shall stand, and I will do all My pleasure'…Indeed I have spoken it; I will also bring it to pass. I have purposed it; I will also do it' Isaiah 46:9-11.

'Seek the Lord while He may be found, call upon Him while He is near, let the wicked forsake his way, and the unrighteous man his thoughts; let him return to the Lord, and He will have mercy on him; and to our God who will abundantly pardon. "For My thoughts are not your thoughts, nor are your ways My ways, says the Lord…For as the rain comes down, and the snow from heaven, and do not return there, but water the earth, and make it bring forth bud, that it may give seed to the sower and bread to the eater, so shall My word be that goes forth from My mouth; it shall not return to Me void, but it shall accomplish what I please, and it shall prosper in the thing for which I sent it" ' Isaiah 55:6-11.

SECTION VI

THE NEED FOR REPENTANCE

CHAPTER NINETEEN
Confessing their Sins (Mark 1:5)

'Search me, O God, and know my heart; try me and know my anxieties; and see if there is any wicked way in me, and lead me in the way everlasting' Psalm 139:23-24.

'Let us search out and examine our ways, and turn back to the Lord, let us lift our hearts and hands to God in heaven. We have transgressed and rebelled...' Lamentations 3:40-42.

Sins of the Nations

Within the United Kingdom, though we rest on a long line of godly ancestral heritage stretching back to the first century AD, we also have committed gross national sin (as have most nations, but especially Western nations who should have known better) throughout the ages whereby ungodly laws have been passed which has resulted in much blood shed and blood accountability resulting in defiled land (Isaiah 1:15-19, Psalm 106:35-39, especially, Leviticus 24:17 and Romans 13:3-4).[1]

Within the United Kingdom, a little over three decades ago the death penalty for murder was abolished, yet murder is legalised amongst the innocent babies in their mother's wombs. Homosexuality has long been legalised and there is a continual push to lower the age of consent. Sexual perversion, blasphemy and general godlessness is daily screened on television and heard on radio. In December 2005 civil partnerships (almost gay marriages) became legal in Britain[2] while in April 2006 it was reported that Britain's spent £50 billion (£50,000,000,000,000) on gambling during the previous year! This is £50 trillion in American numeral terminology, (£50,000,000,000,000) as British and American number terminology differs after the millions.

Pop songs and commercial adverts glorify the god of self-gratification, self-indulgence, excess and the never-satisfied god of materialism. Magazines and daily tabloids write filth, and display scantily clad women or men in provocative poses and boast in adulteries, fantasies and gossip. There is a lack of respect for authority and a general abounding in lawlessness, especially within schools and colleges. These are just some of the sins of Britain that need to be repented of and what is worse, is that many of these sins are even found within the Church. It is the Church who should be setting an example as salt and light amidst a wicked and perverse generation.

Mercy will be granted where proper repentance is sought so that the bowl of judgment can be avoided or delayed (Psalm 106:44-48, Revelation 5:8 and Revelation 8:3-5).[3]

As a place of abiding, humility and humbling, God may lead you into a period of fasting. Fasting is a state of humbling oneself in which we are able to give more time in beseeching God for His mercy, and in the context of revival, repenting of the sins of our forefathers (and the sin that we have committed) and pleading for the outpouring of the Holy Spirit to come and heal our land. Fasting is not necessarily just abstaining from food, but to walk in the statutes of God and to uphold justice and mercy, see Isaiah 1:12-17, Isaiah chapters 58 and 59 and Matthew 23:23.

"As for me, far be it from me that I should sin against the Lord in ceasing to pray for you..." 1 Samuel 12:23. The prophet Samuel speaking to the nation of Israel after King Saul's inauguration.

Edwin Orr wrote: 'No one will suggest that the spiritual poverty and smug self-satisfaction...is the ideal of the Lord for the body of Christ. The antidote is revival, and revival must always be the will of God. To refuse to pray for revival (as hopeless) is like impudently telling the Lord that His power is limited.'[4] 'Away with pessimism. It is the sin of unbelief. The pessimist says that revival is impossible. Such are seldom men of faith. They say that revival is impossible before Christ comes. While the Spirit of the Lord is among us, who *dare* tell Him what is possible and what is impossible. God forgive our unbelief.'[5]

God's Guidelines for Prayer

- 'He [God] also shall be my salvation, for a hypocrite could not come before Him' Job 13:16. You cannot live in sin and expect God to hear your prayers!
- 'As for me, I will call upon God, and the Lord shall save me' Psalm 55:16.
- 'If I regard iniquity in my heart, the Lord will not hear' Psalm 66:18.
- 'One who turns away his ear from hearing the law, even his prayer shall be an abomination' Proverbs 28:9.
- 'The Lord is far from the wicked, but He hears the prayer of the righteous' Proverbs 15:29.
- The formerly blind man (from birth) speaking at the synagogue said, "Now we know that God does not hear sinners; but if anyone is a worshipper of God and does His will, He hears him" John 9:31.
- The apostle Paul writing on submission in marriage, 'Husbands, dwell with them [your wife] with understanding, giving honour to the wife, as to the weaker vessel, and as being heirs together

of the grace of life, that your prayers may not be hindered' 1 Peter 3:7.

- 'Let us search out and examine our ways, and turn back to the Lord; let us lift our hearts and hands to God in heaven. We have transgressed and rebelled; You have not pardoned. You have covered Yourself with anger and pursued us; You have slain and not pitied. You have covered Yourself with a cloud that prayer should not pass through' Lamentations 3:40-44.

- Behold, the Lord's hand is not shortened, that it cannot save; nor His ear heavy that it cannot hear. But your iniquities have separated you from God; and your sins have hidden His face from you, so that He will not hear' Isaiah 59:1-3.

At The Church of England General Synod, 15 November 2005, HRH Queen Elizabeth II said, "For Christians, this pace of change represents an opportunity. When so much is in flux, when limitless amounts of information, much of it ephemeral, are instantly accessible on demand, there is a renewed hunger for that which endures and gives meaning. The Christian Church can speak uniquely to that need, for at the heart of our faith stands the conviction that all people, irrespective of race, background or circumstances, can find lasting significance and purpose in the gospel of Jesus Christ."

Christians and Repentance

For some pastors, ministers, vicars and priests, their job has become a career – I speak as an itinerate speaker who is in full-time Christian ministry. They have disregarded the role of a shepherd and have become hirelings, giving no care to the flock or to their own lifestyle before God; only being concerned with their personal finance. As one minister said, "We cannot expect God to bless us on the Lord's Day, if the devil has use of us on Saturday night!" But all is not doom and gloom, because where sins abound then grace will abound much more, and these leaders are in the minority, whereas the majority are true shepherds living among us, exhorting us to go deeper with God. If any of these abuses concern you; please deal with them in repentance, turn from these wicked ways; repent of this sin of apathy within the Church or of heavy handed shepherding which has led to the abuse of many sheep. Look at the early Church as seen in the book of Acts (and beyond), and model your ministry on that. Reaching out to others, living in harmony, correcting those in opposition with love and humility, and allowing the Holy Spirit to come and move in the meetings as He sees fit. 'Sing to the Lord a new song!'

Within many churches there is a lack of the fear of God, a denial of the Holy Spirit and His gifts which He distributes at will. These precious gifts to the body of Christ are too frequently ignored, denied, abused or neglected and sometimes even despised, brethren this should not be! Many a church congregation love their traditions, more than they love God. They are mere rules as taught by men, yet their hearts are far from God. Outwardly they appear righteous and pious, but inwardly they are full of greed, bitterness, lust, jealousies, anger and the like. They tie heavy burdens to those who are part of the establishment yet care nothing for the lost and hurting outside. Within many congregations there are individuals or groups who ignore each other, yet hypocritically claim to be one in Christ. There is backbiting gossip, slander, and accusations etc. This should not be – we are called to love one another, then all men shall know that we are Jesus' disciples (John 13:34-35).

'Thus says the Lord of hosts: "Return to Me," says the Lord of hosts, "and I will return to you," says the Lord of hosts.' Zechariah 1:3.

Multitudes of Christians daily deny Jesus when they hear Him being mocked, blasphemed or ridiculed and say nothing. Others deny Jesus by being participants to dirty jokes (by listening to them) with work colleagues or friends or join in the gossip. Some will not even mention that they went to church at the weekend when asked what they did, thus being ashamed of the Lord Jesus Christ Himself and His gospel, which is the power of God unto salvation (Matthew 10:33 and Romans 1:16).

Far too many Christians have compromised their testimony, broken God's laws and have therefore publicly dishonoured Him which has led to His name being blasphemed amongst the world (Romans 2:23-24). Bible teacher, Derek Prince said, "Anything that is not righteous is sinful." See 1 John 5:17. Many Christians are no different from the world, they look like them, smell like them, talk like them, act like them and socialise in the same dark places with them. Whilst we live in the world we are not of the world. It is one thing to go into godless places to evangelise, but quite another to socialise. Why do so many people who profess the name of Christ enjoy the company of God haters? What has light got to do with darkness? (2 Corinthians 6:14). Or do you think that the Scripture say in vain, the Spirit who dwells in us yearns jealously? (James 4:5). It is one things to socialise with those who have not yet fully comprehended the truth, but quite another to habitually socialise with those who openly reject the truth.

Jesus said, "He who is not with Me is against Me, and He who does not gather with Me scatters abroad" Matthew 12:30.

Many Christians have not crucified the flesh life, acted in self control, taken up their cross daily and have not been bothered to become a disciple of Jesus, (see Appendix D). Many Christians merely hang around the cross, where in actual fact; you have to get on the cross. Either you deal with your sin in private or when revival comes you will have to deal with it in public! The choice is yours. What God has tolerated in the past He will not tolerate in the future. Let us never forget that judgment begins at the house of the Lord, and if the righteous one is scarcely saved, what about the ungodly?! (1 Peter 4:17-18). You have been warned.

'He who covers his sin will not prosper, but whoever confesses *and forsakes them* will have mercy' Proverbs 28:13, author's emphasis.

It has been stated on many occasions that individuals can always have their own personal revival, a reviving of oneself – by getting the sin out of their lives. The story is told of a man who stood on a beach and drew a circle around his feet and then prayed: "Lord send revival, but start the work in me."[6]

One man with God became the saviour of the nation – Elijah before the four hundred and fifty prophets of Baal and four hundred prophets of Asherah (1 Kings chapter 18). Once the altar was prepared, a complete offering was given, Elijah called upon his God and the fire fell, and the people fell on their faces, crying out, "The Lord, He is God! The Lord He is God!" and then the rain fell which came and healed the barren land! Make sure that you are in a right standing relationship with the Living God and then call upon Him, "Lord send revival, but start the work in me!" From the past we can draw faith for the present and hope for the future.

Decide each day to live your life for God, pray: "Holy Spirit, whatever You are doing today, if I am a part of it,

I ask that You will make it plain to me as I desire to glorify Jesus."

'Those from among you shall build the old waste places; you shall raise up the foundations of many generations; and you shall be called the Repairer of the Breach, the Restorer of Streets to Dwell In' Isaiah 58:12.

The Watchmen Challenge

You are the watchman on the wall who has been called to the kingdom for such a time as this. Rise up mighty warriors and fight the battles that your ancestors believed and prayed for, who did not love their life unto death. Stand in the gap and cry mightily unto God. Give Him no rest, who is the restorer of the breaches, the One who alone is the repairer of the desolate cities. Stand up and take up your position on the battle line over the destiny of the United Kingdom. The land in which many missionaries and revivalist's have been birthed, and raised up to call their children back to their heavenly Father. The Reformation brought about a cataclysmic change to the nation that I love and today I am asking you to be a warrior for this nation. The choice is yours. Will you take up this burden or look to another? Will you wear the sandals of the gospel of peace, clothed in righteousness with the sweet utterance of Jesus upon your lips, permeated with the soaked fragrance of love and compassion; looking unto the blessed Saviour, the redeemer of the nation who shed His blood for all mankind? Whist we are not going to return to the old fashion ways – behold I do a new things, it will break forth into bud, and flower like the rose of Sharon and the fragrance of My knowledge will be as the waters that cover the earth, and My glory will be revealed for all to see.[7]

Epilogue

Now What?

In the process of reading this book the conclusion that has been clearly presented before us is that revival is on God's heart: He takes no pleasure in the death of the wicked and desires to (and will) pour out His Spirit on all flesh. He expects those who have called upon the name of the Lord Jesus to depart from iniquity and lead holy God-fearing lives. Once we are living in obedience to His written word then we can start to call upon Him for the promises that He has made within that word. We want to see revival because God must be glorified in our towns and cities. Without Jesus people will be eternally damned in hell, where the worm dieth not and where there will be weeping and gnashing of teeth.

As a result of God's Spirit coming down on a community people will see their sins (as abhorrent in the sight of God), and will repent, weep, confess their sins and call upon Jesus for their eternal refuge as they will flee from the wrath to come.

But now what? Do we just sit back and wait for revival to come, of course not. It has been estimated that every hour seven thousand people who did not trust in Jesus Christ as their Lord and Saviour die and go to hell.[1] Whilst we believe and pray for revival to come, we are commanded to go into all the world and make disciples of all the nations (and then the end will come – Matthew 24:14 and 2 Peter 3:12) and we must go into the highways and byways and compel people to come in. We must be obedient to the Great Commission of which Jesus spoke about (Matthew 28:18-20)

A. W. Pink said, "It is true that [many] are praying for worldwide revival. But it would be more timely, and more scriptural, for prayer to be made to the Lord of the

Harvest, that He would raise up and thrust forth labourers who would fearlessly and faithfully preach those truths which are calculated to bring about revival."[2] This quote may need to be read several times as for some it may at first appear to contradict what has been written within the book, but this is not the case. Pink does not say that praying for worldwide revival is unscriptural, as God does intend to pour His Spirit out on all flesh. But when the likes of John and Charles Wesley, George Whitefield, Charles Finney, C. H. Spurgeon, Duncan Campbell, Mary Morrison and Steve Hill (to name but a few labourers) preached the truths of the gospel, they saw revival as God poured out His Spirit from on high and people broke down under the conviction of their sin.

You may not be an evangelist, but we are all called to evangelise and if Jesus has changed you, then He can change anyone! We should be preaching the gospel in season and out of season; we should always be prepared to share our testimony and preach the un-searchable riches of Christ Jesus. The apostle Paul was not ashamed of the gospel, knowing it is the power of God to salvation. Outside of Jesus Christ there is no other name by which we must be saved, and those who reject Jesus Christ stand condemned (John 3:18).

'Deliver those who are drawn towards death, and hold back those stumbling to slaughter. If you say, "Surely we did not know this," does not He who weighs the heart consider it? He who keeps your soul, does He not know it? And will He not render to each man according to his deeds?' Proverbs 24:11-12.

The apostle Paul did not shun to declare the whole counsel of God. We must preach: Jesus Christ and Him crucified for our sins; the cross, the blood, the Judgment to come and the ever populating hell and the lake of burning fire for those who refuse to depart from iniquity and reject Jesus Christ as their personal Lord and Saviour. The Law (the Ten Commandments) is our schoolmaster that brings us to Christ, because we can see with greater clarity how we have transgressed the moral law (if you have lied you are a liar, if you have stolen, you are a thief etc. it brings conviction of sin via the Holy Spirit), we are guilty before a holy and just God who demands an account of that which is past. Once we preach the Law it makes the judgment (hell) seem reasonable, and just (as for every cause there is an effect – reaping and sowing) – if I break the law of the land, I will be punished for it, how much more when I break God's perfect law of liberty. After the law which prepares the heart then we can preach grace.[3] The wages of sin is death, but the gift of God is eternal life in Christ Jesus. It was John Wesley who stated that he used to preach the Law (to bring awareness of sin) and then sprinkle it with grace. The reformer, Martin Luther said of the Law, "In its true and proper work and purpose it humbles a man and prepares him – if he uses the Law correctly – to yearn and seek for grace." Charles Finney said, "Evermore the Law must prepare the way for the gospel..."[4]

Never forget that a Christ-less, cross-less, blood-less message will result in spine-less, defence-less and power-less church goers with the nickname Christian. For too long, premature Christians (what the Scriptures call: tares, goats or accursed children) have been birthed who have no real knowledge of salvation or of God and soon become entangled by the cares of this life, the deceitfulness of riches or fall away under trials and tribulations.[5] Other writers call them 'spurious Christians,' 'dummy Christians' or 'adulterous' or 'false converts.' Jonathan Goforth of China called those with a 'give me' attitude, 'rice Christians' as some people are offered inducements to come to Jesus. A. W. Tozer wrote: 'It is in my opinion that tens of thousands of people, if not millions, have been brought into some kind of religious experience by accepting Christ, and they have not been saved!'

We should not preach a false gospel message of 'easy believism' or self-improvement, self-centredness and self-indulgence of 'come to Jesus and all your problems will go away' or 'come to Jesus and receive financial benefits from God.' Whilst there are many benefits in Christ Jesus (of peace and joy, acceptance in Christ, having a lighter yoke etc.), we should preach the entire gospel (not just a 'pick and mix' gospel) and declare that each individual has to take up their own cross daily and follow Him, and that those who live godly in Christ Jesus, will suffer persecution. Steve Hill said, "Ask not what Jesus can do for you, but rather ask what you can do for Jesus."

Far too many people, who call themselves Christians, do not live up to His name. If following Jesus had legal requirements and responsibilities, many British Christians would be charged and fined under The Trades Description Act; they are neither Christ-like nor anointed. If Christianity was a crime, would there be enough evidence to convict you?

Ray Comfort wrote: 'If the average church made as much noise *about* God on Monday as it *does* on Sunday, we would have revival.' He continued, 'If we worship God, yet ignore His command to take the gospel to every creature, then our worship is in vain. It is to draw near to Him with our lips, but to have our hearts far from Him.'[6]

Be warned there are eternal ramifications in this world and the next; we will not only be judged by what we said and did, but also by what we did not say and did not do!

Leonard Ravenhill's epitaph: "Are the things you are living for worth Christ dying for?" – What about you?

APPENDIXES A-E

Appendix A

Author and Bible teacher, Paris Reidhead, in remarking about the ministry of evangelist (and revivalist) Charles Finney wrote: 'Finney was in Rochester, New York, where a blue-ribbon committee of outstanding citizens was appointed by Henry Ward Beecher to study the converts who, a decade earlier, had to come to Christ under Finney's preaching. It was found that eighty-five percent of those who had made professions under Finney's preaching were still faithfully living for Christ.

'In contrast, it is being reported that only one-half of one percent of those who make decisions for Christ in our evangelistic meeting today will be living as Christians two years from now. This is how far we've strayed from the Word of God (*Finding the Reality of God*)'[1]

Ray Comfort in his book, *Revival's Golden Keys* wrote: 'In Leeds, England, a visiting U.S. speaker acquired 400 decisions for a local church. However, six weeks later only two were going on, and they eventually fell away.[2]

Ray Comfort, after citing eighteen examples from across the globe of crusade and denominational (conversion) statistics wrote: 'These statistics of an eighty-four to ninety-seven percent fall away rate are not confined to crusades, but are general throughout local church evangelism.'[3]

Appendix B

Evangelistic Campaigns

In 1954, the Billy Graham Crusade came to London, England. Within three months two million people had heard the good news and tens of thousands committed their lives to Jesus Christ.[1]

In 1957, the Billy Graham Crusade came to New York City. Within sixteen weeks two million people had heard the good news and over fifty-five thousand committed their lives to Jesus Christ.[2]

In 1973, the Billy Graham Crusade came to Seoul, South Korea. On its final meeting one million people attended. The following year an evangelistic crusade sponsored by Campus Crusade for Christ, Explo '74 saw on one evening an attendance of 1.5 million people.[3]

For four nights in August 1980, a cumulative total of 10.5 million people attended the Here's Life, Korea '80 World Evangelization Crusade (HLK-'80 WEC) at the Yoido Plaza, located on an island in the Han River Seoul, South Korea. One and a half million people made a decision for Christ Jesus during the Here's Life campaign. On the final night 2.7 million attended. Including the daytime meetings for six days, the accumulative attendance was 16.3 million.[4]

During 1980, Campus Crusade for Christ blasted and blitzed the Asian Continent and the South Pacific from India to Japan, from Papua New Guinea to Tonga. Frequently and where possible Campus Crusade and fellow labourers would blanket a city with mass media and arouse interest, via the radio, billboards, tract and literature distribution, door to door and using the *Jesus* film which accumulates in a large evangelistic event. Over two hundred million people were confronted with the claims of Jesus Christ and more than eleven million made a profession of faith.[5]

Healing Crusades

At the beginning of the twenty-first century, the evangelist Rhinehard Bonnke, Christ For All Nations (CFAN) held meetings in Lagos, Nigeria where on one night alone, over one million people made a profession of faith and over three million attended. These one million conversions in a single meeting had been prophesied (to him) two decades before.[6]

Rhinehard speaking to *Daystar* Christian TV at the centenary celebrations of the Azusa Street Outpouring stated that since the millennium up until the present (2000 till 29 April 2006), under his preaching, 42,000,000 decision cards had been signed for Christ.

During a three day crusade in February 2004, Pastor Benny Hinn and 4.8 million people gathered at the Bandra Kurla Complex in northwest Mumbai, India, for the Festival of Blessings. In Bangalore, India in early 2005, Pastor Benny Hinn held a three day healing crusade where over six million people attended and hundreds of thousands made a profession of faith and hundreds were healed, in Jesus' name.[7]

The Jesus Film

Bill Bright was founder and leader of Campus Crusade for Christ. He passed into glory in 2003. The organisation in the year of his death had 26,000 full-time staff and more than 225,000 trained volunteer staff in 191 countries in areas representing 99.6% of the world's population. From 1953-2003, Campus Crusade for Christ has seen approximately *6,000 million exposures to the gospel worldwide. *6 billion in American terminology as British and American number differs.[8]

The *Jesus* film was conceived by Bright and funded through Campus Crusade for Christ and was made in 1979. It is the most widely translated and viewed film in the world. Since its use began in 1980-2003, the film has been translated into 812 languages and viewed or listened to by 5.500 million (5.5 billion people in American terminology) in 236 countries, virtually every country of the world. *Gone with the Wind* (1939 American civil war epic) is the second most translated film with only thirty-five translations! By April 2006 there was a cumulative viewing and listening audience of 6,085,804,000 and by May 2006 there was 952 translations.[9]

The *Jesus* film annual budget in 2004 was $38 million (£22 million at 2004 exchange rate) which is made up from sponsorship and charitable donations. Campus Crusade for Christ intends to translate the film into every known language of the world. In 2004 there were about one billion people who could not read and a further one billion who are semi-illiterate – those who attended school but still can not read.

By the end of 2003, over 2,000 million (two billion people in American terminology) have actually seen the film, whether it be on video, a laptop or viewed via a projector powered by the mains or a portable generator, which enables the power of 'television' to be seen in the remotest villages in the remotest parts of the world – even for those who live in caves.

Television Evangelism

In the late eighties the American network, Christian Broadcasting Network (CBN) saw four million conversions when it made block-booking channels for the presentation of the gospel in Latin America. CBN also had a three day media blitz in Guatemala, Nicaragua and El Salvador; thirty-eight percent of 6,500 interviewed in Guatemala City said they received Christ during the broadcast and another nine percent gave their lives to Jesus Christ during the survey interview. In Nicaragua forty percent of 118,000 interviewed had submitted their life to Christ and a further one and a half percent during the survey.

During 1991-1992 more than thirty million people asked for salvation literature when CBN's Soviet Youth TV special, 'What Are You Living For?' was aired all over the former Soviet Union, with a further four million requesting follow up booklets.[10]

In 2005, *The 700 Club* began ministry outreaches in Peru through weekly airings of their Spanish TV programmes. As a result 3.61 million people are projected to have come to Christ. With a population of 28 million and a potential viewing audience of 20.1 million, more than half the viewing country (11.1 million) watched one or more of their programmes in the recent week-long TV media blitz.[11]

Appendix C

Dr. Martyn Lloyd-Jones was speaking one year before the 1960s popular degeneration of Britain's (amongst others nations) general moral standing. In 1961, the contraceptive pill went on sale in Britain, which greatly encouraged promiscuous lifestyles. In 1962, Britain's first legal casino opened in Brighton. In 1965, capital punishment was put on experimental abolition for five years; during those years capital murder rose by 125%. There was a fourfold increase involving shooting and murders committed in the trial course and theft rose threefold. In 1966, John Lennon caused outrage when he stated that the Beatles were probably more popular in their time than Jesus Christ was in His. In 1967, The Sexual Offences Act became law that legalised homosexual behaviour between consenting adults when in private. In 1967, the Abortion Act was introduced in Britain which allowed the foetus (baby) to be terminated (murdered) up to the twenty-fourth week and never past the twenty-eight week. By 2006, there had been over 6.25 million legal abortions (mass genocide which is 10% of the population of the United Kingdom!). Pope John Paul II in His book, *Memory and Identity* (published in 2005) linked legalised abortion with the Jewish holocaust. In 1968 the first theatrical presentation to take advantage of the end of British stage censorship was the musical *Hair* which included one scene where the entire cast was completely nude. In 1969, the death penalty for murder was formally abolished in Britain and crime just rose and rose.

Appendix D

Gwen Shaw wrote: 'Today the Lord needs those who will totally surrender their lives to God and who will "sell out" to God, not counting the cost, for the true revivalist must be ready to burn-out for God.

'He or she will often find that they are very lonely because God will not let them mingle with the crowd or be "one of the gang." They have no time for self or pleasure. Again and again the words come to mind: "Others may – you cannot."

'Because of this separation you will be misunderstood, maligned and held in suspicion. You must keep your eyes on Jesus at all times because if you do not you will become bitter and angry and filled with self-pity and then you will be "finished" and both you and your message will be lost to this generation.'[1]

Those with a divine calling cannot live like those without one. That which God tolerates in some, He will not tolerate in those He has called into ministry. Those with a divine calling should differentiate between what I can do and what I am supposed to do. Deciding what you're not going to do is equally important. A true disciple with a divine calling will say no, especially to the good, in order to produce the best. The prophet Jeremiah was called from a very early age (Jeremiah 1:5-8) and described his test of loneliness as 'bearing the yoke in youth' having to sit alone and keep silent as God had laid it on him, (Lamentations 3:26-28 and Jeremiah 15:17).

If you commission yourself, you will serve yourself and your own agendas, (Romans 12:3). If you go into the ministry without God's calling and appointing, you will go in your own strength and gifting. But when God calls and appoints you, you can go in His authority and see a larger anointing with greater eternal fruit, (John 15:1-11).

Before the apostle Paul was released into the world he had a period of training and testing. Paul was separated to the work that God had called him to, (Romans 1:1). Paul is silent as to what happened in Arabia, but God was dealing with him and eventually God revealed the full gospel to him, (Galatians 1:11-18 and Galatians 2:1-2). Paul submitted to the church at Antioch for a period of testing in whatever duties they wanted him to do, (Acts 13:1). Paul later wrote about the importance of testing and faithfulness, (1 Corinthians 4:2 and 1 Timothy 3:10). Once Paul passed the test in the ministry of helps, he was promoted to the office of teacher, (2 Timothy 1:11 and Acts 13:1-3). Paul's calling and anointing was recognised through his faithful serving, (1 Timothy 1:12). We are all called to be an example, (1 Timothy 4:12).

Brokenness and a contrite heart is a requirement for service and this is what God looks for, (Psalm 51:17, Isaiah 57:15 and Isaiah 66:2). Jesus revealed that you can either be broken by your submission to Him or ground to powder by your rebellion, (Matthew 21:44). To be broken means to submit your will to the Master.

The breaking process deals with submission to all authority, whether it is God's authority or delegated authority, (Romans 13:1-2). It is wrong to submit only when we agree. Those with a calling should be servants (rather than being served) and need to be enrolled in the school of humility. God measures greatness not in terms of status but in service; not by how many people serve you, but by how many people you serve.[2]

Others May...You Cannot

If God has called you to be really like Jesus He will draw you into a life of crucifixion and humility, and put upon you such demands of obedience, that you will not be able to follow other people or measure yourself by other Christians, and in many ways He will seem to let other people do things which He will not let you do.

Other Christians and ministers who seem very religious and useful, may push themselves, pull wires, and work schemes to carry out their plans, but you cannot do it, and if you attempt it, you will meet with such failure and rebuke from the Lord as to make you sorely penitent.

Others may boast of themselves, of their work, of their successes, of their writings, but the Holy Spirit will not allow you to do any such thing, and if you begin it, He will lead you into some deep mortification that will make you despise yourself and all your good works.

Others may be allowed to succeed in making money, or may have a legacy left to them, but it is likely God will keep you poor, because He wants you to have something far better than gold, namely, a helpless dependence upon Him, that He may have the privilege of supplying your needs day by day out of an unseen treasury.

The Lord may let others be honoured and put forward, and keep you hidden in obscurity, because He wants to produce some choice fragrant fruit for His coming glory, which can only be produced in the shade. He may let others be great, but keep you small. He may let others do a work for Him and get the credit for it, but He will make you work and toil on without knowing how much you are doing; and then to make your work still more precious He may let others get credit for the work you have done, and thus make your reward ten times greater when Jesus comes.

The Holy Spirit will put a strict watch over you, with a jealous love, and will rebuke you for little words and feelings or for wasting your time, which other Christians never feel distressed over. So make up your mind that God is an infinite Sovereign, and has a right to do as He pleases with His own. He may not explain to you a thousand things which puzzle your reason in His dealings with you, but if you absolutely sell yourself to be His love slave, He will wrap you up in jealous love, and bestow upon you many blessings which come only to those who are in the inner circle.

Settle it forever, then, that you are to deal directly with the Holy Spirit, and that He is to have the privilege of tying your tongue, or chaining your hand, or closing your eyes, in ways that He does not seem to use with others. Now, when you are so possessed with the living God that you are, in your secret heart, pleased and delighted over this peculiar, personal, private, jealous guardianship and management of the Holy Spirit over your life, you will have found the vestibule of heaven.[3]

Appendix E

John Wesley, in his *Journal* for the 23 June 1755 wrote: 'I was considering what could be the reason why the Hand of the Lord (who does nothing without a cause) is almost entirely stayed in Scotland, and in great measure New-England. It does not become to judge peremptorily; but perhaps some of them may be these:-

1. Many of them became "wise in their own eyes;" they seemed to think they were the men, and there were none like them. And hence they refused God the liberty of sending by whom He would send, and required Him to work by men of learning or not at all. 2. Many of them were bigots, immoderately attached either to their own opinions or mode of worship. Mr Edwards himself was not clear of this. But the Scotch bigots were beyond all others; placing Arminianism (so called) on a level with Deism, and the Church of England with that of Rome. Hence they not only suffered in themselves and their brethren a bitter zeal, but applauded themselves therein; in showing the same spirit against all who differed from them, as the Papists did against their forefathers. No marvel then that the Spirit was grieved. Let us profit from their example.[4]

On the other hand Wesley during the time of the General Assembly in Edinburgh (which drew together ministers, nobility and gentry) on the 29 April 1763 commends the Scots and wrote: 'I spoke as plain as ever I did in my life. But I never knew any in Scotland offended at plain dealing. In this respect the North Britons are a pattern to all mankind.'[5]

In June 1764, John Wesley made the following comment after speaking in a Kirk (Scottish church) in Nairn, 'the bell was immediately rung, and the congregation was quickly in the Kirk. O what a difference is there between South and North Britain! Every one here at least loves to hear the word of God; and none takes it into his head to speak one uncivil word to any, for endeavouring to save their souls. The next day Wesley noted after staying in several inns and inviting the people to join in prayer, that 'among all the sins they have imported from England, the Scots have never learned, at least not the common people, to scoff at sacred things.'[6]

Sources and Notes

Preface
1. Dr. Martyn Lloyd-Jones speaking in 1959, the centenary of the 1859 revival, at Westminster Chapel. Note: Unless otherwise stated all quotes from Dr. Martyn Lloyd-Jones are from the year 1959 when he preached a series of sermons of revivals at Westminster Chapel, London, England.
2. Dr. Martyn Lloyd-Jones speaking at Westminster Chapel.

Chapter One
1. Dr. Martyn Lloyd-Jones speaking at Westminster Chapel.
2. *The Skye Revivals* by Steve Taylor, New Wine Press, 2003, page 142.
3. Dr. Martyn Lloyd-Jones speaking at Westminster Chapel.
4. *When God Came Down an account of the North Uist Revival 1957-58* edited by John Ferguson, Lewis Recordings, 2000, pages 15-16.
5. Dr. Martyn Lloyd-Jones speaking at Westminster Chapel.
6. As quoted by Duncan Campbell in a sermon. Note: Unless otherwise stated all Duncan Campbell quotes are from his recorded sermons which can be purchased from numerous sources in tapes, CD or MP3 formats or listened to online for free at various websites.
7. *Chronicles Magazine* URC Canford Heath Church, September 1997, issue 186.
8. *Revival Phenomena* by Colin Dye, Sovereign World Ltd, 1996, page 12.
9. *Great Revivals* by Colin Whittaker, Marshall, Morgan & Scott, 1984, page 92. Note: a 2005 edition is available from Kingsway. Used by permission of Kingsway Publications, Lottbridge Drove, Eastbourne.
10. Ibid., 105-106. Used by permission of Kingsway Publications, Lottbridge Drove, Eastbourne.
11. *Grace, Grit & Gumption* by Geraint Fielder, Christian Focus Publication, 2000, page 200.

Chapter Three
1. Dr. Martyn Lloyd-Jones speaking at Westminster Chapel.
2. *The History of Revivals of Religion* by William E. Allen (revival series No. 7), Revival Publishing Co., 1951, page 17. And extracts from *The Awesome Work of God* by Jonathan Edwards, Ambassador Publications, 2000.

3. *The History of Revivals of Religion* by William E. Allen (revival series No. 7), Revival Publishing Co., 1951, pages 17-18.

4. *Vignettes of the Great Revival* by E. Paxton Hood, The Religious Tract Society, 1887, page 184.

5. *Great Revivals* by Colin Whittaker, Marshall, Morgan & Scott, 1984, pages 35-36. Used by permission of Kingsway Publications, Lottbridge Drove, Eastbourne.

6. *Wesley His Own Biography, Selections From The Journals*, Charles H. Kelly, 1890, page 109. Note: At least one author states this meeting of Howells Harris with John Wesley with the same quote as of the 5 June 1747 and states Wesley own Journal as his source.

7. Ibid., page 118.

8. *A Lion Handbook The History of Christianity,* Lion Publishing plc, 1996, page 448.

9. *Vignettes of the Great Revival* by E. Paxton Hood, The Religious Tract Society, 1887, pages 12-14.

10. *John Wesley The Hero of the Second Reformation* by Edward Miller, Published by The Sunday School Union, 1906, pages 8-10.

11. Ibid., page 62.

12. *The life of John Wesley by Telford*, The Epworth Press, 1929 edition, pages 115-118 and 129.

13. *Wesley His Own Biography, Selections From The Journals*, Charles H. Kelly, 1890, pages 139 and 157.

14. *The life of John Wesley by Telford*, The Epworth Press, 1929 edition, page 144.

15. *Wesley His Own Biography, Selections From The Journals*, Charles H. Kelly, 1890, page 238.

16. Ibid., page 374.

17. *The life of John Wesley by Telford*, The Epworth Press, 1929 edition, pages 121-125.

18. *Wesley His Own Biography, Selections From The Journals*, Charles H. Kelly, 1890, page 108.

19. Ibid., page 111.

20. Ibid., page 124.

21. Ibid., pages 119-120.

22. *The life of John Wesley by Telford*, The Epworth Press, 1929 edition, pages 122-123.

23. In 1707, Scotland joined with England to become Great Britain and in 1801 with Ireland to become part of the United Kingdom of Great Britain and Ireland. Scotland has always had separate legal and educational system to the rest of the UK, as well as a unique culture.

Chapter Four

1. *Old Time Revivals* by John Shearer, Pickering & Inglis, (undated), page 72.
2. Ibid., pages 65-67.
3. Ibid., page 72.
4. *Vanguard of the Christian Army* by The Religious Tract Society, 1896, page 174.
5. *Old Time Revivals* by John Shearer, Pickering & Inglis, (undated), page 75.
6. *Vanguard of the Christian Army* by The Religious Tract Society, 1896, pages 174-175.
7. *The Half Can Never Be Told*, published by the World Wide Revival Prayer Movement, 1927, page 55.
8. *When the Fire Fell* by George T.B. Davis, Schmul Publishers (undated), page 29.
9. *The History of Revivals of Religion* by William E. Allen (revival series No. 7), Revival Publishing Co., 1951, page 35.
10. *Great Revivals* by Colin Whittaker, Marshall, Morgan & Scott, 1984, pages 73-74. Used by permission of Kingsway Publications, Lottbridge Drove, Eastbourne.
11. *The History of Revivals of Religion* by William E. Allen (revival series No. 7), Revival Publishing Co., 1951, page 37.
12. *Land of Hope and Glory British Revival Through The Ages* by Bruce Atkinson, Dovewell Publications, 2003, pages 259-260.
13. *The Half Can Never Be Told*, published by the World Wide Revival Prayer Movement 1927, pages 55-58 and 62-65. And *The History of Revivals of Religion* by William E. Allen (revival series No. 7), Revival Publishing Co., 1951, pages 36 and 38-39.
14. *When the Fire Fell* by George T.B. Davis, Schmul Publishers (undated), pages 61-62.
15. *The Year of Grace* by William Gibson, Ambassador Productions Ltd, 1989, page 253.
16. (Quoted from Edwin Orr in *Fervent Prayer* from *Evangelical Christendom* 1860) *Great Revivals* by Colin Whittaker, Marshall, Morgan & Scott, 1984, page 81. Used by permission of Kingsway Publications, Lottbridge Drove, Eastbourne.
17. *The Half Can Never Be Told*, published by the World Wide Revival Prayer Movement 1927, (extracts) pages 65-68.
18. *Spurgeon on Revival* edited by Robert Backhouse, Kingsway, 1996, page 7. Used by permission of Kingsway Publications, Lottbridge Drove, Eastbourne.
19. *The History of Revivals of Religion* by William E. Allen (revival series No. 7), Revival Publishing Co., 1951, pages 46-47.

Chapter Five

1. *Land of Hope and Glory British Revival Through The Ages* by Bruce Atkinson, Dovewell Publications, 2003, pages 207-208.
2. *Thomas Birch Freeman, Missionary Pioneer to Ashanti, Dahomey & Egba* by J. Milum, London, S. W. Partridge & Co., 1894, pages 141-149.
3. In 1925 their prayers were fully answered as the Shanghai Revival began, see chapter six.
4. *Missionary Band A Record And Appeal,* London: Morgan and Scott, 1887, pages 22 and 37.
5. Ibid., pages 71-72.
6. *Prove Me Now! 10,000 Miles of Miracle to Moscow* by J. Edwin Orr, Marshall, Morgan & Scott, LTD, 1935, page 36.
7. *Revival comes to Wales The story of the 1859 Revival in Wales* by Eifion Evans, Evangelical Press of Wales, 1995, pages 10-11.
8. *Rent Heavens the revival of 1904* by R. B. Jones, Schmul Publishers (undated), page 40.
9. Note: Rees Howells was challenged by the Holy Spirit to see revival in a village nicknamed Hell-fire Row which had not been touched by the Welsh Revival, for more information on Rees Howells see **www.byfaith.co.uk/paulreeshowells2.htm**. Further detail of the life of Rees Howells and Hell-fire Row can be found in *Rees Howells Intercessor* by Norman Grubb, Lutterworth Press, chapter seven.
10. *Revival Praying* by Leonard Ravenhill, Bethany House Publishers, 1962, page 146.
11. *When the Fire Fell* by George T.B. Davis, Schmul Publishers (undated) pages 70-71.
12. *Rent Heavens the Revival of 1904* by R. B. Jones, Schmul Publishers (undated), page 56.

Chapter Six

1. *The History of Revivals of Religion* by William E. Allen (revival series No. 7), Revival Publishing Co., 1951, pages 54-55. And *Goforth of China* by Rosalind Goforth, Zondervan Publishing House, 1937, chapters ten to twelve.
2. *By My* Spirit by Jonathan Goforth, Evangel Publishing House, (undated), page 25.
3. *Goforth of China* by Rosalind Goforth, Zondervan Publishing House, 1937, chapters thirteen to fourteen.
4. *The Revival We Need* by Oswald J. Smith, Marshall, Morgan & Scott Ltd, 1940, page v.
5. *God's Generals* by Robert Liardon, Albury Publishing, 1996, (factual extracts) pages 145-148.

6. *Azusa Street The Roots of Modern-day Pentecost* by Frank Bartleman, Bridge Publishing, 1980, page xviii.

7. www.azusastreet100.net/history.htm#, used by permission.

8. *Azusa Street The Roots of Modern-day Pentecost* by Frank Bartleman, Bridge Publishing, 1980, pages 56-57.

9. *A Forgotten Revival, East Anglia and North-East Scotland-1921* by Stanley C. Green, Day One Publication, 1995.

10. *Revival Man, The Jock Troup Story* by George Mitchel, Christian Focus, 2002.

11. *The Half Can Never Be Told*, published by the World Wide Revival Prayer Movement, 1927, Part II.

Chapter Seven

1. *All Your Need 10,000 Miles of Miracle Through Australia and New Zealand* by J. Edwin Orr, Marshall, Morgan & Scott, LTD, (undated), circa 1936, (extracts) pages 15-27.

2. Rev. Duncan Campbell preaching. Note: In later age, the Rev. Duncan Campbell when retelling of his experiences would sometimes get place names and the stories muddled up. On more than one occasion, he also stated that not everything that has been written about the Lewis Revival is true. Rev. Campbell also stated the he had had a baptism of the Holy Spirit, though he never spoke in tongues and neither did anyone during the Lewis Revival. He also stated that no physical healings took place. P.S Bristow, who wrote the introduction to *The Lewis Awakening 1949-1953* by Duncan Campbell (1954 The Faith Mission) wrote: 'I have before me Mr. Campbell's own accounts of the work, received from him from week to week, and I can only say that *his much restricted accounts* in these pages gives but a glimpse of the great manifestations of divine power witnessed throughout the island. For personal reasons *the vivid details of experience in the lives of individuals is withheld.* Could they be suitably narrated, they would be thrilling to read.' Author's emphasis, see page 175. The Rev. Gordon I. Thomas, in the foreword to the same booklet wrote: 'Story after story could be told of incidents that are in the realm of the miraculous and which indeed are positively breath-taking to hear. *Practically none of these has been mentioned in this booklet...*' Author's emphasis. I obtained this booklet just as my book was going to print. Due to Duncan Campbell's humility, the culture of the Scots and the fact that it is very difficult to write about ones own experiences immediately after an event, much of what happened during that revival, notably deliverance from demons (often as people were prostrated before the Lord, being delivered by God Himself), under deep conviction of sin has not been recorded in print. This is not presumption to presuppose such a

theory, but a judgment based on revival Church History, mans nature, the devil's shackles and God's power to liberate – just read Wesley's *Journal* and accounts of other revivals within this book. There is nothing new under the sun.

3. Note: Duncan Campbell had never visited this island before and knew no one on the island, but an elder prayed him to the island and was expecting him! For more information about the move of the Spirit on the isle of Berneray, (also known as Bernera) see *Channel of Revival, A Biography Of Duncan Campbell* by Andrew A Woolsey, The Faith Mission, 1982, chapter sixteen.

4. For more information on Rev. Robert Jermain Thomas and North Korea visit **www.byfaith.co.uk/paulkorea.htm**.

5. *The History of Revivals of Religion* by William E. Allen (revival series No. 7), Revival Publishing Co., 1951, page 62.

6. *The Spirit of Revival A first hand account of the Congo Revival of the 1950s* compiled and edited by Norman Grubb, Christian Focus Publications, 2000, page 125.

7. Ibid., page 79-81.

Chapter Eight

1. J. Edwin Orr preaching on a series presented in 1981 at Church on the Way, Van Nuys, California. From a CDR, *J. Edwin Orr Revival Library, The History of Revival,* Orr Latin America, 2005. Orr's preaching can also been heard (or seen) online for free.

2. *Cross Pollination The Miracle of Unity in Intercession, Revival and the Harvest* by Lila Terhune, Revival Press, 1999, pages 15-19. (Lila Terhune was the chief intercessor at Brownsville, A.O.G., Pensacola). And *Great Revivals* by Colin Whittaker, Marshall, Morgan & Scott, 1984, pages 102-104. Used by permission of Kingsway Publications, Lottbridge Drove, Eastbourne.

3. *When God Came Down an account of the North Uist Revival 1957-58* edited by John Ferguson, 2000, Lewis Recordings.

4. Kurt Koch, *The Revival in Indonesia*, Evangelization Publishers, West Germany (undated).

5. *The Rising Revival Firsthand Accounts of the Incredible Argentine Revival – And How It Can Spread Throughout The World* edited by C. Peter Wagner and Pablo Deiros, Renew Books, 1998.

Chapter Nine

1. *Holy Spirit, I Hunger For You* by Claudio Freidzon, Creation House, 1997, page 59.

2. Ibid., pages (factual extracts) 63-65.

3. *CWR TODAY*, (quoting from Joel News) issue 02 Apr-Jun 2006, page 9.

4. Since the end of the Brownsville Revival, the last six years have been difficult for the church, with new leadership (x2) and decreasing numbers. But, it is worth noting that the lasting fruit of the revival can be found in the lives of the millions (no exaggeration) of people who attended its services (and the Awake America campaigns) and were eternally changed (converted and/or empowered for service) and not necessarily within the long-term membership of the church which consistently changes (people die, leave or more away) and develops with new people and leadership teams. Was the Brownsville Revival a first fruit?

As a student and then as a staff member of the Bible College of Wales (BCW), Swansea, on two occasions teams of students from the School of Ministry [Brownsville Bible College] would be ministering in Wales as part of a ministry team. I had the honour of meeting various members of these teams and showed one group of fifty (including other visitors) around the Bible College grounds which were purchased by faith by Rees Howells (**www.reeshowells.co.uk**). These students were on fire for God!

One of the unique things about the revival is that every service has been filmed and videos can be purchased from the church, and as far as I am aware, it is the first time in history that the start of revival (and the continuance of it) has been captured on film in its entirety.

5. Note: for more information on the House Church Movement, read, *The Heavenly Man the remarkable true story of Chinese Christian Brother Yun* with Paul Hattaway, Monarch Books, 2002.

6. During 1959-1961 approximately forty million people died from malnutrition in the Great Famine of Communist China. In part, the famine was a direct result of unsuccessful new farming methods that were introduced by Chairman Mao after the formation of the People's Republic of China in 1949, *Guinness World Records 2002,* Printer Industria Grafica, Spain, page 114.

7. *Jesus in Beijing, How Christianity Is Transforming China and Changing Global Balance of Power* by David Aikman, Monarch Books, 2003, chapter nine.

Chapter Ten

1. Dr. Martyn Lloyd-Jones speaking at Westminster Chapel.

2. Rev. James Robe the leader of the 1742 Kilsyth Revival, commenting in regard to why not all those who were awakened (within the parish of Kilsyth) did not come to a saving knowledge of Jesus Christ, wrote: 'Some of these [having been awakened to their sin] were many weeks, if not months under great terror and distress. Some of those who lost their impressions came to no saving issue, by being engaged too much in worldly affairs. "The

cares of this life choked the word, and they became unfruitful." Some through ignorance, and not being diligent to learn the way of salvation through Jesus Christ [a blasé attitude]; some through the influence of evil company, and consulting with flesh and blood; some through the outcry raised by the Seceders [those who had withdrawn from the established Church], that all their convictions were but delusions and from the devil, one way or another they resisted the Holy Spirit, and provoked Him to withdraw His influences, and so the work of the Spirit upon them ceased, and came to no saving issue.' *When the Wind Blows, The Kilsyth and Cambuslang Revivals factually recorded by Rev. James Robe*, Ambassador Productions LTD, 1985, page 140.

Chapter Eleven
1. *Hot From the Preacher's Mound* by Stephen Hill, Together in the Harvest Publications, 1995, page 7.
2. Note: All quotes or extracts from Charles Finney can be found in numerous sources and editions by various publishers. *Finney on Revival The Highlights of the Sermons on Revival* by Charles Grandison Finney, arranged by E. E. Shelhamer, Dimensions Books – published by Bethany Fellowship, (undated), (extracts) pages 11-13.
3. *Why Revival Tarries* by Leonard Ravenhill, Bethany House, a division of Baker Publishing Group, 1959, (extracts) pages 56-61.
4. *The History of Revivals of Religion* by William E. Allen (revival series No. 7), Revival Publishing Co., 1951, page 4.
5. Dr. Martyn Lloyd-Jones speaking at Westminster Chapel.
6. *When God Came Down an account of the North Uist Revival 1957-58* edited by John Ferguson, 2000, Lewis Recordings, page 16.
7. *The Half Can Never Be Told*, published by the World Wide Revival Prayer Movement, 1927, page 68.
8. *Revival comes to Wales The story of the 1859 Revival in Wales* by Eifion Evans, Evangelical Press of Wales, 1995, pages 97-98.
9. *How Revival Comes, The Two National Broadcasts*, by Colin C. Kerr, Henry E. Walters, 1942, page 3.

Chapter Twelve
1. Dr. Martyn Lloyd-Jones speaking at Westminster Chapel.
2. *The History of Revivals of Religion* by William E. Allen (revival series No. 7), Revival Publishing Co., 1951, page 55.
3. *Revival comes to Wales The story of the 1859 Revival in Wales* by Eifion Evans, Evangelical Press of Wales, 1995, pages 101-102.

4. *Charisma Reports The Brownsville Revival* by Marcia Ford, Creation House, 1997, page 122.
5. Ibid., page 24.
6. *A Box of Delights* complied by J. John & Mark Stibbe, Monarch Books, 2004, page 199.

Chapter Thirteen
1. *All Your Need 10,000 Miles of Miracle Through Australia and New Zealand* by J. Edwin Orr, Marshall, Morgan & Scott, LTD, undated, circa 1936, page 122.
2. *Prayer and the Coming Revival* (first published as The Ministry of Intercession) by Andrew Murray, Ambassador Publications, 1999, pages 16-17 and 19.
3. *Why Revival Tarries* by Leonard Ravenhill, Bethany House, a division of Baker Publishing Group, 1959, pages 59-60 and (extracts) page 152.
4. *When God Came Down an account of the North Uist Revival 1957-58* edited by John Ferguson, 2000, Lewis Recordings, page 10.
5. *Great Revivals* by Colin Whittaker, Marshall, Morgan & Scott, 1984, pages 9-10. Used by permission of Kingsway Publications, Lottbridge Drove, Eastbourne.
6. *Prayer and the Coming Revival* (first published as The Ministry of Intercession) by Andrew Murray, Ambassador Publications, 1999, (extracts) pages 118-122.
7. *God's Harvest The Nature of True Revival* by I.D.E. Thomas, Bryntirion Press, 1997, page 39. Used by Permission.
8. *The Revival We Need* by Oswald J. Smith, Marshall, Morgan & Scott Ltd, 1940, page v.
9. *Great Revivals* by Colin Whittaker, Marshall, Morgan & Scott, 1984, page 97. Used by permission of Kingsway Publications, Lottbridge Drove, Eastbourne.
10. *Market Place Marriage & Revival The Spiritual Connection*, by Jack Serra, Longwood Communications, 2001, (extracts) pages 5, 9 and 11-12.
11. *The life of John Wesley by Telford*, The Epworth Press, 1929 edition, pages 253-256.

Chapter Fourteen
1. *It's Time For Revival! A Bible Study On Revival* by Gwen Shaw, Engeltal Press, 1988, pages 56-57.
2. Dr. Martyn Lloyd-Jones speaking at Westminster Chapel.
3. *Wesley His Own Biography, Selections From The Journals*, Charles H. Kelly, 1890, page 111.
4. Ibid., page 120.

5. *Revival comes to Wales The story of the 1859 Revival in Wales* by Eifion Evans, Evangelical Press of Wales, 1995, page 73.

6. *Why Revival Tarries* by Leonard Ravenhill, Bethany House, a division of Baker Publishing Group, 1959, (extracts) page 59.

7. *The Pursuit of Revival igniting a passionate hunger for more of God* by Stephen Hill, Creation House, 1997, page 133.

8. *Wesley His Own Biography, Selections From The Journals*, Charles H. Kelly, 1890, pages 197-198.

9. *Channel of Revival A Biography of Duncan Campbell* by Andrew A. Woolsey, The Faith Mission, 1982, page 163.

10. *The Spirit of Revival A first hand account of the Congo Revival of the 1950s* compiled and edited by Norman Grubb, Christian Focus Publications, 2000, page 125.

11. *Hot From the Preacher's Mound* by Stephen Hill, 1995, Together in the Harvest Publications, page 100.

12. *Charisma Reports The Brownsville Revival* by Marcia Ford, Creation House, 1997, pages 124-125.

13. *Channel of Revival A Biography of Duncan Campbell* by Andrew A. Woolsey, The Faith Mission, 1982, page 136.

14. Note: All quotes or extracts from Charles Finney can be found in numerous sources, editions and publishers.

15. *Charisma Reports The Brownsville Revival* by Marcia Ford, Creation House, 1997, (extracts), pages 120-121 and 124-125.

16. *The Lewis Revival (Isaiah 64:3)* tape 6, Rev. Duncan Campbell of The Faith Mission.

Chapter Fifteen

1. *The Price And Power of Revival* by Duncan Campbell, Sterling Printing Co., 1957, page 48. Originally preached by Duncan Campbell in 1956 at the Keswick-in-Wales Convention and then transmuted into a booklet.

2. As quoted by Duncan Campbell, *The Fire Of God* CD.

3. *The Revival: An Advocate of Evangelical Truth* No.481, Thursday Oct. 8, 1868.

4. *The Price And Power of Revival* by Duncan Campbell, Sterling Printing Co., 1957, page 49.

5. *The Successful Soul-Winner, A Summary of Finney's Revival Lectures* edited by Commissioner Booth-Tucker, Salvationist Publishing & Supplies, Limited, 1926, (extracts) pages 70-73.

6. *Finney on Revival The Highlights of the Sermons on Revival* by Charles Grandison Finney, arranged by E. E. Shelhamer, (extracts) pages 56-64.

7. *I saw the Welsh Revival* by David Matthews, 1904-Centenary Edition-2004, Ambassador Publications, pages 100-101.

8. *This Is The Victory 10,000 Miles of Miracle in America* by J. Edwin Orr, Marshall, Morgan & Scott, LTD, 1936, pages 67-68.

9. *If Ye Abide 10,000 Miles of Miracle In South Africa* by J. Edwin Orr, Marshall, Morgan & Scott, LTD, undated, circa 1936, page 78.

10. *Feast of Fire the remarkable story of the revival in Pensacola* by John Kilpatrick, Marshal Pickering, 1997, (extracts) pages 126-133.

11. Ibid., (extracts) pages 135-143.

Chapter Sixteen

1. Examples of Steve Hill's hard-core preaching can be found in, *White Cane Religion* by Stephen Hill, Revival Press, 1997 and *The God Mockers* by Stephen Hill, Revival Press, 1997.

2. Note: Earrings for men are a symbol of slavery, bondage and idol worship, see Genesis 35:2-5, Exodus 21:5-6, Exodus 32:1-4, Deuteronomy 15:15-17 and Judges 8:23-27.

3. The author was present at five of the evening meetings at Brownsville A.O.G in the summer of 1997 (during the Pensacola Revival) and has summarised some the main points of Steve Hill's holiness, Christ embracing preaching within this chapter.

4. *The Price And Power of Revival* by Duncan Campbell, Sterling Printing Co., 1957, page 32.

5. *Sinners in the Hands of an Angry God*, Jonathan Edwards Whitaker House, 1997, page 21.

6. *Spurgeon on Revival* edited by Robert Backhouse, Kingsway, 1996, pages 28-29. Used by permission of Kingsway Publications, Lottbridge Drove, Eastbourne.

7. *The Half Can Never Be Told*, published by the World Wide Revival Prayer Movement 1927, page 68.

8. Dr. Martyn Lloyd-Jones speaking at Westminster Chapel.

Chapter Seventeen

1. The prophecy (along with many others) can also be read online at **www.revivalnow.co.uk**.

2. Note: This is a greatly condensed version of the vision using the main facts from *Cross Pollination The Miracle of Unity in Intercession, Revival and the Harvest* by Lila Terhune, Revival Press, 1999, (extracts) pages 213-222.

3. Note: The internet was not birthed until nearly three decades later in 1994 and Christian television first came to Britain via satellite in October 1995.

4. Jean Darnall has shared her vision numerous times over the years, at various churches, conferences and on Christian television. The vision can also be read online at **www.revivalnow.co.uk**.

5. This vision has been shared by Michael Backholer, recreated, and aired on Christian TV, ByFaith 'A Journey of Discipleship,' episode 2, Revival in Britain, available on DVD via **www.byfaithtv.co.uk**.
6. By Paul Backholer, founder of ByFaith Media, **www.byfaithmedia.co.uk**.

Chapter Eighteen
1. The prophecy can be read online at **www.revivalnow.co.uk**. This prophecy was first aired on Christian TV in May 2006, ByFaith 'A Journey of Discipleship,' episode 2, Revival in Britain, available on DVD via **www.byfaithtv.co.uk**.
2. The revelation can be read online at **www.revivalnow.co.uk**.
3. The prophecies for Ireland, Wales, Scotland and England can also be read online at **www.prophecynow.co.uk** and **www.revivalnow.co.uk**.
4. *Derek Prince A Biography, A Teacher For Our Time* by Stephen Mansfield, Derek Prince Ministries – UK, 2005, page 178.
5. Note: Details of some of Britain's past sins, the need for national repentance and the biblical argument for why these sins remain the responsibility of Britain's Church today can be found in the book *Sins of the Forefathers how national repentance removes obstacles for revival* by Brian Mills and Roger Mitchell, Sovereign World Ltd, 1999. History of Britain: **www.xfaith.co.uk**.

Chapter Nineteen
1. Capital Punishment has always been a controversial issue. We cannot do without appropriate penalties as long as crime is rife. In 1965 Britain had five years of experimental abolition of Capital Punishment – murder rose by 125%, (see Appendix C). The lifting of a huge deterrent unleashed more crime. See, *Inspired and outspoken, The Collected Speeches of Ann Widdecombe* edited by John Simmons, Politico's Publishing, 1999, pages 35-36. Whilst 'mercy [imprisonment] is better than judgment [the death sentence]' there is a time and place when those who wilfully commit premeditated murder and show no remorse, (especially armed robbers, terrorists, cop and children killers), after a reasonable period of time (several years minimum imprisonment) should be executed, because, 'God's minister [the governing authority]...does not bear the sword in vain; for he is God's minister, an avenger to execute wrath on him who practices evil' (Romans 13:4). The Book *The Trumpet Sounds For Britain* by David E. Gardner, Volumes 1, 2 and 3 in one edition, Jesus is Alive Ministries! (Undated), circa 2002, covers this topic (amongst many)

from a Scriptural perspective and most other of Britain's sins; history and past in a very comprehensive way.

2. Note: The 21 December 2005, saw the first same-sex civil partnership ceremonies take place in England. Britain's very first gay 'wedding' took place at Derry, Northern Ireland on the 19 December 2005 and Scotland's on the following day.

3. Note: Details of some of Britain's past sins, the need for national repentance and the biblical argument for why these sins remain the responsibility of Britain's Church today can be found in the book *Sins of the Forefathers how national repentance removes obstacles for revival* by Brian Mills and Roger Mitchell, Sovereign World Ltd, 1999. History of Britain: **www.xfaith.co.uk**.

4. *Can God - ? 10,000 Miles of Miracle in Britain* by J. Edwin Orr, Marshall, Morgan & Scott, LTD, 1934, page 121.

5. *This Is The Victory 10,000 Miles of Miracle in America* by J. Edwin Orr, Marshall, Morgan & Scott, LTD, 1936, page 127.

6. The Book *You're a Soldier Now! It's Time For Revival* by John Masters, Sound Books Publishing, 1996, covers the aspect of personal revival, putting sin to death and becoming more disciplined in our walk with God. The booklet *Continuous Revival* by Norman Grubb, Christian Literature Crusade, 1952 enters into this aspect of personal revival (at a deeper level) entailing brokenness, conviction, confessing and cleansing so that each individual can walk in and live in the power of the Holy Spirit. *Rees Howells Intercessor* by Norman Grubb, Lutterworth Press, is a biography of a Welsh coalminer who fully surrendered himself to the Holy Spirit and saw amazing results, including revival in Africa. For an overview of his life see **www.reeshowells.co.uk**.

7. Given to the author as an utterance from the Holy Spirit as a closing word for this section of the revival book, from the 13 -14 June 2005.

Epilogue

1. *God's Great Ambition* by Dan & Dave Davidson & George Verwer, Gabriel Publishing, (undated), inside back cover.

2. *Revival's Golden Keys – Unlocking the Door to Revival* by Ray Comfort, Bridge-Logos Publishers, 2002, page 204.

3. The best book I have ever come across to explain the concept of law and grace in a simple Scriptural manner is *Revival's Golden Keys – Unlocking the Door to Revival* by Ray Comfort.

4. Ibid., pages 47 and 62.

5. In my first book *Mission Preparation Training,* Diggory Press, 2006, (under Section Three) I cover the basics of evangelism, teaching and discipleship in six biblical lessons.

6. *Revival's Golden Keys – Unlocking the Door to Revival* by Ray Comfort, Bridge-Logos Publishers, 2002, pages 182 and 183.

Appendix A
1. *Revival's Golden Keys – Unlocking the Door to Revival* by Ray Comfort, Bridge-Logos Publishers, 2002, page 73. (From *Finding the Reality of* God, By Paris Reidhead, Reidhead Publications, Box 556, Denton, MD 21629).
2. *Revival's Golden Keys*, Ibid., page 68.
3. Ibid., page 71.

Appendix B
1. *Derek Prince A Biography, A Teacher For Our Time* by Stephen Mansfield, Derek Prince Ministries – UK, 2005, page 178.
2. *Six steps to Spiritual Revival* by Pat Robinson, Multnomah Publishers, 2002 page 11.
3. *Awakening in Asia* by Bailey Marks with Shirley Mewhinney, Here's Life Publishers, Inc., 1981, page 23.
4. Ibid., page 20.
5. Ibid., pages 7, 9 and 30.
6. Rhinehard Bonnke speaking on Christian television.
7. Benny Hinn 2005 calendar.
8. British and American terms for numbers are identical through the millions, but thereafter they differ significantly. One thousand million in English equals one billion in American, and one billion in English equals one trillion in American.
9. www.jesusfilm.org.
10. *Revival its Principles & Personalities* by Winkie Pratney, 1994, Huntington House Publishers, pages 187 and 194.
11. *The 700 club* magazine, May 2006.

Appendix D and E
1. *It's Time For Revival, A Bible Study On Revival* by Gwen Shaw, Engeltal Press, 1988, pages 57 and 59.
2. *Mission Preparation Training*, by Mathew Backholer, Diggory Press, 2006, pages 51-52.
3. Public Domain.
4. Ibid., page 278.
5. Ibid., page 322.
6. Ibid., page 330.

ALSO FROM BYFAITH MEDIA

Mission Preparation Training

The book, *Mission Preparation Training*, by Mathew Backholer covers 29 topics in 35 lessons. Most people will spend hundreds or even thousands of their hard-earned savings to go on a short-term mission trip, yet still go unprepared – well now there is no excuse. Mathew Backholer has been on more than thirty short-term mission trips in over twenty countries on four continents. He co-presents ByFaith TV 'A Journey Of Discipleship,' writes for www.byfaith.co.uk and is author of *Revival Fires and Awakenings,* www.revivalfire.co.uk.

Jesus said, "Go into all the world and preach the gospel to every creature" Mark 16:15.

The book in conjunction with the full use of Scripture will aid the reader to discern the voice of God, finding His will and direction and how to implement and prepare for the call on their life as part of the Great Commission. The book covers the practical application of preparing for a short-term mission trip, to include: servant-hood, implementing a God-given vision and the financial, emotional, physical and spiritual preparation.

On the mission field (or your own home town) the book covers the various aspects and approaches which can be used in evangelism and shows the biblical methods of teaching other believers the truths of God's word and how they can enter into the fullness of God, by being set free and delivered from past bondages and afflictions; (in practical hands on ministry) being made whole in body, soul and spirit, whilst being built up in the most holy faith.

For more information please visit **www.byfaith.co.uk**.

ALSO FROM ByFAITH MEDIA

ByFaith - A Journey Of Discipleship - DVD's

The adventure of a lifetime begins when two British brothers step out of their comfort zone, to embark on several unique worldwide missions. Join them on their extreme missions in Europe, North Africa and through Asia. In each country they have to put their faith into action and learn from their experiences.

In twelve episodes and fourteen nations, armed with their backpacks, Bibles and a video camera, Paul and Mathew Backholer share their successes, failures and jubilation as they seek to win people to the message of Christian discipleship. They see the wonderful hand of God, but also face many challenges, especially in the developing world, as they experience many trials which bring them to their knees.

On the missions they give an insight into their *Journey Of Discipleship* in the realm of reality TV and tell stories of God's work around the world today. ByFaith TV is a fast paced, engaging programme with a Christian worldview and radical message, which is safe for the whole family. The complete series deals with twelve biblical subjects through the experiences that the guys have encountered whilst on mission.

The 4 DVD's contain: 12 ByFaith episodes. A total of 300+ minutes of video footage! Over 150 scene selections! The DVD's are authorised to be used in churches, cell / youth groups, with free downloadable Bible studies for each episode.

ByFaith TV is aired on various networks around the world. Watch the trailers at **www.byfaithtv.co.uk**.

NOTES

www.byfaith.co.uk - www.revivalnow.co.uk
www.reeshowells.co.uk - www.byfaithmedia.co.uk
www.xfaith.co.uk - www.prophecynow.co.uk - www.revivalfire.co.uk

Printed in the United Kingdom
by Lightning Source UK Ltd.
112850UKS00001B/73-249